STAGING TRADITION

MUSIC IN AMERICAN LIFE

*A list of books in the series
appears at the end of this book.*

MICHAEL ANN WILLIAMS

Staging Tradition

JOHN LAIR AND
SARAH GERTRUDE KNOTT

UNIVERSITY OF ILLINOIS PRESS

URBANA AND CHICAGO

Publication of this book was supported by a
grant from Western Kentucky University.

Library of Congress Cataloging-in-Publication Data
Williams, Michael Ann.
Staging tradition : John Lair and Sarah Gertrude Knott /
Michael Ann Williams.
    p.   cm. — (Music in American life)
Includes bibliographical references and index.
ISBN-13: 978-0-252-03102-1 (cloth : alk. paper)
ISBN-10: 0-252-03102-4 (cloth : alk. paper)
ISBN-13: 978-0-252-07344-1 (pbk. : alk. paper)
ISBN-10: 0-252-07344-4 (pbk. : alk. paper)
1. Lair, John.
2. Knott, Sarah Gertrude, 1895–1984.
3. Impresarios—United States—Biography.
4. Music—Social aspects—United States.
5. Music festivals—United States—History.
I. Title. II. Series.
ML429.L25W55   2006
791.092'273—dc22   2006003050

For my mother,

Josephine Rice Williams,

who began her radio career at KFBI, Wichita

Contents

Preface

As biographers often note, writing about a person's life is akin to developing a long-term relationship. That has certainly been the case for me. At times I felt annoyed with either Sarah Gertrude Knott or John Lair; other times I felt admiration. Finally I felt that I could just accept them for who they were, the endlessly complicated human beings who refused to give up on their dreams. In writing this book I also came to realize that I love messy history, those instances when individual narratives defy grand theories and common assumptions. Knott and Lair provided plenty of complications for me to ponder.

Scholarship on the politics of cultural representation informed my understanding of Lair and Knott and also gave me something against which to react. Not that I think scholars should only deal with idiosyncratic facts and individual biographies, but they need to guard against constructing straw men and women. Furthermore, as essential as the writing on cultural representation has been, it has the potential to breed sanctimoniousness. Rather than prompting, as it should, a more critical look at our own practices of cultural representation, what if it instead encourages a certain self-congratulatory assurance that we have come a long way?

To a large extent, Bascom Lamar Lunsford, folk entrepreneur of western North Carolina, brought me to the lives of John Lair and Sarah Gertrude Knott. In pondering Lunsford's career in writing my book on the folklife of the Great Smoky Mountains, I found him difficult to pigeonhole according to assumptions of cultural representation in southern Appalachia. David Whisnant, who had written insightfully about Lunsford's career a few years earlier, largely excluded him from his ground-breaking study of the politics of culture in Appalachia, *All That Is Native and Fine*. Was it simply that Lunsford did not fit the mold of interloper? At times in his career he worked closely with both Lair and Knott, and it was through consideration of Lunsford's career that I began to understand the ties that bound early folk festivals and radio barn dances.

The more I pursued Knott and Lair the more delighted I became with the parallels of their careers. Not only were they from the same state and almost exact contemporaries, but they also seemed driven by the same passion—the need to be center-stage. They drew from different theatrical models, but their careers intersected at various crucial points. Through them I could meditate on the theatrical nature of the representation of tradition. The recent literature on the construction of authenticity helped me avoid simplistic contrasts between Knott and Lair and folk festivals and barn dances. Both individuals desired the approval of academic folklorists, but they also firmly knew they were in the entertainment business. Rather than hold up their careers to the yardstick of today's construction of the authentic, it is more productive to see how both negotiated their visions of authentic tradition within the demands of theatrical staging and economic survival.

At the beginning of this study I was also intrigued by the similarities between Knott's and Lair's ascribed places in the history of cultural representation. There seemed to be grudging acknowledgment of their significance coupled with an undertone of dismissal. They pop up in this study or that, but oddly, especially considering the wealth of primary documents they left behind, they have seldom been treated in-depth. As with all constructions of the past, contemporary views of Lair and Knott have been shaped by current needs and desires rather than any clearheaded examination of their lives. I could not help but think that history would have treated both of them better had they retired some time in the 1950s and disappeared happily from sight. That is especially true of Knott. Imperious old ladies in evening gowns did not fit well into the folk festival scene of the Age of Aquarius.

Beyond the gross intolerance of older people held by baby boomers (my generation) who came of age during the 1960s and 1970s (we did make exceptions for aged blues musicians and fiddlers), it is also necessary to look to the full flight that the emerging profession of public folklore took from the inescapably theatrical nature of Knott's and Lair's endeavor. Significantly, studies of the antecedents of public folklore focus on the work of the folklorists of the New Deal, whose productions were largely literary, rather than the first generation of folk festivals. Based on a scholarly study of a single festival they have all been painted with the same brush, and in doing so folklorists used the guise of politics to distance themselves from theatrics. Ironically, as Barbara Kirshenblatt-Gimblett and others have suggested, rather than escape the theater, the development of the modern folk festival parallels that of avant-garde theater.

It is not necessary to embrace the now distasteful pageantry of Knott's National Folk Festival to recognize her achievements. Nor is it necessary to celebrate the artifice of Lair's radio shows in order to appreciate his passionate interest in folk traditions and understanding of the interplay of traditional and popular musical forms. Instead, critical assessments of Lair's and Knott's attempts to accommodate authenticity, as they saw it, to theatrical vehicles should be tempered with self-realization of how modern constructions of authenticity shape today's assessments.

I hope this point of view will be seen in part as a self-criticism. I grew up in Washington, D.C., and regularly attended the the Smithsonian's Festival of American Folklife and the National Folk Festival when it was held (sans Sarah Knott) at Wolf Trap Farm. I was probably among the great unwashed that horrified Knott loyalists. Later, during the early 1980s, I worked as a public folklorist and organized folk festivals in southwestern North Carolina. I would have been no less dismayed by the antiquated pageantry of Knott's earlier festivals or the corny Appalachian stereotypes of Lair's media shows than my compatriots. But in understanding the history of the enterprise of being folklorists or other presenters of culture, I now feel that it is critical to seek to understand, not simply dismiss, my predecessors.

In the days of writing this book I was sometimes glad that I did not have to deal personally with either John Lair or Sarah Gertrude Knott. They could be self-obsessed, overbearing, and some times downright delusional. But in the end, I felt they were old friends or close relatives whose flaws were beside the point. If what motivated them was a human need to be center-stage rather than a clear political agenda, I suspect that they share that trait with the majority in public presentation and academia.

Acknowledgments

My greatest debt of gratitude is to the long line of graduate assistants who worked on this book. David Baxter and Hillary Glatt Kwiatek helped me finish *Great Smoky Mountains Folklife* and begin this study. They also conducted the first round of interviews and transcribed John Rumble's earlier interviews. Andrew Lee made the first pass through the Sarah Gertrude Knott Collection in the Folklife Archives at Western Kentucky University.

Larry Morrisey made the Lair project his own, locating and interviewing individuals who knew John Lair and combing the John Lair Collection in the Southern Appalachian Archives at Berea College. Brian Gregory followed up in the Lair Collection and transcribed taped interviews. I benefitted from the careful research of both as well as from their ideas about Lair and Renfro Valley.

Hayden Roberts proved to be a history sleuth extraordinaire, finding many facts about Knott I might otherwise have missed. Tracy Boyarsky chased down numerous loose ends and proved a cheerful companion on our monthly trips to Princeton, Kentucky.

Debbie Loveless Everly developed an extraordinary ability to read Knott's handwriting. Both she and Tony VanWinkle read early drafts of this project, and Rachel Baum brought her wonderful intelligence and careful eye to helping prepare its final versions.

A number of other former graduate students helped in various ways. Thanks to Michele Pezutti, Ardell Jarratt, Jon Kay, Teresa Hollingsworth, and Jim Nelson. Thanks also to Stuart Burrill for helping to prepare the scans of the photographs and Christie Burns for the final reading.

Two extraordinary archival collections formed the backbone of this study: the John Lair Collection, donated to Berea College by Lair's daughters, and the Sarah Gertrude Knott Collection at Western Kentucky University. Thanks so much to Harry Rice at Berea for helping us negotiate the Lair Collection and to Pat Hodges at WKU for giving me the freedom to comb through the Knott Collection.

Oral history also provided an important source of information. The Kentucky Oral History Commission funded the interviews we conducted as well as the transcription process. They also funded transcriptions of oral histories on Renfro Valley conducted by John Rumble of the Country Music Foundation.

Thanks to John Rumble as well as Lisa Yarger and Kevin Mooney for sharing their research, and a special thanks to Yvonne Dodge for opening the Little Green House and sharing its treasures. And to all the family members, friends, acquaintances, and former co-workers of John Lair and Sarah Gertrude Knott who agreed to be interviewed, thanks so much for making them come alive. Thanks as well to Joe Wilson and Tim Lloyd for their helpful reading of the manuscript.

Finally, as always, thanks to my "reference spouse," David Carpenter, for always quickly and willingly chasing down answers to questions.

STAGING TRADITION

1 *Tradition, Ambition, and the Theater*

> How 'ya gonna keep 'em, down on the farm, After
> they've seen Paree?
> How 'ya gonna keep 'em away from Broadway; jazzin'
> aroun', And paintin' the town?
> —Sam M. Lewis and Joe Young, 1919

Born at the tail end of the nineteenth century, John Lair (1894–1985) and Sarah Gertrude Knott (1895–1984) lived to see most of the next century pass. Knott, founder of the National Folk Festival, and Lair, creator of the Renfro Valley Barn Dance, both devoted their lives to staging traditional culture. Seemingly, their visions turned back toward the century they left, and it would be easy enough to label their lives' work as antimodernist. Typical of the generation that came of age during the watershed years of World War I, however, they eagerly lived lives that differed substantially from those of their parents. They saw enough of the past century to know its ways and regret the passing of a way of life, but Knott and Lair were firmly citizens of the twentieth century.

If Lair and Knott straddled two centuries, they also came from border regions. A slave state that did not secede during the Civil War, Kentucky hovers perennially in a mode of regional identity crisis. Neither Knott nor Lair hailed from the two easily identifiable regions within Kentucky, the wealthy horse country of the inner Bluegrass or the poor, coal-mining towns of Appalachia. Lair spent most of his life in the hills of Rockcastle County on the western edge of the eastern part of the state, where the Bluegrass meets the eastern coalfields. Knott grew up in the region known as the Jackson Purchase. Paducah served as the big city of that far western area, and St. Louis was the closest metropolis. Throughout her career Knott often seemed frustrated that she did not come from a distinctive place such as Appalachia, Acadia, the Ozarks, or the Southwest whose regional cultures she often featured onstage.

Despite the three hundred miles that separated their home communities, Knott and Lair had similar upbringings. Both came from respectable rural families. Although hardly elite, their families produced schoolteachers and local politicians as well as farmers. Knott's father, Clinton Isbel Knott, a well-respected farmer, served several terms as a magistrate in the fiscal court. His obituary labeled "Squire Knott" as a successful farmer and "one of the best known men of McCracken County."[1] Clinton Knott apparently had at least one powerful political connection, Alben Barkley, who later became one of Kentucky's most influential politicians of the twentieth century and vice president under Harry S. Truman. In a letter written long after her father died, Knott, the inveterate name-dropper, referred to Senator Barkley as "my father's friend from Kentucky."[2] Lair's grandfather, Jerome Burke Lair, also dabbled in local politics and served as a county judge.

Although both families produced locally prominent citizens, the Lairs and the Knotts stayed firmly rooted in their communities. In 1880 Clinton Knott married Ella Wren, the eldest daughter of L. D. Wren, whose lands were located just southwest of the Knotts' property. Elsewhere, Lair's parents, Thomas Burke Lair and Isabelle Coffey, were also neighbors. Grandfather Lair owned much of the land lying along the Little Renfro Creek, and John Lair's maternal grandfather, Thomas Jefferson Coffey, held a substantial portion of the land bordering Renfro Creek. Aptly enough, Lair's parents eventually purchased a farm at the fork of the two creeks. Until Lair constructed it on-air, a community named "Renfro Valley" did not, however, exist.[3] Lair spent his first five years in the town of Livingston, Kentucky, where his father worked as a carpenter and repairman for the Louisville and Nashville Railroad, and then the family moved back to the farm along Renfro Creek.

Although neither obtained college degrees, education was an important influence on both Knott and Lair. Both mythologized the small rural schools of their youths. The young Gertrude (as she was known in those days) attended the one-room, frame Knott School located on land between the farms of her two grandfathers, Atlas Knott and Levi Wren. By her own account, Knott showed early aptitude for organizing others. She recalled that the "games I remember best were the ones of which I was often the leader, taking my little playmates up and down the 'Clark's Line' road (presently Highway 60) to neighboring homes, to sing or play imaginary musical instruments."[4] Lair received his early education in an even more romantic setting, the one-room, log Redbud School, which he later moved to the Renfro Valley complex. Lair and Knott progressed from these small rural schools to new consolidated high schools. Knott graduated from McCracken County (Heath) High School, established in 1910 as the first rural high school in the county.[5] Lair completed his education in 1914 with the first graduating class of Mt. Vernon High School.

Although both her sisters became teachers, Sarah Gertrude Knott's ambitions eventually took her far beyond the expected role for women raised in rural western Kentucky at the turn of the century. She was inspired to pursue dramatics by a high school teacher and a visiting lecturer: "We had a teacher of dramatics who came down to the McCracken County High School . . . I took this dramatics from her. And people thought I was pretty good and I thought I was pretty good, too. . . . I acted in the plays you know, there at high school, and in giving readings and things like that. And then Dr. King came over to La Center—that's a little town out from Kevil. And he was advertised at Paducah and round about. And I went down to hear him. He had been a teacher who believed in the type of acting you had to feel, you know. He was a wonderful actor." Knott subsequently enrolled in the Kings School for Drama in Pittsburgh.[6]

Along with these theatrical influences and her own strength of character, the support Knott received from women in her family and community enabled her to break with tradition. Sarah Gertrude, the second youngest in a family of three girls and three boys, was four when her mother, Ella Wren Knott, died. The task of raising her and their youngest sister, Gladys, fell to Lannie, the eldest sister, who not only served as a surrogate mother but also taught her younger siblings at the Knott School.

The only Knott sister to marry, Lannie wed Ernest Ransdell and settled nearby. Sarah Gertrude Knott's closeness to her sisters endured throughout her life, and "home" was always where they lived. In 1941 Gladys Knott moved sixty miles east to Princeton, Kentucky, to teach. Lannie Ransdell joined Gladys several years later, after the death of her husband. In 1951 the two sisters built the "little green house" where Sarah eventually spent her retirement years.[7] If Lannie held the position of surrogate mother, Gladys, two years Sarah Gertrude's junior, was her closest friend and ally. While Sarah picked a less conventional career choice, Gladys sought a better education, obtaining a B.A. from Western Kentucky State College and a master's degree in recreation from George Peabody College. As close as Gladys and Sarah Gertrude were, they were also strikingly different in looks and temperament. Both independent and strong-willed, the practical and athletic Gladys contrasted with the flamboyant and dramatic Sarah Gertrude. Later in life they jokingly told their friends and neighbors in Princeton, "We are Knott sisters."[8]

Aside from the Knott sisters, Kevil produced other independent and ambitious women. After high school, Sarah Gertrude and about seven of her close friends formed the Local Talent Club, which met during the summers even after several moved away from Kevil. Among the group was Mary Lanier Magruder, a freelance writer for the *Paducah Sun Democrat* and the *Saturday Evening Post.*[9] In 1929 Knott produced and directed a dramatized story by Magruder about Kevil, using local people as actors.[10] Magruder also helped Knott understand that western Kentucky was rich in folk traditions.[11]

After her father's death in 1918, Sarah Gertrude pursued her dramatic interests. She attended Kings School for Drama in Pittsburgh, the Elias Day Bush Conservatory in Chicago, and Georgetown College back in Kentucky. Although she apparently did not earn a degree, in 1923 she landed a position as an "instructor of expression" at Chowan College, a small Baptist women's school in Murfreesboro, North Carolina. The inscriptions in her volume of the 1926 yearbook indicate that the students held the beautiful young instructor in high esteem. One wrote, "I love you for your beauty, your independence, your sense of humor."[12] The tiny school could not easily contain the high-spirited Knott. As she recalled late in life, "I was hard to hold down in that little college of Murfreesboro, because they tried to get you in at eight o'clock but they couldn't get me in at eight o'clock."[13]

Knott's ambitious dramatic program for Chowan brought her into the sphere of Frederick Koch, creator of the influential Carolina Playmakers. This contact with the dean of the "folk drama" movement opened a new universe of possibilities for Sarah Gertrude Knott. At Chowan, Knott produced *Fixin's,* written by Koch's former student Paul Green, and invited Koch to attend: "I stayed [at Chowan College] for three years and I kicked up a little fuss. We had a traditional drama contest. . . . We'd just got a new cyclorama and auditorium and everything and we paid for everything with the dramatic groups we had there because there wasn't anything that anybody had done that amounted to anything and I worked so hard that it sort of showed, you know. And Proff Koch came down there the first time and we filled the auditorium."[14]

After she produced her first folk festival in 1934, Sarah Gertrude Knott avidly documented her career. She seldom accounted for her first thirty-nine years in detail, however, aside from noting that she trained in the dramatic arts. Knott became so invested in her persona as "founder and director" of the National Folk Festival that she had a difficult time conceiving of who she was before that time. Later in life she decided that she was a "product of folklife" and offered up snippets of her early childhood as evidence. Although she spent most of her adult life far away, her ties to her home community remained strong throughout her life. Even when they were older, Sarah and Gladys Knott continued to visit Kevil and reaffirm their strong connection to their birthplace. A friend who went along noted, "I remember when I made my first trip down to the [Spring Bayou] cemetery and that area, they showed me the creek where their sins were washed away, the well where they used to stop and get a drink of water, the school, Knott School."[15]

Far more than Knott, John Lair intensely mythologized his childhood, using it as a central theme of his writing, radio productions, and even the complex he built at Renfro Valley. Lair often said that he designed his radio programs to appeal to plain country folk like his parents, who both died before his radio career took off. Lair, however, did admit that neither his father nor his paternal grandfather approved of fiddle music or public dancing. Ballad singing did fall within the family's range of acceptability, and Lair noted the influence of the singing of his great-grandmother, Matilda Dalton Coffey, and his grandmother, Ann French Lair, in shaping his interest in traditional music.[16] Late in life he confessed that as a young boy he actually feared his ancient great-grandmother: "[She] sang and played a little concertina. And she scared the heck out of me. And I'd just stand rapt and afraid to move and she thought I was so taken with her music, you know. . . . She had an old handwritten copy of a song called 'The Silk Merchant's Daughter' that her sweetheart had written down for her and gave it to her the night he left there to go down and join Andrew Jackson at the Battle of New Orleans. Well, he never came back, but she always kept that song and she told the folks before she died she wanted me to have it."[17]

Similar to Knott, Lair had more aptitude for organization than performance. Although he developed an early interest in string-band music and attempted to learn the mandolin, he soon found that his talents lay elsewhere. Of his school days he recalled, "I never could play an instrument but I could always scrounge around and furnish the instruments and the meeting places and rehearsals and do that sort of thing . . . I could strike any tune but I could never get good at it. So I was just sort of a hanger on, trying to find my way into it."[18] Despite his later glorification of rural life, Lair possessed no fondness for farm work. According to family stories, he, like Tom Sawyer, was adept at persuading friends to do his chores for him.[19]

Lair's major break from home came with induction into the army during World War I. He never saw conflict but instead found himself stationed in Washington, D.C., where he became part of the production staff for a theatrical show, *Atta Boy.* Captain Frank Tinney, a popular comedian and actor before the war, starred in the production. The *New York Times* review of the show's opening at the Lexington Theater noted that although the production contained the usual burlesques of camp life, "The music of 'Atta Boy' is unusually tuneful, and no doubt Broadway will be whistling 'Strolling 'round the Camp with Mary,' which seemed particularly to please the good-sized first-night audience which greeted the soldier-actors."[20] A program from a Camp Meigs production lists Lair as one of many performers. By his own account, however, he wrote one of the sketches and managed to write himself into the act when the Ziegfield Follies incorporated the show into one of its productions.[21]

Lair also demonstrated other talents when during the war's final days he produced *Lest We Forget*, a small book of poetry and drawings about army life. According to Lair, the prominent actress Helen Ware read one of the poems onstage at a theater in Washington and introduced Lair to the audience.[22] Although Lair would subsequently have plenty of opportunity to explore his skills at sentimental and humorous writing, later in life he expressed regret that he had not further pursued a career as a cartoonist.[23] In any case, serving in the military opened a new world of opportunity for John Lair. As his daughter Barbara Smith has said, "I remember Mother saying one time that after they were married, or around that time, that the government gave the veterans of World War I a bonus, a small bonus, and Daddy sent his back with a letter saying he had the best time he'd ever had in his life . . . 'I should pay you,' you know, because he probably never would have gotten out of the county . . . without that experience."[24]

Similar to many young men of his generation, Lair must have found it difficult to settle back into rural life after the war, even if he did not "see Paree." In his narrative about the creation of the Renfro Valley complex, Lair suggests that return from the army inspired his commitment to preserve Renfro Valley history. Disturbed by changes that had occurred during his absence, Lair hoped that Renfro Valley "could always be the way I first saw it and best remembered it."[25] His schoolboy days at Redbud, the dances at the neighbor's barn, and the Sunday morning gatherings all served as memories around which he reimagined his community as the valley where time stood still. "If before the tale is told you begin to get the idea that this is more a history of John Lair than of

Renfro Valley," he wrote, "it will be because I cannot write it any other way. I don't know how to tell either, leaving out the other."[26]

After his army service, Lair taught briefly at a small school in Livingston, Kentucky, and then at Mt. Vernon High School, where his students included Virginia Crawford, seven years his junior.[27] The future Mrs. Lair found his talents as a teacher more theatrical than intellectual. According to their eldest daughter, Ann, "[Mother] said, 'I could tell the first day he didn't know what he was talking about. Because he was making a game out of mathematics.' See, that's the way he did everything, you know, everything was kind of a show or a production. So she said, 'I knew right then he didn't know anything about mathematics. But a lot about dramatics.'"[28]

Lair soon left teaching, moving on to a newspaper job at the *Corbin Tribune* and then on to Louisville to work in advertising. Apparently, while in Louisville he found opportunity to dabble in the entertainment industry, booking acts for the Continental Lyceum.[29] In 1922 the Liberty Mutual Insurance Company hired Lair, first as an investigator and later as a medical director. The job took him far from Kentucky, first to Boston, then to New York, and finally to Chicago. Although Lair found little outlet for his theatrical interests at the time, the dramatic bent of his personality revealed itself to those close to him. The Lairs' daughter Nancy Griffin remembered how her mother described Lair when he arrived by train for a visit: "'He always was sitting by the window posed.' She says, 'We could tell he was posed.' Because, he was, I guess, quite the glamorous, romantic sort of figure, coming back to the little town after he was making his mark in the city."[30]

In 1924 Lair married the beautiful, blue-eyed Virginia Crawford. At the time, the shy Virginia could probably not have anticipated how public a life they would live. During their Chicago years a number of the performers John Lair brought to the city lived with the Lairs for a time. Later at Renfro Valley, Virginia Lair worked quietly behind the scenes at the post office and in small shops, putting up with constant interruptions of family life from fans who saw the Lair family home as part of the public complex. Although many of his acquaintances later believed that the dollar was always John Lair's bottom line, the couple's daughters insist that it was their mother who possessed practical business sense. "Mother had a business head on her," maintained Barbara Smith. "Daddy probably couldn't have carried Renfro Valley as long as he did without mother. . . . Any profit or any money realized, daddy put right back into the business. Mother, pretty much, with her souvenir shop and frugalness or whatever, put four girls through college and clothed them."[31]

Three of the four Lair daughters were born during the family's years in Chicago: Ann in 1927, Virginia Lee (Ginalee) in 1932, and Nancy in 1935. Lair announced the birth of their youngest child, Barbara, from the stage of the Renfro Valley Barn Dance in 1940. Although frequently occupied with his career, Lair's love for staging extended to relationships with his daughters. As Nancy recalled, "He did a lot of things together with us, and one of our favorite things, he made us corn cob pipes one time. And we went out into the woods, and we found Brer Rabbit's briar patch. And he got Brer Rabbit tobacco, and put it in our little pipes. Now we were seven or eight years old, and he told us stories while we sat in the middle of the briar patch."[32] Barbara seemed a bit more immune to her father's showmanship. One Christmas, Lair set up a speaker system in the living room and, out of sight, pretended to be Santa Claus. "Ho, ho, ho, Barbara. Do you know who this is?" he asked. Little Barbara, more interested in opening presents, ignored him until her older sisters finally urged her to respond. "Who is that?" they asked. Barbara responded, "Sounds like John Lair in the *Sunday Morning Gatherin'* to me."[33]

Nancy Griffin, who insisted that her father restage some of their special childhood events such as storytelling by the fireplace, apples and potatoes cooking in the ashes, for her own children, felt that his stagings for family paralleled what he wished to accomplish professionally: "I think daddy always had in mind, even dealing with us, and with everybody, to make something a memory, to build a memory. That this would be something you would look back on and remember, and so let's make it very special."[34]

Appropriately enough, the traditional music of John Lair's childhood, as well as the traditions of burlesque and vaudeville he encountered during his military experience, shaped his career. Country music radio would weave American vernacular music with the traditions of American popular theater, and the emergence of this new form of media entertainment seems to have been custom-made for Lair's talents and interests. Although the basic technology had long existed, commercial radio did not emerge until after World War I. At first conceptualized as a service enterprise, the practice of "selling time" for advertising did not become fully established until the end of the 1920s.[35] Ironically, the new media soon found that it could market a salve for nostalgia.

John Lair could hardly have picked a better city than Chicago to enter country music radio. In 1924 the Sears Roebuck Agricultural Foundation established its own radio station in Chicago, WLS, which catered primarily to rural listeners. In its first year WLS hired George Hay and soon thereafter established the National Barn Dance, one of the first successful radio shows to feature old-time music. Hay served as the show's first announcer, but the following year WSM lured him away with an offer of a job as the radio director in Nashville, where he developed the program that became the Grand Ole Opry.[36] Despite the departure of Hay, WLS continued to program old-time music. In 1928 Sears sold the station to the Prairie Farmer Publishing Company, which, under the direction of Burridge Butler, set out to make WLS the "Station of the Common People."[37]

Lair, "quite by accident," discovered the music being broadcast from his local Chicago station. The act that first attracted his attention was that of a Kentucky-born ballad singer: "I was in Chicago and I noticed on WLS some very unusual people, just like home folks. . . . And I heard Bradley Kincaid at his height. And Bradley was one of the most popular things in the country. And I wanted to go over and give him a lot of old songs that he wasn't singing."[38] Already hugely popular, Kincaid acted none too interested when Lair approached him. Still, Lair saw a business opportunity for himself in radio: "I thought, well hell, I'll get somebody to sing my songs. I'll get them on the air after all."[39]

Lair convinced several musical acquaintances from Rockcastle County to relocate to Chicago and then attempted to sell them to WLS. His first success came with a mandolin and guitar duo, Karl Davis and Hartford Connecticut Taylor. Karl and Harty, the Renfro Valley Boys, became the stable nucleus of Lair's first successful group, the Cumberland Ridge Runners. Lair soon added his childhood friend Doc Hopkins, who sang and played guitar. After the initial three members of the band, Lair looked further afield. He recruited Gene Ruppe, a Tennessean, to play fiddle and banjo, and when Hopkins departed the group, Lair replaced him with Hugh Cross, the "Boy from Smoky Mountain." Ruppe soon proved unsatisfactory, and Lair hired an odd-looking fiddler from Indiana, Slim Miller, solely on the basis of his comic appearance. As Lair would explain, "I was willing to take Hugh's word for it that he was a fiddler, I just knew that I didn't want to lose a boy that looked like that."[40]

Lair's final two additions to the Ridge Runners became the most successful. His sister told him about a local boy from nearby Berea who sure could sing, and in early 1931 Lair contacted Clyde Foley, telling him that he was his first choice to replace Hopkins, who had received an offer from NBC.[41] Negotiations apparently stalled, and Hugh Cross filled the position instead. The following year, however, Foley did move up to Chicago to join the act. Lair changed his nickname from "Grump" to "Red" and had Foley learn the bass fiddle. Cross departed the following year, leaving the male vocal lead to Foley. Finally, Lair found Jeanne

Meunich, a beautiful young nightclub singer (the "Redheaded Bluebird"), dressed her in gingham, stuck a bonnet on her head, and rechristened her as Linda Parker, the "Sunbonnet Girl." The first of many female acts Lair developed, Parker became hugely popular. Never one to work solely behind the scenes, Lair often included himself in photographs of the Cumberland Ridge Runners. The publicity shots often pictured Lair blowing the jug for the group, and sometimes he sang backup vocals, although Lair admitted that he had no talent for singing. He brought far more than his paltry musical talents to the Ridge Runners, serving as manager and announcer, for which he took 20 percent of earnings.

Later in life John Lair took partial credit for two revolutionary changes in the National Barn Dance—moving the program from the studio to a live stage show and convincing the management to feature dancing.[42] Whether or not it did so on the advice of Lair, a part-time employee, in 1932 WLS relocated the National Barn Dance to the Eighth Street Theater, where it played to packed audiences for the next two decades. Shortly thereafter the NBC network picked up the show's last half hour.

Whatever his influence on WLS, Lair's genius lay in his ability to transcend the aural nature of the media. He could envision that the radio audience might want to hear the sounds of a "real" barn dance, including dancing, just as later it occurred to him to set a barn dance in a real barn. As the concept of selling radio time became fully entrenched, Lair also perceived the appeal of developing programming that integrated the message of the sponsor into the theme of the show.

Country music histories often depict Lair as a traditionalist. In keeping with Burridge Butler's predilections, he distanced himself from the perceived lower-class elements of the emerging commercial "hillbilly" genre and connected his groups to "traditional" folk music. Yet he was also an innovator and bragged that he helped introduce the bass fiddle and Hawaiian guitar to string-band music. In his later years, Lair voiced strong opposition to drums and electrified instruments in country music, but the early Renfro Valley Barn Dance included the steel guitar and electric mandolin.[43] Lair also later objected to the westernization of country music but did, however, include western acts in the early days, most notably the Girls of the Golden West, a duet of singing sisters from Illinois. He also had a life-long interest in the stories and songs of the Old West. The growing fascination of the country music audience with cowboys, however, posed a business threat to Lair, who invested heavily in the upland South context of his enterprise. He also invested in country comedy. Although the emergence of radio, the recording industry, and motion pictures spelled an end to various forms of live entertainment, it also provided jobs for displaced performers. The comedic traditions of vaudeville, as well as vaudevillians themselves, soon found their way into radio and ultimately to country music shows.

Although early country music entrepreneurs had relatively little constraint in altering tradition for entertainment value, several, including George Hay of the Grand Ole Opry and John Lair, recognized their roles in preserving folk tradition. Both men saw through the artificial lines between folk and popular forms of music drawn by some of the scholars of the day, and Lair actively researched the roots of American songs.[44] Early in his career he positioned himself as an authority on folk music, and throughout his life he interacted with academic folklorists as well as those in the folk festival movement. While Hay, Lair, and others fashioned the barn dance format, another group of entrepreneurs developed a different way to present American traditional music. The modern "folk festival" emerged, in part, from the nation's fascination for the regional culture of southern Appalachia.

The first Appalachian folk festival was directly connected to the growth of tourism in western North Carolina during the 1920s. The Asheville Chamber of Commerce discovered that it could market local culture as a commodity, and in 1928 the Chamber asked a local lawyer to present a program of folk dances and music as part of the Rhododendron Festival. The following year the program's director, Bascom Lamar Lunsford, created the Mountain Dance and Folk Festival, over which he would preside for the next forty-five years. Unlike many folk music collectors in Appalachia, Lunsford's musical interests extended beyond ballads, and his festival always included string-band music and dance. Although he conducted some fieldwork among African Americans and the Cherokee, Lunsford's festival was predominantly monocultural, focusing on Anglo-American Appalachian music and dance.[45]

The second Appalachian folk festival seemed to have a more purist approach, although at the same time it relied more on artifice. Jean Thomas caught the show business bug early in life and worked in both New York and Hollywood. In the mid-1920s she returned home to Ashland, Kentucky, and soon thereafter met a fiddler and balladeer, James William Day. Thomas transformed "Blind Bill Day" into an old mountain character named "Jilson Setters" and herself into the "Traipsin' Woman." In 1930 Thomas held an informal folk festival in her backyard for an NBC radio personality. The event proved so successful that two years later she staged the first American Folk Song Festival near Ashland. Thomas stressed the supposed Elizabethan roots of Appalachian culture and wrote that in her festival "only those mountain minstrels to whom the ballads had been handed down by word of mouth should participate. Only those untrained fiddlers and musicians who had learned their art from their for-bearers should take part."⁴⁶ Not one to eschew mass media when it served her purposes, however, Thomas used a popular radio performer, Bradley Kincaid, as emcee for the American Folk Song Festival for a number of years. The event continued until 1972, when Thomas retired.

In 1931, the year between Thomas's informal backyard festival and her first official American Folk Song Festival, Appalachia gave birth to yet another folk festival. Annabel Morris Buchanan created the White Top Folk Festival in southwest Virginia in uneasy alliance with attorney John Blakemore and Richmond composer John Powell. Although the White Top Festival initially included a range of string-band music, it became increasingly purist each year. Still, the event attracted national interest, and in 1933 First Lady Eleanor Roosevelt attended. Others from Wash-ington had less positive reactions. Visiting three years later, musicologist Charles Seeger labeled the festival "reactionary to the core."⁴⁷ Unlike the Mountain Dance and Folk Festival and the American Folk Song Festival, however, White Top did not have a long life. Tension among its three organizers, as well as bad weather atop White Top Mountain, ultimately led to its undoing, and the festival did not survive into the next decade. Although often characterized as typical of the early folk festivals, White Top was the most short-lived and the most anomalous.⁴⁸

David Whisnant suggests that the three Appalachian festivals, as well as Knott's National Folk Festival, were apparently created to encourage public appreciation of true folk music over the "vulgar commercial imita-tions" represented by early radio barn dances and the recording companies' production of hillbilly records.⁴⁹ That assumption may be more true of the White Top Festival, which Whisnant examines closely, than of the others, and deserves a closer look. A number of folklorists and collectors of the day did see commercial recordings and radio as detrimental to folk traditions, yet early festivals developed as much in tandem with as in opposition to early country music radio. Buchanan explicitly condemned the "type of folksong heard continually over the radio" as crude and degrading.⁵⁰ Lunsford, although disliking hillbilly stereotypes, did not dismiss radio itself and collaborated on a number of projects with John Lair. Thomas, for all the purist sentiment she expressed, had a show business heart and did not shy from promoting Jilson Setters on the radio or having a popu-lar radio celebrity emcee her festival. Sarah Gertrude Knott always used the mass media when it served her purpose. As Knott's career suggests, the folk festival, whether or not organizers acknowledged the fact, was yet another form of theatrical production, working either together with or in opposition to mass-media forms of entertainment.

Knott's National Folk Festival, established in 1934 in St. Louis, in many ways radically departed from previous festivals. Most significantly, it possessed an adamantly multicultural and multiregional focus. Knott, however, did not create her festival in opposition to existing festivals; both Lunsford and Thomas participated in the National Folk Festival, and Buchanan served on its advisory board for a number of years. Knott never publicly criticized the other events, but if she did not create her festival in opposition to earlier, monocultural ones then neither did they directly influence her decision to create a national festival.

Folklorist Archie Green once conjectured, and it has often been repeated as truth, that Lunsford's Mountain Dance and Folk Festival inspired Knott.[51] When a revision of Green's article on the creation of the National Folk Festival appeared in the program for the 1975 National Folk Festival, however, Knott wrote an emphatic "No" alongside his speculation.[52] She brought in Lunsford as a consultant before the first National Folk Festival in 1934 but did not attend the Mountain Dance and Folk Festival until 1935. Later in life, in a letter to Buchanan, Knott stated, "White Top was the first I attended."[53] A letter from 1936 indicates that Knott first attended White Top in 1934, four months after staging the initial National Folk Festival.[54] Apparently, Knott attended no folk festivals before the debut of her own, other than the Ozark mini-festivals she organized as a means to identify participants for the festival in St. Louis.

The independent invention of four major folk festivals in six years is surely indicative of larger cultural influences. Although the festivals clearly benefited from the depression era's fascination for the "art of the common man," enthusiasm for all things folk predates the 1930s. The emergence of folk festivals has been tied to the earlier American enthusiasm for historical pageantry. Of all the early events it is the National Folk Festival that most clearly shows direct lineage to this earlier phenomenon. Pageantry flourished in American cities and towns during the early years of the twentieth century, but by the end of World War I the movement began to splinter into separate groups: recreation workers, dramatists, and members of patriotic or hereditary societies. Knott would later use the arguments of recreational reform to support her festival, but the dramatic offshoot of the pageantry movement more directly shaped her vision.

Frederick Koch, one of the most influential dramatists the pageantry movement spawned, began his academic career at the University of North

Dakota, teaching English and producing historical pageants and "Native Prairie Plays." In 1918 he accepted a position at the University of North Carolina, where he would establish the influential Carolina Playmakers.[55] Inspired by involvement with historical pageantry as well as by Ireland's Abbey Theater, Koch developed the concept of "folk drama." The plays written by his students and associates were "folk" in content but not composition. As he noted, they were "the work of a single artist dealing consciously with his materials."[56]

Similar to the folk festival, the ideology behind historical pageantry could be either reactionary or progressive. A number of southern pageants during the 1920s openly glorified the Ku Klux Klan. The work of Koch's students, however, dealt progressively with topics such as labor unrest and race relations. Koch encouraged students to write from their own experiences, and he also suggested that they explore African American music and folklore. One of his earliest followers, philosophy student Paul Green, responded directly to this encouragement. Green's plays about African American life soon received national attention, and in 1927 he won the Pulitzer Prize for *In Abraham's Bosom.* By this time Green had joined the faculty at Chapel Hill and emerged as a central figure in a literary renaissance blossoming in the South. Unlike the nucleus of literary activity forming at Vanderbilt University, the circle at Chapel Hill held decidedly liberal views, and Green actively worked for civil rights for African Americans and Native Americans throughout his career.[57] Koch's concept of the importance of regional and folk culture and Green's progressive opinions on race relations would deeply shape Sarah Gertrude Knott's views.

Although Koch devoted many of his efforts to his student group, the Carolina Playmakers, he also encouraged theater in high schools, at other colleges, and in community groups. In 1923 he established the Bureau of Community Drama under the university's Extension Division and hired former pageant director Ethel Rockwell to head it. Through these outreach efforts Knott became familiar with the work of Koch and Green. After joining the faculty at Chowan College, she became involved in the Carolina Dramatic Association, serving as its vice president in 1926 and executive secretary treasurer the next year. In the wake of conflicts with Rockwell, Koch turned to the energetic Gertrude Knott for help. As Knott would recall, "Proff Koch and the University of North Carolina and Miss Rockwell who preceded me had set up a wonderful program of community drama there and she couldn't get along with Proff Koch and I said that I could because I didn't know anything and she did."[58]

In 1927, and at Koch's invitation, Knott left Chowan College to take Rockwell's former position.

Although Knott's actual work with "Proff" Koch lasted only two years, she would credit his and Green's influence the rest of her life. After thirty years of producing folk festivals she wrote to Green that Koch had inspired her dream of the National Folk Festival and that the festival was still "based on what I consciously and unconsciously learned from you & Proff."[59] Fourteen years later, as she reviewed her career near the end of her life, Knott wrote to Green again: "Since I have been at home studying the situation, I feel sure that Proff Koch and the influence I received during the time I was at the University of North Carolina, under the Carolina Dramatic Association and of course from you, and others there, introduced me to the folk activity field of a different nature and gave me the insight to use folklore and folklife in the performing arts scene, which really developed along lines that I couldn't quite analyze then. But looking back and looking through the material I can see it now."[60]

Driven by the restlessness that infected their generation, both John Lair and Sarah Gertrude Knott left the rural communities that had nurtured them in order to seek fortunes far from home. The new developments in theater and entertainment that each discovered during the 1920s led them to careers that fed a personal need to be center-stage. A passion for the theater, far more than concern for preserving the past, led them to discover their callings in life, although both keenly understood the countercurrent of nostalgia that emerged in the thoroughly modern 1920s. Perhaps happenstance dictated which theatrical model each stumbled across to use as a vehicle for staging tradition. They both spoke candidly of the accidental nature of their careers, and despite the ultimate differences between their creations neither authenticity nor commerciality seemed to much influence their choices. Both early barn dances and folk festivals had roots in popular entertainments of the early twentieth century, although radio drew more from the theatrical forms with strong comedic traditions that were largely absent in the more sober pageantry movement. Whether or not by accident, Lair and Knott perhaps found themselves drawn to the theatrical models that best suited their temperaments.

2 "Something Big": The Birth of the National Folk Festival

As the frog said to the tick, you've got hold of
something big.
—Paul Green, letter to Sarah Gertrude Knott, 1933

While John Lair slowly tested the waters of a radio career, holding on to the security of his day job, Sarah Gertrude Knott plunged headfirst into festival work. Knott did not start small. Having never attended
a folk festival, she set out to create one national in scope. Perhaps it was
just as well that the preexisting festivals did not unduly influence Knott,
for she was not tied to a glorification of Anglo-American culture. Instead,
the principles of Frederick Koch and Paul Green shaped Knott's vision,
and the festival embraced multiculturalism from the outset. Still, she
took a giant leap away from her mentors in conceiving of folk art as a
form of theatrical performance rather than as source material for theatrical presentation.

Whatever Knott's reasons for moving to St. Louis in 1929, she must
have left her position on good terms with Koch and Green. A few years
later she would ask for their help and receive it. Knott became prominent enough in her new city by 1930 that the *St. Louis Globe-Democrat*
carried a long story on her, saying she wished to "bring the theater back
to the people" through the promotion of amateur drama. As executive
director of the Dramatic League, she brought together and assisted more
than forty clubs and fifty individuals interested in community theater.
Although Knott emphasized the need for "local plays by local writers and

actors, all of them truthfully reflecting the historical or modern character of the place and people," no specific mention is made of the folk arts.[1]

How did a self-described "non-scientific folklorist, non-scholar, non-musician, non-anything much" become one of the most influential folk festival organizers of the mid-century?[2] Knott herself often seemed at a loss to answer that question. In one version of a manuscript, "The National Folk Festival USA," she wrote, "What gave you the idea for a National Folk Festival? I was often asked during the first years of the Association. . . . Usually I did not answer this question. I did not know! Finally M. J. Pickering, Business Manager of the Association from St. Louis, started speaking for me. 'It's because she is from Kentucky,' he answered. I denied it. 'We don't have this kind of music in Kentucky,' I told him."[3]

Later Knott did realize that folk traditions in far western Kentucky did exist although her interests always tended to focus on the cultures of others. In 1971 she told an interviewer that although she was "not particularly exposed" to Anglo-American folk song and dance as a child, she did choose to attend "Negro churches kind of against what would've happened to most people there in our section of Kentucky."[4] No single epiphany catapulted Knott into the folk festival movement, but over her lifetime she offered a variety of origin narratives. Appropriately multicultural, they seemed crafted to suit the particular audience she addressed.

Knott began the Dramatic League in St. Louis on the eve of the Great Depression and soon began to tailor its activities to address the problems spawned by the economic crisis. The Federal Emergency Relief Administration, an early New Deal program, supported at least some of Knott's activities.[5] As she described her activities, "For two years, from January until May, we presented programs five nights a week in the underprivileged sections where people could afford no other kind of entertainment. At first we drew our talent altogether from the dramatic clubs in universities, colleges, high schools, and churches, which made up The Dramatic League, or from cooperating musical groups."[6]

One version of events that led up to the National Folk Festival, published in 1939, describes an old man who asked to go onstage during a performance of Knott's "Strolling Players" in a city park. "Miss Knott, touched by the little old man's enthusiasm, sandwiched his fiddling in between the acts of the play. He played 'Turkey in the Straw' and sang, to his own accompaniment, 'The Wreck of the Old 97.' The impromptu act almost brought down the house literally, for the audience stamped and applauded so vigorously and enthusiastically that a five hundred–pound bale of cotton fell loose from the stage."[7] In another account Knott recalled, "To our surprise, audiences liked folk music and folk dances better, it seemed, than the dramatic offering or the more classic or modern music by trained musicians. As the weeks passed, there could be no doubt of the hold the old tunes and dances had on many people who now lived in the city."[8]

Knott's Dramatic League included "The Theater of Nations" that brought together recent immigrants to present plays in their native languages. Some participants, however, wanted to take part in the citywide recreation project. The result was a "Festival of Nations," possibly the first festival Knott would organize. Exposure to the traditions of recent immigrants had led her to wonder, "What are the songs and dances that bind us all to this country which is now home?" Soon Knott's ambitions grew, and she began to think, "Why not a National Folk Festival, bringing together groups from the different sections of the country with their folk music, dances, and plays, to see what the story would tell of our people and our country? My part would be small; merely to find and bring together those who had specialized in the various forms of folk expression, and their groups to demonstrate."[9]

After conceiving of a national festival, Knott approached several influential St. Louis businesspeople, including her "special friend" Charles Hatfield and millionaire Maurice Weil.[10] Through them, she joined forces with a veteran showman, "Major" M. J. Pickering, manager of the Coliseum, and received the support of the local Rotary Club, which provided her with office space. Through her Rotary contacts Knott also met Ralph Hubbard, who had come to St. Louis to stage an Indian pageant, and Native Americans soon become a central part of the National Folk Festival.[11]

Sarah Gertrude Knott never shied from asking for help. Of the basketful of letters she sent, the most important proved to be the one she sent to Paul Green. She did not know whether Green even remembered her, but on June 25, 1933, she told him of her marvelous idea.[12] "As the frog said to the tick, you've got hold of something big," Green replied in folksy vernacular. "If I can be of any help to you whatever," he added, "please call upon me."[13] Green may not have known what he was getting into. Unwilling to overlook an offer of help from a nationally prominent playwright, Knott offered—and Green accepted—a leadership position in the National Folk Festival Association.[14]

President Paul Green and Business Manager M. J. Pickering both served in their respective positions in the National Folk Festival Association for almost two decades, and one can only wonder how Knott managed to reconcile the advice she received from this odd couple. Pickering worked the business angle, and although the event never developed into a commercial success, he kept it financially afloat. Green, for his part, tried to steer Knott away from commercialism. In his first response to her idea, he objected only to the planned tie-in with the opening of the new Keil Municipal Auditorium. "There seems to be a little smacking of over-civic pride and gratulation. I mean that the dress looks finer than the wearer, for the generation of a national thing around a local building suggests something of the cart before the horse." In a postscript, Green added, "One of the problems will be to keep local merchant commerce out of your plan but it can be done."[15]

Getting "local merchant commerce" into the plan, however, stood at the center of Pickering's mission. Although Knott tended to follow Pickering's lead in matters of business, she listened to Green's gentle persuasion. In December 1933 she visited Green in Chapel Hill to go over her plans for the National Folk Festival. The following month he complained about the new stationery that "put the representatives of folk-culture on the back of the stationery and the representatives of finance on the front." In this matter Green prevailed. Only Knott's, Green's, and Maurice Weil's names appeared on the front, while the folklorists and business leaders were printed on the back.[16]

Other commitments often prevented the prolific Green from actually attending the National Folk Festival, but he recognized that his name and influence served Knott's cause better than his physical presence would. In February 1934, Green wrote to President Franklin Roosevelt, requesting a statement on "the importance of conserving the folk traditions on which a nation's culture ultimately rests." Roosevelt did not attend the first festival, but he replied to Green with words that the National Folk Festival Association would subsequently quote frequently:

> We in the United States are amazingly rich in the elements from which to weave a culture. We have the best of man's past on which to draw, brought to us by our native folk and folk from all parts of the world.
> In binding these elements into a National fabric of beauty and strength, let us keep the original fibres so intact that the fineness of each will show in the completed handiwork.[17]

While Knott relied on Major Pickering more often for practical advice, Green served as moral rudder for the National Folk Festival Association; his values helped shape Knott's attitudes toward folk culture. Green also served as a confidant, and although not a hands-on president he willingly lent a sympathetic ear to Knott's concerns.

Knott formulated her general procedure for organizing a folk festival during the planning stage of the first National Folk Festival. As she succinctly stated her modus operandi more than twenty years later, "I'm no authority, myself, but I know who the experts are—and I go to them first."[18] Frequently, Knott did not directly select participants for the festival but relied instead on intermediaries whom she cajoled into doing her bidding. Knott often chose academic folklorists or folklore collectors as go-betweens, but she also called on government agencies, schools and churches, social workers, and others to help identify festival participants. That the procedure made for strange bedfellows did not concern Knott as long as their beliefs did not actively work counter to the folk festival's agenda.

Two participants in the First National Folk Festival, George Pullen Jackson and Zora Neale Hurston, embody the range of academic perspectives found among Knott's advisors. One of the first scholars to study religious folk song in the South, Jackson, a professor of German at Vanderbilt University, held an active role in the festival from its beginning until his death in 1953. He served on the board and regularly brought groups of shape-note singers to the festival. Much to Knott's consternation, some scholars later dismissed Jackson's work because of his contention that African American spirituals were derived from white folk music.

The folklorist and novelist Zora Neale Hurston added an important African American presence to the first National Folk Festival. Although Hurston received academic training in anthropology and folklore under Franz Boas and teetered on the verge of success as a novelist, she, like Knott, yearned to be onstage. In 1933 Bethune-Cookman College in Daytona Beach offered Hurston an opportunity to establish a school of dramatic arts. Although she quickly decided that the job at the college did not suit her, she accepted an invitation to participate in the first National Folk Festival and took a group of students to perform folk songs and a folk play she had written. Hurston acknowledged that self-interest motivated her participation. "I am invited to come to St. Louis to the National Folk Festival of which Paul Green is the head," she told a friend. "Walter Prichard Eaton, Gertrude Knott and lots of *grand* folks behind the thing. It will bring me no money to take my dancers there, but it will give my books a push—especially 'Mules and Men,' in that it will increase my standing as a Negro folk-lorist outside of calling attention to me generally." Hurston added, "I know you'd love it. Ozark Mountaineers, lumberjacks, Indians, and Aunt Hagor's low visibility chillum. Even Pres. Roosevelt is steamed up about it."[19] Hurston and her group performed several games and folk songs, a dramatized folktale "De Fiery Chariot," and what Hurston labeled an "African Survival Ritual." Aside from Hurston's troupe, the only other African American folklore presented at the first festival was a "Negro Chorus of Three Hundred Voices."

Hurston apparently did not participate in the next few National Folk Festivals. In 1938, however, while working for the Federal Writers' Project in Florida, she organized a group of dancers and singers and took them north to perform at the National Folk Festival held at Constitution Hall in Washington, D.C.[20] In the 1940s Hurston served on the national committee of the National Folk Festival Association. Her later involvement with the festival possibly resulted from collaborations with Paul Green. Despite her complaints about the efforts of white playwrights who wrote about African American life, Hurston saw benefits to working with Green. After participating in a play-writing seminar at Green's home in 1939 she wrote to him, "I see no reason why the firm of Green and Hurston should not take charge of the Negro playrighting [*sic*] business in America, and I can see many reasons why we should."[21]

Another academic who staged folk plays at the First National Folk Festival, Arthur Campa of the University of New Mexico, developed a life-long involvement with Knott's event. While other writers of his time glorified a mythical Spanish culture in New Mexico, Campa instead explored its multicultural makeup.[22] At the 1934 National Folk Festival he presented Spanish folk songs and a religious mystery play. Campa not only became the festival's leading authority on southwestern culture but he also became one of Knott's closest academic advisors. In 1946 he moved to the University of Denver, where he chaired the Department of Modern Languages and Literature and helped develop a folklore program during the 1950s. Although Knott only once staged her festival west of Texas and Oklahoma, Campa's presence for almost forty years assured representation of the Southwest.

The prominent writer Constance Rourke also brought a group of performers to the First National Folk Festival. In 1931 she had published *American Humor: A Study of National Character*, and the folk roots of American literature held particular fascination for her. Hearing of the festival, Rourke contacted Knott, who invited, at Rourke's suggestion, a group of lumberjacks from Michigan under the direction of folklorist Earl Beck. During the early years Rourke remained an influential advisor, serving in the capacity of vice president of the National Folk Festival Association. She also helped bring national publicity to the festival with articles she wrote in *The New Republic* in 1934 and 1935.[23]

A number of other academic and applied folklorists worked primarily as advisors. Before the 1934 festival Knott managed to identify and contact, probably with Paul Green's help, most of the prominent individuals in the discipline. She later claimed that the first response she received came from the eminent Harvard folklorist George Lyman Kittredge, who wired his acceptance to a position on the advisory board. Although no record exists of his active participation in the National Folk Festival Association, Kittredge served on its board until his death in 1941. Louise Pound, a ballad scholar at the University of Nebraska, was more actively involved. Pound, who nicknamed Knott "Go Gettin' Gertie," attended and actively promoted several festivals.[24]

Probably the most influential of Knott's advisors among the folklorists, Ben Botkin, an assistant professor at the University of Oklahoma in 1934, actively assisted in the initial planning stages of the first festival. In 1937 Botkin moved to Washington to conduct research as a fellow at the Library of Congress. Subsequently, he became the first national folklore editor of the Federal Writers' Project and was later head of the library's Archive of Folk Song. Botkin became best known for his popular books, especially *A Treasury of American Folklore*. Although dismissed by some as a popularizer, in more recent years folklorists have recognized his innovative work in the areas of multiculturalism, urban and occupational folklore, and applied folklore.[25]

The list of other notable folklorists who served on the national committee of the National Folk Festival Association during its first decade includes Frances Densmore of the Bureau of American Ethnology, an early researcher in American Indian music; Martha Beckwith, president of the American Folklore Society from 1932 to 1933, known for her research in Jamaican, Native American, Portuguese, and Hawaiian folklore; ballad scholar H. M. Belden of the University of Missouri; and Indiana University's Stith Thompson. Notably absent from this list, John and Alan Lomax never involved themselves in Knott's festival. John Lomax's name apparently appeared on an early list of advisors, but he either declined to serve or did not receive an invitation. Knott was undoubtedly familiar with Lomax's well-known publications, but he also had personal conflicts with a number of the prominent members of the National Folk Festival Association's board during the 1930s and 1940s. His son, Alan, recorded at least one of Knott's regional festivals and corresponded with her but also never served on the board. Many years later, after retirement, Knott told Bess Lomax Hawes, "I will send you a few things about the over-all National Folk Festival Association. Your father knew about it and so does Alan. I am not sure how much they agreed, but I think they did respect the plan."[26]

Despite Knott's considerable successes in alliance-building, neither the earlier or later manifestations of the Washington folk establishment ever fully accepted her. Her political views during the 1930s, however, remained in tune with the spirit of the New Deal. Although some members of her advisory board valued only Anglo-American folk culture, the academics to whom she listened were those with liberal and pluralistic views. When, at a meeting in Nashville before the second National Folk Festival in Chattanooga, advisors from Tennessee urged her not to include Indian and Spanish American traditions because they were "doomed to die" and not part of the cultural pattern of the United States, Knott ignored them.[27] Throughout her career she credited three individuals as her most influential advisors: Paul Green, Arthur Campa, and Ben Botkin.

Knott's main strategy for finding performers consisted of contacting experts, but she employed a secondary strategy as well: staging small, regional festivals. She designed these preliminary festivals to identify folk artists who would "win" a chance to perform at the National. The mini-festivals also generated publicity for the National Folk Festival, and Knott used the small admission fees charged to offset the costs of bringing the "winners" to her big festival. As Knott formulated the plans for her first festival she knew she wished to feature traditions of the "great seedbed of Anglo-Saxon lore" that lay in St. Louis's backyard. She did not select an academic folklorist to direct the Ozark festivals but rather chose a popular local journalist, May Kennedy McCord, who wrote a column entitled "Hillbilly Heartbeats" for the *Springfield Daily News.*

Of the first preliminary festival, held in Eureka Springs, Arkansas, on March 15, 1934, folklore collector Vance Randolph recalled, "I attended this meeting myself, and heard plenty of good singers, fiddlers and banjo-pickers." Randolph bragged that the National Folk Festival did not originate in St. Louis, but instead, "The truth is that the whole thing began in Arkansas." He also noted the success of subsequent small gatherings of local folk in the Arkansas Ozarks after "Miss Knott's national organization had shown the way."[28]

Vance Randolph had ulterior motives for participating in the Ozark festivals—his attraction to Sarah Gertrude Knott. Whatever his intentions, however, the appearance on the scene of the courtly and charming Bascom Lamar Lunsford apparently thwarted his plans. Lunsford and Randolph both acted as judges for an All-Ozark festival held in Springfield, Missouri, in mid-April. Whether Lunsford and Knott actually felt mutual attraction or were merely excited about each other's work cannot be known; throughout her life Knott remained tight-lipped about relationships with men. Whatever the case, the attention she paid to Lunsford, who had a much greater role than Randolph in the First National Folk Festival, inspired considerable jealously on Randolph's part.[29]

Randolph also received the brunt of antifestival feelings growing among some Chamber of Commerce members in the Ozarks who feared that the festival might impair the image they nurtured of the region as being progressive. At the opening dinner of the Ozark Folk Festival in Springfield, a local Chamber member, although claiming support for the festival itself, delivered a scathing attack on those who wrote about the Ozarks. Randolph, among the honorees at the banquet, refused to respond that night to the attack, although McCord and others came to his defense.[30] McCord also used her column to battle those who opposed the festival. In one article she noted that the Chamber of Commerce in Asheville, North Carolina, planned to pay Lunsford to bring a cross-section of his Mountain Dance and Folk Festival to St. Louis for the National. She also stressed the national publicity that the folk festival attracted: "If Hillbilly isn't taking the map right now, then I'll eat my hat. Folk Festival news everywhere—Reporters running around photographing everybody. . . . A reporter from the United Press cornered me for an hour and a half to learn all about square dancing!"[31]

McCord elicited active participation from readers of "Hillbilly Heartbeats." Reporting that the Russell Sage Foundation would be sponsoring an exhibition of crafts, she stated, "I want us in the Ozarks to show that we have old stuff." The next week, after writing a column on old shape-note books, McCord asked, "Now do any of you folks have groups or know of groups of people anywhere who would sing some of these old religious songs, as group, quartette or any ensemble form, in the coming Ozark festival? Will anyone sing old folk songs alone or accompanied by guitar or fiddle or banjo or dulcimer? Or no other way, I'll play the guitar accompaniment for you myself. Will you, Mrs. Adams at Miller?"[32]

Of course, not all who showed up at the Ozark festivals had what the organizers wanted. Knott later noted that participants "had never before been faced with a problem of separating their songs and dances into any special categories," and she and the other organizers "sometimes had to sit through tap dances, or listen to popular songs."[33] In her column, McCord wrote of a similar problem. A group who had an act similar to the Weaver Brothers could not understand why the organizers could not use them. "Finally, after talking with Miss Knott and Vance Randolph and myself, a light broke in upon them and they began to sing the songs we wanted, but they didn't dream would ever be sung . . . I kept softening down their lovely accompaniments, and 'working them over.'"[34] When the same group performed at the National Folk Festival, the *St. Louis Daily Globe-Democrat* described them as singing "a mournful, bucolic ballad of the type heard in hillbilly programs on the radio" but hastened to add that the song had "been sung in Ozarks [sic] since before the civil war and is indigenous rather than manufactured."[35]

Previous folk festivals already established the tradition of folk festival organizers shaping performances to their own tastes rather than those of the performers. Knott, to her credit, at least struggled with some of the distinctions and held more open-minded (or, to some, less discerning) views than her more purist colleagues. Her encounters in the Ozarks began a lifetime struggle with distinguishing between folk and hillbilly music. "What does the word 'hillbilly' mean?" she asked several years later. "Does it refer to the kinds of songs or music or is it the style of singing or playing? What is its place in the folklore field?"[36] In 1956 Knott advised Maud Karpeles of the International Folk Music Council, who believed that radio was destroying American folk singing, "While there is no doubt that the new and cheapened versions of many of our folk songs are much in vogue everywhere—still many of the so-called 'hillbilly' singers alos [sic] still know the genuine traditional British ballads and our own real folk songs—if we can dignify them, and I believe we are doing that in a number of ways now, I doubt that it is necessary for our folksong tradition to pass."[37] Knott's reading, after retirement, of Bill Malone's *Country Music, U.S.A.* finally made the pieces fall into place. In April 1972 she told Malone, "You sold me on Country Music!"[38] "I have been studying the book—Country Music USA by Bill Malone," she informed folklorists D. K. Wilgus and Wayland Hand. "This book makes sense to me."[39]

According to Knott, more than seventy participants selected from Ozark festivals performed songs and dances, retold legends, and described other traditions at the First National Folk Festival. Local Ozark folk did not open the program, however; Knott gave that privilege to Native American performers. As the *St. Louis Post Dispatch* stated in an editorial the day after the opening, Knott "recognized that the Indian had developed a high order of folk art long before the white man came by giving a first place to the native music and dances of members of the Kiowa tribe in Oklahoma."[40]

The First National Folk Festival opened on April 29, 1934, and ran for four days. Along with the Kiowas and the many Ozark performers, the event included Lunsford's contingent, George Pullen Jackson's shape-note singers, Jean Thomas presenting Jilson Setters, and a program of Vermont folk songs. Along with Hurston's presentations of African American lore and Campa's Hispanic traditions, groups from Vincennes, Indiana, and St. Genevieve, Missouri, represented French American culture. Ironically, Knott did not invite the recent immigrants who helped inspire her to create the festival. Although the policy changed after a few years, she included only ethnic groups with a long established presence in America in the initial festivals.

The festival also featured three occupational groups, including retired seamen from the Sailor's Snug Harbor on Staten Island who performed chanteys. Years later Knott described her fortuitous discovery of these performers: "I was in New York—at a newspaper. . . . They said you ought to have the sailors from Snug Harbor. And I went up there. I called up . . . and I said, 'I'd like to come out.' And they said, 'Well, we're glad to have you.' And I remember what they said. They said, 'But we ain't no society people.' I said, 'Well, I'm not either.'"[41] Along with the sailors, Romaine Lowdermilk and Jack Widmer presented cowboy songs and traditions, and Constance Rourke presented the lumberjacks from Michigan. Cowboys, sailors, and lumberjacks, as representational occupational groups, might now seem hopelessly romantic or even corny, but Knott should be credited as the first person to present occupational lore as a part of a folk festival.

Finally, in keeping with the festival's roots in folk drama, Knott staged three plays by the Carolina Playmakers, including Paul Green's *Quare Medicine.* Her other theatrical mentor, Frederick Koch, attended the festival and introduced one of the plays. Knott's early festivals typically included the production of these folk plays, but they were eventually phased out because of production costs. Exhibitions of folk art and crafts were a standard part of the National Folk Festival from its outset. The festival in St. Louis included the Southern Highland Handicraft Guild's first major traveling exhibit, "Handicrafts of the Southern Highlands," curated by Allen Eaton.[42] There was also an exhibition of paintings by Kiowa artists.[43]

The inclusion of sessions for academics and other "practitioners" stands as another important innovation of Knott's festival. Although open to the general public, these sessions do not appear in the printed programs of the first two events. In planning for her third national festival, however, Knott directed, "There should be morning sessions during at least three of the mornings during the Festival, in which leaders from the various folk fields in the United States would meet in conference for discussion and interchange of ideas. Our morning conferences have given the leaders a more genuine national viewpoint and broader conception of the American folk expressions."[44] The "forenoon folklore discussions" in St. Louis featured most of the folklore presenters and included a paper on "Folk Arts and Crafts at the Folk Festival."[45] As well as providing intellectual exchange among folklorists, the morning conferences explored forms of folklore such as material culture and belief that were less amenable to presentation on the stage.

To a remarkable degree the First National Folk Festival set the mold for Knott's subsequent presentations. In the printed program she included brief contextual notes to some performances (often with snippets of quotations from the experts) and the names of some, but never all, performers. Knott tended to be far more scrupulous in listing the presenters and the sponsors. Although not formalized, the first festival also set the policy for not paying most performers. Performers at the preliminary festivals "won" the opportunity to perform at the National, and Knott used the small proceeds of the regional festivals to help defray travel expenses. She and many intermediaries also worked to secure funding from a variety of external sources, including educational institutions and private businesses. Sources of support for the First National Folk Festival included the Chambers of Commerce in Ft. Worth, Texas, and Asheville, North Carolina; the Michigan Tourist and Resort Association sponsored the lumberjacks. Nor did Knott pay the expenses of folklorists and other festival presenters. Some, such as Zora Neale Hurston and later John Lair, came because they thought the festival could further their careers. As their reputations grew, their interest in helping Knott dwindled. She charged an admission fee for most of her festivals, but it was modest. Even with the policy of not paying performers or presenters, the early festivals consistently lost money.

Overall, the First National Folk Festival appears to have been a popular and critical success. After the opening day the *St. Louis Post-Dispatch* described the event as "not only pleasantly diverting, but richly informative and truly cultural." The coverage particularly emphasized the more exotic performers such as Native Americans, lumberjacks, and sailors.[46] The *Globe-Democrat*, which almost two decades later became the National Folk Festival's sponsor, put more emphasis on local performers, although not without some condescension. One subheading characterized the singing of participants from the Ozarks as "nasal vocal offerings."[47]

After the festival was over the National Folk Festival Association took a more formal shape. As Knott recalled, "Seems to me the original plan was written down with suggestions by George Pullen Jackson (who actually wrote it), Campa, and Botkin, especially."[48] The final version of the "General Plan" stated: "The National Folk Festival has as object the bringing together of groups from various sections of the United States, with their characteristic folk expression, in the faith that national incentive gives encouragement to regional festivals, and that continued participation in such festivals keeps alive the fine traditional customs associated with the founding of this nation." Moreover, the festival provided "basic cultural leisure-time activity" and presented material that "may inspire future artistic creations." The document articulated the genres presented at the festival: folk music (both traditional and "compositions, choral and individual, based on American folk music"); folk dances; folk plays ("suitable plays, which utilize native folk material"); folk arts and handicrafts; and legends and superstitions ("told in special sessions"). The plan also specified the inclusion of conferences of "participants and authorities" as part of the program.[49]

The First National Folk Festival lost several thousand dollars. "Chances are," Knott later wrote, "that it made little difference with this group of men, who for years had guaranteed the necessary money for the Municipal Opera." She added, "We were conscious of the loss, and though it had not been our gain, we did not feel like asking them to continue the financial risk for the continuation of the festival which they had undertaken for its creation. Then, perhaps, we thought it might be wise anyway to move from city to city."[50]

Knott and Major Pickering saw a fresh opportunity when a group from Chattanooga contacted Pickering, asking if he could help them with a spring festival. Pickering suggested instead that they sponsor the second National Folk Festival.[51] Knott was thrilled to be going to "another state rich in the same Anglo-Saxon traditions we had found in the Ozarks." They had much less time to prepare for the event than they did in St. Louis, however, and did not find the "broad shoulders of specialists upon which to lean" in Tennessee. Knott planned preliminary festivals for Birchwood, Crossville, and Chattanooga as well as an impromptu festival at Soddy, which she described as "just a neighborly gathering, and to me it was more interesting than any of the other Tennessee festivals because of its naturalness."[52]

As in the Ozarks, Knott found some local citizens sensitive to the fact that the promotion of folk traditions could be linked to negative regional stereotypes. The following year she recalled, "In the Tennessee mountains a picture of a very disreputable mountaineer was put in the Chattanooga Times as representing the type of mountaineer who would participate in our National Folk Festival. This caused quite a furor among the mountain people, and did not build us up in a dignified way with the people who would make up our audience."[53] Subsequently, Knott attempted to have absolute control over the photographs released to the press for the promotion of the festival.

The second National Folk Festival, held in Chattanooga from May 14 to 18, 1935, featured many of the same performers and presenters as the previous year. Chattanooga's festival also included for the first time the folklore of an industrial occupational group, Pennsylvania's anthracite coal miners, as well as a new ethnic group, Pennsylvania Germans. After reading *Songs and Ballads of the Anthracite Miner* Knott decided to invite its author, George Korson, to bring a group to the festival, and Pickering met with him to suggest the idea. Korson, in turn, secured funding from John L. Lewis of the United Mineworkers. Inspired by the idea of a folk festival, Korson organized the first Pennsylvania Folk Festival, which was held less than two weeks before the festival in Chattanooga. As well as bringing performers to Tennessee, Korson also read a paper at the morning session at the second National Folk Festival.[54]

Zora Neale Hurston did not attend the festival in Chattanooga. Instead, Knott worked through African American religious, educational, and social organizations, the "uplifters" Hurston wryly referred to as "Negrotarians."[55] This time the chorus, locally based in Chattanooga, had a thousand voices. The Bonny Oaks School provided spirituals, and the Girl Reserves of the YWCA presented African American games. The festival also featured a performance by the Fisk Jubilee Singers. During the same year, Thomas E. Jones, president of Fisk University, a traditionally African American institution, joined the executive committee of the National Folk Festival Association.

Knott's uncritical eagerness to recruit any and all representatives of American folk culture reflected a degree of naiveté on her part, particularly in the representation of African American culture. In 1935 she repeatedly tried to recruit an all-white and racially conservative Charleston group, the Society for the Preservation of Negro Spirituals (SPS), to perform at the Chattanooga festival. When rebuffed, she asked whether they could not instead send "a few of the Gullahs." Others saw the SPS as a legitimate preserver of African American tradition as well. Earlier the same year the group performed for Franklin and Eleanor Roosevelt and their guests at the White House.[56]

Although the Kiowas once again opened the program, the National Folk Festival in Chattanooga also included representatives of the Eastern Band of Cherokee. The great dance leader Will West Long, who actively promoted the revival of Cherokee dance, performed in Chattanooga along with his half-nephew Walker Calhoun. The Cherokee dancers shared the same part of the program as Lunsford's square dance teams. In fact, one of the two groups Lunsford featured, Arnold Cooper's Great Smoky Mountains Square Dance Team, consisted primarily of Cherokee performers.[57] Other performers brought by Lunsford included Sam Queen and the Soco Gap Dancers, who four years later performed at the White House for the queen and king of England, along with Lair and the Coon Creek Girls; fiddler Bill Hensley; and the legendary banjo player Samantha Bumgarner.

Although the festival once again lost money, Knott and her advisors developed ambitious plans to establish a permanent home for the festival. She and Pickering formed a small executive board that included Paul Green as president and Constance Rourke as vice chair; Thomas E. Jones of Fisk and Louise Pound of the University of Nebraska also served. Nonacademic members of the board included F. W. Reeves of the Tennessee Valley Authority and Charles F. Hatfield from St. Louis. The group planned to establish a year-round, permanent organization to carry on the National Folk Festival and cooperating regional festivals.

Surprisingly, the plan placed great emphasis on a strong tie-in with academic institutions. Noting the support already received for the festival from various universities and colleges, the authors wrote that the National Folk Festival should be permanently located in a city that was "a strong university center and is interested in developing a folk-lore program." Other specifications included location in a region rich in folklore and a city with "general cultural interests" and "proper radio facilities." The executive committee planned to apply for foundation funds to start "courses in research for students on a five year plan." That plan would include a foundation course taught by Knott assisted by "such men as" G. L. Kittredge, Arthur Campa, Ben Botkin, and Bascom Lamar Lunsford. The class would include methods for developing community and state festivals. Other folklore courses offered by teachers in regular departments of the school, working in cooperation with the National Folk Festival, would accompany the foundation course. At the beginning of the second year a course in the "Organization of Courses of Study and Technique of Presentation" would be added to the curriculum.

The plan proposed an annual budget of $40,000. Foundation funds would be used for leadership training and for research to be carried on at the cooperating university. A local citizen's committee and the board would assume financial responsibility for the festival itself. At the time of its writing, the board assumed that the next festival would be held again in Tennessee, with the opening scheduled for Norris to correspond with the dedication of the Tennessee Valley Authority's dam. They hoped that the latter location would ensure the presence of the president or first lady. Proposed sites for the festival itself included various venues in either Knoxville or Nashville, including the Ryman Auditorium, which later became home to the Grand Ole Opry. Although unstated, the executive board probably hoped that the proposed academic program would be housed at either the University of Tennessee or Vanderbilt University. Thomas E. Jones served on the executive board, but the document made no specific mention of the involvement of Fisk University.[58] The ambitious plan did not reach fruition; the early proposal was decades ahead of its time. Some academic programs in English and anthropology offered folklore courses in the mid-1930s, but no academic folklore programs yet existed. Furthermore, no folklore programs integrated an applied dimension until the 1970s and 1980s.

Although plans for another National Folk Festival in Tennessee fell through, Knott continued to search for support. After the Chattanooga festival she traveled to Washington and New York, where she met with representatives from the American Council on Education, the Federal Bureau of Education, and the Carnegie and Rockefeller foundations. While in Washington she visited the White House at the invitation of Eleanor Roosevelt. Later the same year she returned to the East Coast, this time meeting with interested parties at Columbia University and with John Collier of the Bureau of Indian Affairs.[59]

Sarah Gertrude Knott eagerly furthered her education about folk traditions and the organizations that supported their preservation. With her eyes now open, folk performances seemed to spring up all around her. After her first trip to New York and Washington, Knott sailed to London to attend the First International Folk Dance Festival in order to compare the National Folk Festival Association's plan with those of other countries. According to an account written on her return, she thought that while at sea she would have a chance to forget about folklore for a while. That was not to be the case. "It was a moonlight night in July; we were all on deck, wondering what to do when suddenly a group of twelve men made the decision and burst into song and dance." The group was a Maccabee motorcycle team headed home after a goodwill tour for the Zionist movement. A Greek woman from Chicago then began to sing, and "these unexpected finds gave me the idea of a folk festival at sea. . . . We sent out notices to every deck and just after the sun went down, on the last night out, the crowd began to gather for a folk festival, which was to include the folk expressions that they had carried on here in their new homes."[60] The story may seem a bit fanciful, but it probably accurately indicates the energy and enthusiasm (as well as compulsion to organize) that Knott brought to her new mission in life.

After returning from England, Knott spent a month at Fisk University, studying African American folklore, and then another month in Oklahoma on "Indian research."[61] While in Oklahoma at the invitation of Ben Botkin, she read a paper at the Southwest Cultural Conference at the University of Oklahoma and apparently drummed up quite a bit of enthusiasm for her festival. On November 20, 1935, Botkin informed John Gould Fletcher in Arkansas that Knott had come over to discuss the possibility of holding the next National Folk Festival in Norman. Botkin noted that despite the fact that enthusiasm ran high for the idea, he doubted whether the university would be able to cooperate financially. Dallas, he wrote, seemed to be the likely site for the next festival.[62]

Dallas was indeed a likely locale. In 1936 Texas would celebrate its centennial, and Pickering and Knott actively campaigned to be included in the festivities. As usual, Knott's dreams were expansive. Following up on a visit a few days earlier, she advised Frank Watson, director of promotion for the Texas Centennial Commission, not only of her proposed plans for the festival but also of the possibility of "developing a permanent organization which might make our Festival alternate each year between the Southeastern and Southwestern regions."[63] Two days later Pickering also wrote to Watson, outlining a budget and stating that they would not object to a "dignified" sponsor such as Ford, General Motors, or Sears-Roebuck. Noting Henry Ford's personal interest in American folk dancing, Pickering added that they had already made contact with the Ford organization as well as with the Agricultural Foundation, a Sears-Roebuck–supported agency.[64] Sponsorship apparently did not materialize, but the commission gave the festival a relatively generous budget if not fully what Pickering requested.[65]

The surviving draft of the contract between the National Folk Festival and the Texas Centennial Exposition specifies "American Indians, Spanish Americans, Pennsylvania Germans, French Americans, Cowboys, Mountaineers, Country people, anthracite coal miners, lumberjacks and sailors" but makes no mention of African Americans. The centennial committee had little interest in representing this group, and, in fact, the federal government separately funded a "Hall of Negro Life." Knott, however, did not disguise from the organizers her interest in having strong African American participation in the festival. In early January 1936 she produced a four-page memo, "Things I Have Done," for centennial representatives and reported that she had been in touch with A. Maceo Smith, leader of the Dallas Negro Chamber of Commerce, and was going to call a meeting of "about fifteen outstanding Negroes from Dallas." She also hoped to stage African American festivals throughout Texas in order to select participants for the National Folk Festival.[66] A subsequent press release stated that Knott discovered "a greater wealth of Negro material in Texas than in any other part of the country" and was receiving "splendid" cooperation from "Negro educators and leaders."[67] Among the members of the Dallas Negro Folk Festival committee was the African American folklorist John Mason Brewer, who thirty-five years later joined the executive committee of the National Folk Festival Association.

In a memo of May 6, 1936, Sarah Gertrude Knott responded to Smith's inquiry about the National Folk Festival's plan for "Negro Day," scheduled for June 19. Knott had already planned to feature a statewide chorus of five thousand in the Cotton Bowl, a presentation of Paul Green's play *No Count Boy,* and "singing games, square dances, cakewalks, slave tales, etc." In addition, "We should like very much your co-operation in bringing the Fisk Jubilee Singers to Dallas on Negro Day to top off our program of negro spirituals. We believe that the contrast between Cab Calloway and the type of program that we are representing would be a fine thing for your day, adding to the dignity of the spiritual along with the gaiety of Cab Calloway."[68] The printed program for the third National Folk Festival did not specify June 19 as Negro Day, although it listed a large number of African American performances scheduled for that day.

Knott used extensive networks of contacts in arranging for the performance of African American folklore, but some forms did not need searching. They appeared before her eyes. "One morning," she wrote, "I heard peculiar rhythmic chants and looked around to find a group of Negroes tamping ties for the street car track that was to run in front of the Administration Building. These were just the songs we had been looking for."[69] Knott also found singers among African American women employed in a Works Progress Administration (WPA) sewing project. After a day of sewing, more than two thousand would gather to sing together before leaving for the day. "As the serious procession moved out," Knott remembered, "we imagined that the economic struggle for existence in these depression days made them sing with genuine understanding the songs another oppression brought into being."[70]

Despite Knott's enthusiasm, Dallas posed difficulties that she had not encountered in St. Louis or Chattanooga. In planning the festival, she acceded to some degree to the segregated nature of Texas society, both by staging separate preliminary folk festivals for African Americans and by featuring African American folklore in the Hall of Negro Life. Yet the printed program for the festival clearly indicates that all races performed on the main stage every night.[71] As with other difficult issues, in the matter of race Knott charged ahead with deliberate naiveté. Probably not by chance, however, she avoided the Deep South for decades in staging the National Folk Festival.

The real success of the Texas undertaking lay in the regional festivals. Knott later referred to Texas as the "happy hunting ground" for the extent to which folk traditions survived in daily life. Before the third National Folk Festival in Dallas, Knott staged thirty community festivals, including large ones in Fort Worth and Houston sponsored by local recreation departments and a number of more intimate gatherings. German language and lore dominated the festival in Fredericksburg, whereas the San Antonio festival emphasized Hispanic lore. West Texas festivals featured cowboy culture. As a result of the smaller events Knott created a National Folk Festival rich in Texas lore.

Knott's plans also called for regional festivals in adjoining states. Before the festival she made extensive contacts in New Mexico, Arkansas, and Oklahoma. In particular, her work in Oklahoma expanded the representation of Native Americans. In November 1935 she stated that she had already laid plans for a possible "Five Tribes Festival" to be held in Muskogee.[72] Significant additions to the National Folk Festival roster also came from Louisiana. Under the direction of Lauren C. Post, the Louisiana Folk Festival sponsored by Louisiana State University selected participants for the National Folk Festival. Louisiana performers in Dallas included an Acadian band from Lake Arthur, consisting primarily of members of the Broussard family; the Evangeline Band of St. Martinville; and an African American male quartet from Southern University. In his memoir, the aspiring folklorist William A. Owens singled out the performance of "J'ai passé devant ta porte" by Elmore Sonnier of Scott, Louisiana, as one of the moments of beauty at the festival. Writing of Irene Whitfield and her group from Lafayette, Owens also recalled, "In the long stretches between shows I often sat with them listening to a kind of singing and playing that never got on the stage—too spontaneous, not professional enough."[73] The best music may have been performed off-stage, but the 1936 National Folk Festival gave Cajun music national exposure that it had never before received.

In her more than thirty-five-year career the Dallas festival was the most ambitious that Knott undertook. She was used to confining the festival to a single building, and the centennial grounds provided a huge challenge. The formal evening program would be held in the band shell, and daytime activities were scheduled at seven other sites. Square dancers and cowboy bands performed outside the Texas State Building, the Hall of Religion served as the venue for sacred harp singing, and the Domestic Arts Building Plaza featured mountain bands and fiddlers.[74]

The Horticultural Building contained the "Handicraft Exhibition of the National Folk Festival." Apparently one of the more successful aspects of the festival's undertakings in Dallas, Major Pickering made arrangements to leave most of the handicraft exhibit for the remainder of the centennial celebration. Noting that tens of thousands of women had visited the exhibit and reacted positively to it, Pickering suggested to the centennial committee that Knott remain to act as the exhibit's director at a suggested salary of $40 a week plus two paid assistants.[75]

The Horticultural Building also included a display of books written by members of Knott's national committee. The academics and collectors themselves convened in the Artists Auditorium. Over the course of several afternoons Ben Botkin, Louise Pound, George Korson, Bascom Lamar Lunsford, and Jean Thomas as well as a number of regional collectors read papers. Frederick Koch was on hand to speak on "Making an American Folk Drama." As usual, no record exists of how many people actually heard the papers, but Knott's stage directions call for seating for two to three hundred, with "no amplification necessary."[76]

Notably, the opening night of the festival lacked any emphasis on Anglo-American traditions. The evening began as usual with Native American music and dance, an honor accorded to a Tigua group from El Paso. Other performances included music and dance from a *tipica* orchestra, the singing of early Spanish mission hymns, songs performed by the El Paso County Colored Pioneer Club, and spirituals sung by a local group from Booker T. Washington High School. Squeezed in the middle of the program was a square dance by the "Centennial 8 of Dallas Figure Eight."

Perhaps Knott, in her ambition, had bitten off more than her organization could chew. In *Texas Folk Songs* William A. Owens left an account of his experience as stage manager for the performances in the band shell. Although all folk festivals are a bit chaotic behind the scenes, Owens, in his introduction to "professional folkloring," was taken aback by the lack of preparation: "The Centennial was in its first days a rather disorganized affair, and the National Folk Festival was the most confused event of all. A great number of real folk had come from far and near to sing ballads, dance reels, and tell tales. The National Folk Festival was unprepared for so many, and the folk were unprepared for the lack of attention they received." Nor, as Owens discovered his first night, did the promise of racial understanding always emerge from such a climate. When a group of women from Dallas's music clubs, invited to sing Stephen Foster songs, grew indignant when an African American choir went onstage first, they began to sing, in competition with the choir, from their seats. The same night, a Mexican tipica orchestra and a group of Kiowa dancers almost came to fisticuffs when the musicians, seated onstage during the dancers' performance, started mocking the Kiowas.[77]

Knott would never admit to racial strife erupting at her festival, but she did admit that the Dallas festival had a chaotic side, later referring to it as a "three-ring circus." "This was the second week of the Centennial," she recalled, "and things had not settled down. Although much interest had been around in communities throughout the state, most on the Centennial grounds had never heard of the National Folk Festival and to them it was just another show—a free one at that. Since there was no admission fee, those who made up the audience came and went at will." In the end, Knott was not sure whether the third National Folk Festival had either educated or entertained. The consolation was in the success of the regional festivals: "Time proved that the emphasis put on folk traditions throughout the state that year bore fruit. The strong revival of interest in many localities dates back to 1936."[78]

With Dallas under their belts, Knott and Pickering stepped up efforts to find a permanent home for their festival. In December they wrote to Marcus Weil and Charles F. Hatfield, noting that they could not continue to maintain the festival's headquarters in St. Louis at their own expense. Knott and Pickering went on to mention that several cities had expressed interest in the 1937 festival, including Richmond, Chicago, Cleveland, and Charleston, South Carolina.[79] At the same time, they approached W. Roy Mackenzie, head of the Department of English at Washington University, about a possible plan of cooperation between the university, the Rockefeller Foundation, and the National Folk Festival. Charles Hatfield contacted the university's chancellor, George R. Throop, to endorse the plan. Referring to Knott as the "outstanding genius and wonder-woman in this folk festival movement," Hatfield noted that he knew of no other event in the previous three years that had brought such positive publicity to St. Louis, and it was too valuable a national organization to lose.[80] Throop also received a letter from Henry J. Gerling, superintendent of instruction, endorsing Washington University's support of a permanent Folk Festival headquarters.[81]

On New Year's Day, Pickering again wrote to Hatfield and Weil, this time more explicitly laying out the financial picture. Pickering outlined his and Knott's various activities of the past four years, as well as the money they spent for travel and maintaining an office at the Coliseum in St. Louis. He noted that they had resisted commercializing their work because doing so would be "fatal" to their endeavor, but they could not continue without some financial return. So far, Knott had used an inheritance from her grandfather, and he had run through his savings. Finally getting down to dollars and cents, Pickering asked for a minimum salary of $5,000 per year each. He indicated, however, that he and Knott were willing to wait for plans to mature if they could receive drawing accounts of $75 per week as well as ordinary office and traveling expenses. Pickering noted that if commercial prospects developed, they would also ask for recompenses for past services totaling $12,500 for Sarah Gertrude Knott for work completed between 1933 and 1936 and $9,500 for himself for work between 1934 and 1936.[82]

Whether or not the request for $22,000 in compensation for past services played a role, the deal with St. Louis fell through. Chicago became the site of the fourth National Folk Festival. Sponsored by the Adult Education Council, the fourth National Folk Festival took place as part of the Chicago Charter Jubilee celebrations. As with Chattanooga, Knott and Pickering rushed to get the festival onstage by May. As usual, Knott called on the individuals and groups who had previously performed at the National Festival or the many regional festivals, but she also wished to include folklore of the surrounding region. On a radio program in April, Knott characterized the festival as the first "north of the Mason-Dixon Line." She admitted that people who lived in the South thought that the "chief traditional American expressions are to be found in that section," but added, "we may have to revise our ways of thinking." Knott reported that she had just returned from a trip to Wisconsin and later in the week would be traveling to Indiana and downstate Illinois.[83]

Arguing that "certain racial groups have integrated more in the American cultural life than others," Knott tended to expand with new regional representatives of groups that had already performed at the festival. In Chicago this included Germans from Milwaukee and Winnebago Indians who would perform along with "our Kiowas from Oklahoma."[84] Knott also found southern folklore surviving in urban Chicago. "Why, right here in this city," she informed the *Chicago Daily News*, "it has been a pleasant surprise to find that there are many nonprofessional Negro singers who have learned from their parents or grandparents the real songs of the cotton fields and southern camp meetings."[85]

Knott also hoped to include more lumberjacks, this time adding a group from Wisconsin. She enlisted the help of a cafe owner, Otto Rindlisbacher, who had previously assisted ballad scholar Franz Rickaby in his study of lumber-camp songs. Unlike the predominantly Anglo-Celtic lore presented by Michigan lumberjacks, Rindlisbacher's program for the National Folk Festival emphasized the ethnic diversity of the camps and included Scandinavian music and dance, French Indian fiddle tunes, and French Canadian dialect stories. Through Rindlisbacher's efforts the Wisconsin

lumberjacks slid representation of recent immigrant groups through the
back door of the National Folk Festival.[86] Rindlisbacher also represented
a different kind of presenter than Knott commonly used. Although Knott
often used educated outsiders such as academically trained folklorists as
presenters, she also began to use insiders like Rindlisbacher, especially
as she added "new Americans" to the National Folk Festival roster.[87]
Although the policy had not yet officially changed, the high profile of
more recent immigrants in Chicago led to some rule-bending. Another
soon-to-be National Folk Festival stalwart, Vyts Beliajus, who led a group
of Lithuanian dancers, also joined the ranks in Chicago.

Knott allowed groups such as Rindlisbacher's to construct their own
representations of their region or occupation, but she still leaned heavily
on scholars and nationally prominent authors. In her radio broadcast for
WCFL, Knott credited "three outstanding authorities in the folk field"
who helped in the National Folk Festival Association's understanding
of Chicago and the upper Midwest.[88] No other record confirms that poet
Carl Sandburg was involved with the National Folk Festival Association. The other two, Frances Densmore and Stith Thompson, both academic folklorists, joined the national committee. Although Thompson
had reservations about the festival's format, he served on the committee
for more than two decades.

Throughout her career Knott always made efforts to court academic
folklorists and frequently took stands that she felt would please them.
This included occasionally making statements about the detrimental
effects of mass media. In a 1939 article for the *Southern Folklore Quarterly*, for example, she observed, "With the picture show, radio and other
forms of newer entertainment now within the easy reach of most, many
of the forms that served an older, simpler America will pass unnoticed
unless stimulus is given to those who carry in their hearts these fine
traditions."[89]

Knott and Pickering eagerly exploited the mass media, however,
when doing so furthered their goals. In his January 1937 letter to Hatfield and Weil, Pickering maintained that over the previous three years
he and Knott had learned how to use the local and national media. On
a recent trip to New York they had visited again with NBC officials and
made a contact at CBS. Most important, they had opened negotiations
for commercial sponsorship of a "National Folk Festival of the Air."[90]
This virtual festival never came into being, but four months later Knott,
rather than distancing herself from one of the nation's foremost purveyors
of hillbilly music, enlisted WLS's help in locating and sponsoring talent
for the National Folk Festival in Chicago.

The Redbud Schoolhouse before John Lair moved it to the Renfro Valley complex. (Southern Appalachian Archives, Berea College)

The Knott family, circa 1901. Sarah Gertrude stands to the left of her father, with her younger sister, Gladys, and older sister, Lannie, on the right. (Yvonne Dodge Collection)

Gladys (left) and Sarah Gertrude Knott. (Yvonne Dodge Collection)

The Knott sisters later in life. Sarah Gertrude is left, Lannie is seated, and Gladys stands behind her. (Yvonne Dodge Collection)

John Lair as a soldier in World War I. (Southern Appalachian Archives, Berea College)

A man about town: John Lair in 1922. (Southern Appalachian Archives, Berea College)

Sarah Gertrude Knott and Bascom Lamar Lunsford, 1930s. (Bascom Lamar Lunsford Scrapbook Collection, Appalachian Archives, Mars Hill College)

What You'll See and Hear at the National Folk Festival

INDIANS of the Kiowa and Cherokee tribes in their tribal rituals and war dances.

COWBOYS in authentic ballads of the plains.

SAILORS singing sea chanteys.

MOUNTAIN PEOPLE from Tennessee and surrounding states in songs, dances and play-party games of the hills.

LUMBERJACKS from Michigan in songs and stories of the timberlands.

NEGROES from Tennessee, singing their spirituals and other folk songs.

MINERS from Pennsylvania presenting the songs of their dangerous life.

Many OTHER entertaining and educational features, Spanish singers, Pennsylvania Germans, Fisk Jubilee Singers, etc.

Advertisement for the second National Folk Festival. (Department of Library Special Collections, Folklife Archives, Western Kentucky University, Bowling Green Kentucky)

Lair at the American Folk Song Festival, mid-1930s. George Biggar appears in other photographs of the festival from the same year. (Southern Appalachian Archives, Berea College)

John Lair with Bascom Lamar Lunsford, 1937, probably at the time of the Chicago National Folk Festival. (Southern Appalachian Archives, Berea College)

Lair onstage, 1930s. (Southern Appalachian Archives, Berea College)

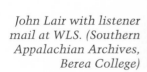

John Lair with listener mail at WLS. (Southern Appalachian Archives, Berea College)

3 John Lair, Student of the Origins of American Folk Music

I suppose Bascom showed you this letter-head and the
very high-brow way in which we have included you on
our National Committee
—M. J. Pickering, letter to John Lair, 1938

The fourth National Folk Festival in Chicago brought together
John Lair and Sarah Gertrude Knott in May 1937. WLS had watched the
event's development closely; the previous two years its weekly magazine, *Stand By*, ran effusive articles by WLS promotional director George
Biggar on the National Folk Festivals in Chattanooga and Dallas. Both
articles emphasized the diversity and scope of the music. "If I had had any
idea that American 'folk' music and songs originated only in the cabins
of our southern mountains and around the 'bunkhouses' of our western
ranges, I learned differently while attending the National Folk Festival
in Chattanooga, Tennessee, in May," Biggar began his first article.[1]

Just weeks before the Chicago festival, Knott asked Biggar for the
station's help in locating fiddlers, dancers, and harmonica players to represent Illinois. WLS agreed to sponsor several individuals, and John Lair
arranged for special features to be held on the *Dinnerbell* program each
festival day. On May 23 the station broadcast a fifteen-minute segment
featuring Knott, Lair, and Elsie Mae McGill, who presented old songs
from the Kentucky mountains. On other days the program featured lumberjacks, anthracite miners, a Spanish quartet with Arthur Campa, and
Bascom Lamar Lunsford. Despite his earlier articles, however, Biggar
apparently possessed reservations about the festival. He informed Pro-

gram Director Harold Safford that Lair would speak to Knott to ensure that WLS and *Prairie Farmer* received credit on the program for the acts they supplied. He added in the next paragraph, however, that WLS should work as much as possible with Knott but not "assume too much credit" because the festival was "often rather disappointing to the public from a showmanship standpoint."[2]

Whatever reservations Biggar may have had about the quality of the festival's showmanship, a number of performers could comfortably appear on either the National Folk Festival or the WLS stage. Appearing at the Chicago festival courtesy of radio station KOY, Phoenix, cowboy Romaine Lowdermilk, one of the mainstays of the National Folk Festival, was already a WLS regular. In fact, Biggar may have discovered him at the Chattanooga festival because he wrote of his great popularity there. WLS performers Lulu Belle (Myrtle Cooper) and Scott Wiseman performed with Lunsford at the Chicago National.[3] The station also sent two other employees, Floyd "Salty" Holmes and Check Stafford, both harmonica players, to perform on the folk festival's stage.

If WLS had reservations about the entertainment value of the folk festival, it expressed no reservations about the multicultural programming. In fact, several years before the creation of the National Folk Festival, WLS described its musical mission in words that would greatly resemble Knott's. The *1931 WLS Family Album* stated, "In building the musical programs at WLS, we have followed many trails and made many interesting discoveries. These mountain songs, the plaintive and humorous cowboy ballads of the West, the Negro spirituals and work songs as sung by the Metropolitan Church Choir of one hundred Negro voices, native Indian music—these are all part of WLS. They are a basic part of American life and culture."[4] Of course, WLS's actual presentation of Native American and African American music was quite limited, but its public stance toward the presentation of American music could be characterized as inclusive, at least during the 1930s.

John Lair acted as a go-between for the National Folk Festival and WLS in 1937. Possibly, he and Knott had met by that date, perhaps at Lunsford's festival, which Knott attended in 1935. Lair also attended the White Top Festival in southwestern Virginia in 1935 and found that show, which he labeled a "folk festival by the folk and for the folk," impressive. In his article for *Stand By,* "High Jinks on White Top," Lair wrote, "Generally these folk music festivals are anything but exciting with the time principally taken up in dry, scholarly discourse on music by collectors and authors whose aim seems to be to impress their colleagues rather than to interest the masses." Lair did note that the White

Top participants included John Lomax, "tireless searcher after strictly American folk songs," and George Pullen Jackson, "whom I strongly suspect of having just a bit the clearest conception of certain phases of American folk music of any man in the country." Despite the favorable slant of the article, Lair could not, at the end, resist the suggestion that the population around White Top more eagerly embraced WLS than it did the folk festival. According to his story, as he left the region Lair encountered "a courtly old gentleman from the valley below," and the old man said, "I'd a-walked ever step of the way up ole White Top jest to shake hands with somebody frum ole WLS."[5]

By 1937 Lair had struck up a friendship with Lunsford, who, as a festival director and self-styled folk entrepreneur represented a middle ground between Knott and Lair and would work collaboratively with both throughout his lifetime. Lunsford, as always, attended the National Folk Festival in 1937, as did Wiseman, his friend and fellow western North Carolinian. According to Wiseman, during Lunsford's visit to Chicago for the festival the two men got together with Lair to play songs and reminisce. After their session Lunsford sold Wiseman the rights to his song "Mountain Dew" in order to pay for the trip home. Wiseman added verses, and the song became a hit for Lulu Belle and Scotty although WLS viewed its content as not wholesome enough for its programming and forbid its performance.[6]

Lair's involvement with the National Folk Festival lasted only a few years, but the relationship fortified his image as an expert in American traditional music. Throughout the early and mid-1930s John Lair worked to build that reputation at WLS. The station's management first recognized his skill for bringing "authentic" talent to WLS and soon discovered as well that Lair had a knack for writing and announcing. The Aladdin Lamp Company wanted to sponsor a country music program and invited the Cumberland Ridge Runners to audition. As Lair recalled, "I got the afternoon off or just took it off. I was working on the street and [the insurance company] never knew where I was anyhow . . . so I decided that it would be a novelty to let one of them announce the act instead of having a regular station announcer. So I picked on Karl, Karl Davis, and I was going over the thing and telling him what to say and how to say it, you know. And the station manager came in, called me off to one side, says, 'The sponsor's already here and he's in the audition room and he wants you to announce it.'"[7]

The Aladdin Barn Dance Frolic, broadcast immediately before the National Barn Dance, premiered on December 6, 1930. At first the shows consisted of songs strung together with commercial patter. For his introduction to the song "Lost John," Lair wrote, "This is about a feller named John that got lost out in the mountains one night, and when you're lost in them mountains you're plum lost. If thedy [sic] had a Aladdin Lamp to set out on the front porch John coulda found his own way home without all this destirbance."[8] Shows soon became more thematic. On January 10, 1931, Lair began, "Tonight we're going back to school, down in the little ole Red Bud schoolhouse in Rockcastle County, Kintucky, where we used to go when we wuz kids. Want to come along?"[9] The following month he demonstrated his emerging genius for tying his radio fantasy world to real life by arranging for a local Aladdin dealer to provide light for the Rose Hill Meeting House in Renfro Valley and for some local boys to rig up a radio in the church for a special broadcast. The radio audience could not only listen to Lair telling the history of the Rose Hill Meeting House but also imagine the congregation, at that very moment, being lit by an Aladdin Lamp, listening to their own story.[10]

The Aladdin program also included play-party "games" that in Lair's childhood were acceptable among some religious people who forbid outright dancing. Despite the lack of visuals in radio, this aspect of the show proved popular and spawned Lair's first publication, *Swing Your Partner*, in 1931. "The tunes and verses to the games in this collection," Lair advised, "are recorded here just as I knew and played them some fifteen years ago in the Renfro Valley region of the Kentucky hills. If they are not in accord with your own version of them, please remember that they have been passed along, orally from person to person, from community to community, from state to state and even, in some instances, from country to country, and have naturally undergone considerable change in so much handling." A two-page essay by Lair on "The Play Party in the United States" followed the introduction.[11]

Lair billed another of his early sponsored programs specifically as a folk music show. The original broadcast on April 4, 1931, opened with an announcement: "These boys—the Cumberland Ridge Runners—whom you will hear tonight for the first time on the program of Olson Rug Folk Songs, bring to you the only pure strain of American folk songs and folk lore, mixed with a staunch but simple philosophy, reminding us of the strength and simplicity of their native hills." Renditions of "Sally Goodin'" and "Cripple Creek" followed. A few weeks later the Ridge Runners did a special Abraham Lincoln edition of the show broadcast over WABC and a Columbia network.[12]

Although a self-styled authority on Appalachian music, Lair continued to explore other musical genres, but those ventures tended to be framed to remind the audience of the performers' (supposed) origins. After

Slim Miller and Hugh Cross performed a rendition of "San Antone" on a noontime show in 1932, Lair chimed in, "That's a might good song, Boys, but it's kinda takin us out of our territory a little. We'll have folk thinkin we're cowboys 'stead of mountaineers. Cowboys is alright, but it's too late fer us to change now."[13] The previous year Lair framed his experiment with virtual blackface comedy with an explanation of why he had "sut" on his face: "Some of us wuz over to town lass week testifyin in a lawsuit an we seen what they call a minstrel [*sic*] show." The boys noticed that the show took in a "heap of money" and decided it might be a way to raise money for a bell for the meeting house. Afraid that the audience might not like the show, "We figgered we bettr let you lissen to us practice tonoght fore ye spent yer quarter fer a ticket."[14] In both instances such framing allowed Lair the safely to explore other genres without having performers truly abandon their on-air personas.

From their beginning in 1930, the Cumberland Ridge Runners were a success and established Lair's reputation at WLS. As he told Clyde (soon to be Red) Foley in February 1931, "We have made a big hit on this station. Our Aladdin program went over so big that I have a separate contract with Aladdin to put on their program next year, so I think steady work is assured for several months to come." With the departure of Bradley Kincaid, Pie Plant Pete, and Doc Hopkins, WLS was left, in Lair's words, "without a single first class voice for old-time stuff." He added, "Somebody could step in here now and be the headliner in a few months. I have a year's contract with the station for this act and I want to fill Dock's place with someone who can work up a lot of popularity during the year." As was usual, Lair offered Foley a room in the Lairs' own home so Foley would not have hotel expenses.[15]

Even before the inclusion of Red Foley and the popular Linda Parker (Jeanne Meunich), the Cumberland Ridge Runners developed a large following. In a short piece at the end of the 1931 *Swing Your Partner*, George Biggar noted that the Ridge Runners' fan mail "has run in excess of eleven thousand letters on a single broadcast."[16] At the time, radio stations gauged a performer's popularity on the volume of fan mail received, and Lair paid particular attention to listeners' correspondence.[17] Later in life he admitted that he paid a janitor at WLS to let him sift through mail that others had thrown away so he could gauge what the audience wanted. He recalled, "I thought I could learn the people's minds and wishes that way better than any other."[18]

Lair constantly sought new talent. A letter to a potential performer laid out his deal with the musicians. "You would not be on salary. W.L.S. would use the entire orchestra every Saturday night, paying twelve dollars per man, and if you could do specialties they could use you occasionally through the week. The real money comes from theatre and party work through the week when we could get as much as thirty dollars per man per night. I would manage the act, look out for booking etc. and handle you as I do the other boys—that is, retain half of what you make above fifty dollars per week—or, if you prefer, take twenty percent of all your earning."[19]

Even during the early 1930s Lair must have been looking for ways to be more than a small cog in the WLS machine. Some inspiration may have come from his friend Steve Cisler, a radio announcer who left WLS for Cleveland just before the Ridge Runners' big break with Aladdin. In January 1931 Cisler contacted Lair about ambitious plans he was developing with Aladdin. The letter proposed a series of recorded programs produced in New York by Lair and Cisler, featuring the "Renfro Band" with "leading recording artists of old time music" such as Bradley Kincaid, Jimmie Rodgers, and the Carter Family serving as guest entertainers. "We would try to reproduce an old time get together up in the mountains for each program, giving it an original setting," Cisler wrote. Then he proposed a second, even more ambitious, scheme for a radio show featuring "genuine folk music" each week from different parts of the United States. The scope included Kentucky mountain dancing, Alabama sacred-harp singing, a Swedish American barn dance, a Memphis jug band, and a Louisiana plantation frolic. Cisler stated that he did not want to discourage Lair's work at WLS, although he clearly indicated that he did not think the management could be trusted. "I know you boys are anxious to get somewhere in radio work," he added, "and it is my sincere belief that we can make money on old time music programs for radio advertisers who look for something different."[20] If Cisler's grand plans came to naught they certainly must have pointed a way for Lair, still a novice in the profession, to pursue his destiny.

Despite Lair's success developing artists and programs for WLS, the station did not employ him on a full-time basis during the early 1930s. The *1933 WLS Family Album* listed his occupation as "medical director of a large insurance company."[21] With the reorganization of WLS's music library in 1935 he secured a position as the station's music librarian and left the insurance business for good. The entry on Lair in the *1936 WLS Family Album* reflects his greater role: "Outstanding authority on American folk music. John has studied mountain music far back in the hills, and has proved that many of the mountain ballads are centuries old. Has written a good many songs himself. Often been heard announcing. In charge of WLS music library."[22] John Lair's position at WLS had become prominent enough for him to be featured on the front cover of the February 8 issue of *Stand By.*

During the mid-1930s Lair publicly addressed the relationship between "authentic" folk music and "hillbilly" radio. The March 16, 1935, issue of the *New WLS Weekly* (named *Stand By* two weeks later) included the article "No Hill Billies in Radio; Ballads Are Still Written Says John Lair." Noting that the term *hillbilly* characterized a manner of singing rather than the origin of a song, Lair stated that Tin Pan Alley hung the name on a certain type of entertainer and might well be responsible for the death of this style of music. Well before it became accepted doctrine among folklorists, Lair noted the arbitrary line often drawn between folk and popular songs. Many songs labeled "folk" appeared in print years before, but as they were handed down, words were changed to fit local conditions. He also noted that ballad writing had not died out but still continued, especially in response to current tragedies. Seven months later Lair broadly defined folk music as "any music long popular with the common folk of a country."[23]

As manager of the WLS music department, Lair held responsibility for developing the station's collection. Through his column "Notes from the Music Library," begun on August 24 he elicited donations of old music and songbooks from listeners and answered questions about old songs. Months later Lair submitted a plan to extend the activities of his department. He began by acknowledging that much of WLS's popularity was due to the use of a "certain type of music." He went on to note, "'Hillbilly' music, as a fad, is subject to decline in due course, but the basic folk music on which it is founded improves with age and we can consider that we are building for the future when we do anything to increase it's [sic] importance in the minds of our listeners." Lair proposed a fifteen-minute program to be broadcast five days a week, plus a half-hour Saturday show. The show would feature Lair discussing the origins and history of certain songs and answering questions about music from any source. Thus, Lair suggests, the station could direct attention to the fact that "WLS is a leader in the field, an authority on the subject and in possession of a remarkable collection of old songs." Lair went on, "I would use a variety of talent on these programs, attempting to bring in all types and classifications of folk music, as well as such better class music as our artists are capable of delivering. I would try, in so far as possible, to devote most time and attention to that type of music which is sincere and friendly without being flippant or trashy, working on the basis that 'hillbilly' does not have to be poorly done to be appreciated. A major aim of the series of programs would be to discredit the synthetic,

Tin-Pan-Ally type of folk song and build appreciation of the traditional music from which these later adaptions [sic] are made."[24]

The commercial angle of his plan lay in selling sheet music by mail order. This marketing would emphasize the type of music played on WLS, including "old popular music up to 1925, original compositions of [our] artists and the old traditional songs never sold in sheet music form," all of which were difficult or impossible to find. Lair envisioned that the primary market would be rural listeners who could not easily obtain sheet music.[25] Another plan Lair submitted suggested a way for WLS to circumvent paying fees to the American Society of Composers, Authors, and Publishers (ASCAP). Lair had access to two collections of musical compositions, one of which he privately owned, that contained thousands of songs on which copyright had expired. This collection, he noted, represented "more than fourteen years research into all realms of music." Lair proposed that WLS could make arrangements from the originals, avoiding payment to ASCAP, and earn additional money by making the collection available to other radio stations.[26]

Lair knew that just because a song was labeled "folk" the issues of ownership and copyright could not be ignored. The previous year, a challenge to the notion of collective ownership of folk music came to WLS in the form of a registered letter from American Folk Song Festival director Jean Thomas. She advised that J. W. Day (Jilson Setters) had sent a copy of the ballad "The Rowan County Troubles," which he had written, to a Mr. O. H. Harris. Thomas later discovered that Harris's son-in-law performed as a member of the Cumberland Ridge Runners, and she emphatically stated that Day had not given him or anyone else permission to use the song. Thomas, however, also indicated that she and Day could be mollified by the offer of a gig at WLS. She concluded by stating that they had appeared on NBC together, and if WLS "would be interested in a program of ancient Elizabethan music which he fiddles and sings, I should be glad to bring him to Chicago, if financial arrangements can be made."[27] For all her purist sentiments, Thomas would not pass up an opportunity to promote herself or Day on a station as powerful as WLS.

Lair's plans for the WLS music department did not always reach fruition, but he never ceased to search for ways to make extra money for himself or pursue his interests. Following a strategy that had proven successful for Bradley Kincaid, Lair marketed songbooks to his radio audiences, and WLS also underwrote his various research projects. As musical director, he said, "I had a lot of time on hand and a good expense account, [and I] could go wherever I wanted to, so I set out to trace these old songs down."[28]

Songs associated with outlaws and other western characters particularly fascinated Lair, and on his trips he collected oral histories from relatives of Frank and Jesses James and John Wesley Harding. His song research continued throughout his life and frequently was the center of family vacation trips. "He always disguised it real well, so that you didn't know it until you were in the middle of the vacation that this is what we really came for," recalled daughter Ann Henderson.[29] Lair also spent weekends haunting old book stores for sheet music, adding to a collection started by his great-grandmother when she bequeathed him her handwritten copy of "The Silk Merchant's Daughter."[30]

During his years at WLS Lair paid particular attention to developing female talent, giving the station three of its most popular acts. Linda Parker grew up in an industrial section of Indiana although the radio station emphasized her supposed "Kentucky roots." Before Lair discovered her in 1932 she struggled along as a nightclub singer. Lair transformed her into Linda Parker, the Sunbonnet Girl, and she rose to fame performing sentimental songs such as Lair's own "Take Me Back to Renfro Valley."[31] Soon after Linda Parker became a hit, another young woman, Myrtle Cooper, began to hang around the station, looking for a break. At first she failed to impress WLS's management, but Lair saw some potential: "She'd been down there to audition three or four times, trying to sing Linda Parker songs, they wouldn't pay any attention to her. And I heard about her; George Biggar and I talked about it, I told him I thought I could do something for her. So I had her come down to the house and listened to her. I told her, I said, 'Now you, I can't do anything for you with the straight ballads because I've got Linda doing that.'" Lair encouraged her to study the act of a hillbilly vaudevillian, Elviry Weaver, and develop a bold and sassy persona. Rechristened Lulu Belle, Cooper became an instant success, and WLS promoted her as the Radio Queen. Her quick rise to success sparked some jealousy. Lair later admitted, "The rest of my act, oh, they didn't like her at all. They were loyal to Linda, you know, and Lulu Belle just took the show away from her."[32]

Neither woman remained under Lair's management for long. Lair initially partnered Lulu Belle with Red Foley, presenting her as his girlfriend from back home. When Foley married Eva Overstake of the Three Little Maids in 1933, however, his new bride insisted that the act be broken up. The station then matched Lulu Belle with newcomer Scott Wiseman. The partnership succeeded, both onstage and off, and Wiseman took over the management of Lulu Belle and Scotty. In December 1934 they married. Linda Parker's brief career came to an end the following year when she died of appendicitis at the age of twenty-three.

Her death brought an outpouring of grief from the radio audience, and many sent in poems, songs, and other tributes. One "true W.L.S. Friend," Esther M. Koehler, sent in the handwritten lyrics and music of a song dedicated to Linda Parker. In her song "Silent Singer" Koehler wrote of her hope to some day meet Parker in heaven.[33] The song brought a less divine if still sought-after encounter. Two years later, when John Lair put together his first all-girl string band, Esther Koehler became Violet of the Coon Creek Girls.

After losing his two top female acts, Lair went looking for another and found a young girl who, he thought, was "even more real than Lulu Belle." Lily May Ledford hailed from the Red River Gorge area of eastern Kentucky. In 1935 Lily May auditioned at WLS with her band, the Red River Ramblers. The Ramblers, which included Ledford's sister, Rosie, were much in demand for square dances back in Kentucky, and Lily May was already a veteran of many fiddle contests. The young fiddler impressed Lair but not program director Harold Safford. As usual, Lair found a way to circumvent the WLS hierarchy. He encouraged Lily May to enter a talent contest the following summer, which Safford planned to attend. The second time around Safford was sold. Lair then took Ledford aside and advised her not to sign with WLS. Instead, she signed a five-year manager's contract with Lair.[34]

Unlike Linda Parker or Lulu Belle, Lily May Ledford had spent her life in the southern mountains and, perhaps for that reason, she had difficulty seeing her radio persona as an act. After arriving in Chicago she wished to look less like a hick, whereas Lair wanted her to keep and enhance her country persona. As part of the promotion for Lily May, *Stand By* ran a comic strip entitled "Lily May, the Mountain Gal" that was sponsored by Pinex Cough Syrup. Although the strip made use of many Appalachian stereotypes it depicted Lily May as spunky and resourceful.[35] The photograph that *Stand By* ran of her looking "collegiate in a bright red sweater with a turn-over collar, worn with a gray tweed skirt" probably better represented the image the young woman sought.[36] Although Lair presented Lily May Ledford as a solo act on WLS in 1936, the following year, when he moved on to Cincinnati, he fashioned an all-girl group, the Coon Creek Girls with her at its center.

Uncharacteristically, Lair let one noted female country performer slip through his fingers. Cynthia May Carver (Cousin Emmy) grew up in central Kentucky. When she was young she toured with the Carver Family, and in 1935 she became the first woman to win the National Old-Time Fiddlers Contest in Louisville. In 1936 Carver and her partner Frankie Moore contracted with Lair to have a music book published.[37]

Lair, however, must have discussed a far more extensive business relationship with Cousin Emmy. The following year, on the eve of his departure from Chicago he released her from any actual or potential contractual arrangement. "If I had gone ahead and advertised you or started a campaign to boost you in any way," he said, "I would expect you to go through with me, but since nothing has been done you are not obligated to me in any way, so go ahead with the deal and maybe we can get together some other time."[38] Five years later Cousin Emmy, now at WNOX in Knoxville, still hoped that Lair would help make her a star. "Mr. Lair," she wrote, "I will cut you in any way you see fit. Now is our chance to make some money." Lair responded that he could not afford to buy time but perhaps could arrange a sponsor or make a songbook deal with the station.[39] Soon thereafter Cousin Emmy reached the height of her fame at KMOX in St. Louis.

During the early to mid-1930s John Lair began developing an on-air presence for his semimythical home community. In March 1935 the grueling weekday morning schedule that began at 6 included many permutations of Lair's acts such as the "Cumberland Ridge Runners in Old-Time Melodies," "Linda Parker in Mountain Songs," "Renfro Valley Boys," "Ramblin' Red Foley in Folk Songs," and the "Cumberland Ridge Runners and Linda Parker."[40] On Saturday nights before the National Barn Dance, WLS broadcast the *Cumberland Ridge Runners and John Lair in "Mountain Memories."* The following year brought *Coon Creek Social,* which Lair emceed, and *Front Porch Serenade with John Lair.*[41]

In the fall of 1935, Lair's Renfro Valley began its presence on network radio with the Sunday afternoon broadcast of *Pine Mountain Social* over NBC. An announcement for the program cast the show as a reliving of the weekly meetings of "Kentucky mountain folk" who, beginning in 1798, assembled in Renfro Valley for entertainment and to exchange ideas. The announcement went on to note that "John Lair of WLS, authority on American folk music and legends of the hill country, will be heard as narrator, giving continuity to the weekly rural community gatherings and presenting origins and histories of many of the songs included in the broadcasts. The original Renfro Valley homestead, scene of the series, is still standing. It was built by Lair's great-aunt."[42]

Although Lair fixed his programs in a distinct geographical location the appeal of John Lair's programs to WLS audiences seems to have been found more in their old-fashioned quality. A fan from Illinois wrote, "I like the old-time kind of programs, especially John Lair and his type of life programs. . . . I wish I could have lived back in the good old days when we were not always in such a hurry and had time to visit with our neighbors and made real friends."[43] Lair's shows may have found an audience among dislocated Appalachians, but they also appealed to a broader sense of loss of place and times gone by rather than a longing for a specific region. Lair used his home community as the stand-in for whatever loss of the past his listeners felt. Even as he moved programming to Kentucky, a large portion of the audience remained north of the Ohio River.

In September 1936 *Stand By* announced that Lair had departed WLS "to do free-lance radio work in Cincinnati."[44] With "more guts than sense" and a borrowed sum of $500 Lair struck out to build a business at Renfro Valley, stopping first at WLW in Cincinnati.[45] Lair's stories about building the Renfro Valley Barn Dance vary, whether from his youthful wish to "see the valley go back to its original form," to noting that if rural audiences would come to the city to see a barn dance then perhaps city audiences would come to the country for a show.[46] In a 1971 interview Lair recalled going home for a vacation and being told by a man who ran a nearby station that people stopped by daily to ask about Renfro Valley. "And I thought," Lair said, "'well heck, I'm building up something for this guy, I might as well go down and build it up for [myself].'"[47]

Although not the first to sell nostalgia by means of the radio, Lair pioneered a way for country music radio to capitalize on the budding automobile culture in America. Time had not stood still in the "valley where time stands still." During the 1920s, U.S. Highway 25 bisected Rockcastle County as part of the Dixie Highway, the first major American road system to run north and south and connect Michigan to Florida. Lair clearly saw the potential for automobile tourism, and the land purchased for the Renfro Valley complex straddled the highway. Much of the complex was visible from the road, including its central icon, the barn, with "Home of the Renfro Valley Barn Dance" emblazoned across its roof. Renfro Valley would become country music's first auto-tourist site.[48]

The two-year sojourn in Ohio allowed Lair time to construct his complex at Renfro Valley and build the radio show. More than halfway home from Chicago, Cincinnati gave the Lair family a foothold back in Kentucky. They settled into Covington, Kentucky, immediately across the river from Cincinnati. More important, however, Cincinnati sported the most powerful radio station in the country, WLW. In 1934 the Federal Radio Commission had granted a special temporary experimental authorization to WLW to broadcast at 500 kilowatts, making it the first and only radio superstation in the United States. Ultimately, WLW lost its special authorization and in March 1939 returned to a normal power of 50 kilowatts, but for five years the "nation's station" was ten times stronger than stations such as WLS and could be heard throughout most of the United States.[49]

Lair did not hold a position at WLW, but he sold a packaged show, complete with sponsors, to the station. The Renfro Valley Barn Dance began broadcasting on October 9, 1937. The program also toured local theaters, schools and auditoriums through dates set up by a booking agency. According to Lair, between January 1938 and June 1939, the Renfro Valley Barn Dance played to more than a half million paid admissions. Most appearances took place in Ohio and Indiana, with additional stops in Kentucky, West Virginia, and Illinois.[50]

While Renfro Valley grew from an individual dream of a single man, Lair needed help to make the project a success. His original partners included Red Foley and Whitey Ford (the Duke of Paducah) as well as Foley's brother Cotton, a businessman from Berea, Kentucky. Behind the scenes, hand firmly on the purse strings, was Freeman Keyes, an advertising executive in Chicago who lined up sponsors for Lair's shows and was responsibile for overall financial management. The long-time correspondence between the two indicates that Lair had far less financial control over his organization than many imagined. Both being strong-minded, Lair and Keyes could not resist telling each other how to run their side of the business. On June 8, 1938, Keyes reminded Lair that they both worked for the Russell M. Seeds Company, an advertising firm in Chicago, and suggested that they stop "these criticizing letters going back and forth." Although Keyes assured him that he believed Lair knew "more about hill-billies than anybody else in the country," he also asked Lair to "give me credit for using good judgment in handling clients."[51] The intent of the letter seemed to be to delineate the responsibilities of the two men, with Keyes in charge of the money and Lair in charge of producing the shows, yet Keyes began another letter less than two weeks later, "If it's humanly possible, we need an accordian [sic]."[52] Keyes also conveyed sponsors' personal preferences to Lair. At the end of 1938 he advised, "Mr. Noll of the Pinex Company liked the electric guitar very much last week. Will you please make the necessary arrangements."[53]

John Lair built his cast of the Renfro Valley Barn Dance from seasoned performers doing familiar acts, experienced performers who had new radio personas, and total newcomers. The freshest new act, the Coon Creek Girls, was billed as the first all-woman string band. Their success grew from Lair's skill at recognizing talent, his construction of a radio image, and sheer good luck. Evelyn Lange, like Lily May Ledford, began her musical career with a youthful passion for the fiddle. Unlike Ledford, who learned her music first in the context of her home and community in eastern Kentucky, Lange, an Ohio farm girl, picked up her style from the early barn dances on the radio. In 1937 Evelyn Lange placed first in a talent contest, which won her a spot on WLS where she met Lair. In August of 1937, she told Lair that she was "still craving a job" and noted, "In this last issue of your Standby Magazine we read in the 'Listeners' Mike' article an item suggesting an all-girl program. If you take up this lady's nice idea we would like for you to stop and think about us, and please give us a break if you can."[54] When she subsequently found out that Lair had moved to Cincinnati, Lange and her mother took a bus there and dropped in on Lair. Perhaps he admired her spunk, or maybe, as Lange later suggested, Lair, pressed for time, simply wanted to get rid of her, but he told her to meet him at a certain date at his sister's house across the river in Covington.[55]

Surprisingly, Lair seems to have exerted little control over the initial meetings of Lily May and Rosie Ledford, Evelyn Lange, and mandolin player Esther Koehler. Neither did he have to engineer the chemistry among the young performers. He did, however, control most other aspects of their lives. Earlier Lair had encouraged Lily May to take up the banjo as her main instrument rather than the fiddle. Now he had fiddler Evelyn Lange learn to play the bass. With the Ledford sisters already sporting flower names, Lange became Daisy and Koehler was Violet. When the girls requested that the group be called the Wildwood Flowers to match their names, however, Lair insisted instead on the Coon Creek Girls, who supposedly hailed from Pinchem Tight Hollow. Again Lair mixed fiction and reality. There was no Coon Creek in the Ledford sisters' native Red River Gorge, but a Pinch-Em-Tight Mountain and Holler did exist near where they grew up. Lair had already used "Coon Creek Social" and "Coon Creek Literary Society" in the titles of his Renfro Valley–themed programs on WLS, and perhaps he wished to tie the girls to the image he had already constructed. Or, as Lange has suggested, he simply wished to signal that the group played hillbilly music. Lair watched closely over the activities of the four young women, though. As Lange later admitted, his paternalism was not totally uncalled for: "Boss watched us carefully, we were all very young and very dumb."[56]

To the Coon Creek "family," Lair added a comedy act. As a foil to the "authenticity" of the girls, he hired an old vaudeville trouper who had yet to break into radio. Margaret Lillie began her career in dance halls and the vaudeville circuit in the Oklahoma Territory and, in the 1920s she performed with the successful hillbilly vaudevillians, the Weavers.[57] In January of 1937 she informed Lair that she would very much like to try radio: "I have a blue's voice also can sing hillbilly songs." Lair replied,

"I am reasonably certain that I can place you to advantage around next September or October." In August Lair wrote that he was about to relocate to Cincinnati: "As I told you once before it is doubtful if I can get much money for you in the beginning but am certain that I can build you up in a 'Lum and Abner' type of show to the point where you can command a good price."[58]

For Lillie, Lair constructed the persona of A'nt Idy Harper, also from Coon Creek. Lair paired the character with his large, baby-faced nephew Harry Mullins, who played her son, Little Clifford. The act became a smashing success. In October 1938, Lair described A'nt Idy and Little Clifford as "the hit act of the Renfro Valley Barn Dance."[59] Some fans contacted Lair before buying a ticket to make sure Idy would be performing. "We will have to drive better than three hundred miles so we want to be sure we could see Aunt Ida when we come," wrote a woman from Mattoon, Illinois.[60]

The WLS veterans on the Renfro Valley Barn Dance included two former members of the Cumberland Ridge Runners, Red Foley and Slim Miller, as well as Millie and Dollie Good, billed as the Girls of the Golden West. Announcer Bill McCloskey, Millie Good's husband, also moved from WLS to WLW. Members of the Cincinnati Renfro cast performed on two other radio programs, the fifteen-minute *Pinex Merrymakers*, which aired on weekday mornings, and the *Plantation Party*. Implementing an idea he had formerly pitched to WLS, Lair appeared on the latter show with his "Notebook of American Folk Songs" in which he discussed the origins of particular pieces of music.

The meeting between John Lair and Sarah Gertrude Knott at the 1937 National Folk Festival in Chicago had been fortuitous for both parties. Each saw how they could use the other. Knott, of course, always sought out people who could bring new performers to her festival. On the eve of his new business venture, Lair saw the National Folk Festival as a way of boosting his national reputation. After the Chicago festival Knott placed Lair on the National Folk Festival Association board as a "Student of the Origins of American Folk Music." In February 1938, M. J. Pickering, the National Folk Festival business manager, told Lair about a woman who owned handwritten copies of music used in dances when her father was a pioneer in Nevada. Pickering, using the National Folk Festival Association's new letterhead, pointed out to Lair the "very high-brow way in which we have included you on our National Committee."[61]

In March 1938, Lair and Lunsford, at the request of Knott, organized the Ohio Valley Folk Festival to select participants for the fifth annual National Folk Festival, scheduled to be held in Washington, D.C. With

Lair's hands full developing new radio programs, Lunsford did most of
the promotion for the festival. On stationary printed during his time in
Cincinnati, he listed his various positions, including "Folk Dance Director" of the Renfro Valley Barn Dance, founder and director of the Annual
Mountain Dance and Folk Song Festival in Asheville, and member of the
executive committee of the National Folk Festival.[62]

With sponsorship from radio station WCKY in Covington, Lair and
Lunsford held the Ohio Folk Festival on March 27 at the Cincinnati Music
Hall.[63] The Library of Congress sent youthful folklorist Alan Lomax to
make recordings for the Music Division.[64] Lomax, who at that period
clearly distinguished between authentic folk and radio hillbilly, found
the festival not to his liking:

> The Ohio Valley Folk Festival turned out to be largely hill-billy and
> very little folk. Obviously Mr. Lunsford, who was in charge, acting as
> master of ceremonies, had done very little preparation and, just as obvi-
> ously, was afraid of his audience, his performers, and of what he thought
> they wanted. As a result, the folk singers present were pushed to one
> side, and the festival dragged on hour after hour from one "Uncle Zebe
> and his Hill-Billy Harmonizers" to the next. Almost every fiddle tune,
> almost every song was the ordinary [sic] stuff that comes over the air
> from Nashville, Covington, Cincinnati and the other radio stations that
> feature mountain music.[65]

Lunsford, Lomax believed, had been under pressure "from his connections in the radio world in Cincinnati" to include professional groups,
"notably the Coon Creek Girls (sponsored by Mr. Lahr [sic]) and those
performers set the tone of the whole entertainment. . . . No question
that 'hill-billy' music is following a vigorous development of its own,
more or less apart from folk music, and this group of performers thoroughly vindicated its independence with tremendous vigor," Lomax
concluded.

Not surprisingly, one of the two acts winning a spot to go on to Washington was Lair's Coon Creek Girls. Robert L. Day, who performed with
his grandchildren, won the other. Knott, also present at the festival, had
not been troubled by the professionalism of the Coon Creeks, but she did
wish to tone down the hillbilly artifice in their footwear: "I think they
are very attractive in the dresses that they wear and I think the shoes fit-
ted in fine on the Barn Dance program, but I believe it would be better if
they would wear some kind of slippers." Knott added, "I surely like these
girls, I met them as I went home and walked with them to the hotel."[66]

Even the *Washington Post* bought Lair's hype about the authenticity of the Coon Creeks. Despite the fact that only two of the four girls

came from Kentucky and that Lily May Ledford had already become a radio sensation, the newspaper's festival issue presented them as straight from the mountains. According to the caption of a picture of them in long dresses and high-top shoes and in front of a log house, "These Kentucky mountain girls make up one of the winning teams from the Ohio Folk Festival held in Cincinnati in preparation for the National Festival. Each plays all four instruments shown in the picture and sing ballads known in their families for generations."[67]

Lair's letters to Knott, written just before the 1938 National Folk Festival, reveal his usual combination of wheeling and dealing and sincere interest in the folk process. Lair adamantly stated on April 11 that he could not personally sponsor other groups, and he wrangled for control of his own performers: "If you want to invite other groups which came to your personal attention at the [Ohio Valley] Festival it would of course be perfectly alright, and you could use them if needed, however for our own particular spot I would like to confine entirely to the Coon Creek Girls and the Day family." Lair also responded to Knott's concern about costuming. Although he expected to bring the Coon Creek Girls in ordinary street clothes, "If you feel that their gingham dresses are permissible, I know that would make a very colorful spot on the program and the dresses are carefully made so as to be just the type of thing they used to wear at home." Moreover, Lair seemed to relish his role as advisor to Knott on matters of folk music. In the same letter he told her, "Without having time to do any research work on the questions you asked, and answering only on the spur of the moment, I would say that the 'Martins and McCoys' and 'Zeb Turner's Girl' are not the type of numbers you would want to use, as both are popular sheet music numbers."[68] In his next letter, however, Lair suggested a provocative use of a popular song: "[Day's] three grand children will sing 'We Sat beneath the Maple on the Hill.' This is a rather peculiar thing to bring to a folk program, but I have an object in selecting it. It is a very good example of how songs began changing in the hands of folk singers. I have the original and sheet music form published several years ago, but the way it is now being sung around the country is quite different from the original, illustrating the changes which take place in a song when transmitted orally."[69]

For reasons of budget, Day's grandchildren did not attend the National Folk Festival, but Lair's suggestion did represent a revolutionary step in presenting folk music, especially for 1938. He also submitted an article, late, on the "Origins of American Folk Music" to use in the program but declined to arrange an exhibit of old music because of his time on the road. Lair scheduled his musicians to play two dates en route as well as broadcast from a Washington radio station the same evening as their festival performance.

Although Lair benefited from his association with the National Folk Festival, Knott's approach to doing business rankled. Before the festival he complained to her, "After paying all expenses, etc., [of the Ohio Valley Folk Festival] we had exactly $92.00 left with which to bring our group to Washington. If I bring the Day family and the Coon Creek Girls along with me, it will mean that I will have to pay a small part of their expense at least, out of my own pocket."[70] Later in life Lair recalled, "We were invited [to the National Folk Festival] every year, but I don't like their method. They want you to pay all your own expenses and come up and they keep the gate, you know."[71] Because the National did not pay Lair or his performers, even for travel expenses, his interest in the event quickly dwindled as his other projects grew. In 1943 Pickering recommended that Lair be dropped from the board for lack of interest.[72]

The Coon Creek Girls' legendary 1939 performance for the king and queen of England at the White House may have resulted directly or indirectly from their participation in the National Folk Festival. King George VI and Queen Elizabeth were the first British monarchs to visit the United States, and the Roosevelt White House planned an elaborate evening of American music. Charles Seeger of the Federal Music Project and Adrian Dornbush of the Resettlement Administration directed the folk portion of the show, but it is unclear who actually suggested that the Coon Creek Girls perform. Any number of the Washington folk establishment would have had the opportunity to hear them at the National Folk Festival in 1938, as would have Eleanor Roosevelt, who served as the event's honorary chair. Lily May Ledford believed that Mrs. Roosevelt personally asked for them, but Daisy Lange thought that Lunsford, who brought a group of square dancers to the program, might have had some influence in the selection.[73] Late in life, however, Lair recalled, "Our invitation came from a young man who was in the government work of some sort, I don't remember exactly what. But he was stationed at Cincinnati and he was on rather familiar terms with the White House."[74] The description of the "young man" would seem to fit Alan Lomax, who had been earlier put off by the Coon Creeks' professionalism. Perhaps the group's performance at the National Folk Festival changed his mind, because four years later Lily May Ledford performed in a musical production written and arranged by Elizabeth and Alan Lomax.

According to stories told by Lily May Ledford and Daisy Lange, Lair encountered trouble getting into the White House because, unlike Lunsford, he did not perform with the group. As the story goes, he finally convinced the guards that he was essential to carry the bass fiddle. The guards, however, denied entry to Lair's wife, Virginia, who had bought a new outfit for the occasion.[75] Lair may have indeed had trouble with the White House guards, but his name appears in the printed program. The entry for the Coon Creek Girls read, "From Pinchem-Tight Hollow in the Renfro Valley of Kentucky. They led the normal hard life of the mountaineers of the State until 1937 when they were 'discovered' by Mr. Lair and started their radio career."[76] Of the Coon Creeks' four songs listed in the program, only one, "The Soldier and the Lady," was an English ballad. The other three—"Cindy," "Buffalo Gals," and "How Many Biscuits Can You Eat?"—can be attributed partially to minstrel or African American sources. That may have reflected the New Deal ideology of the concert organizers, but it also indicates Lair's interests.[77] Whatever his shortcomings, he did not insist on the Anglo purity of American folk music.

If his involvement with the early years of the National Folk Festival was short-lived, Lair's plate was full with many other projects. The broadcast power of WLW provided a potentially enormous audience, and letters, some remarkably personal, came from fans across the country. Eva Travis, an "old lonesome mother" from Iowa, wondered if that was her son "Verle" playing on the *Plantation Party*, to which Lair promptly responded that the performer, a native Kentuckian, was named Merle.[78] A listener from Connecticut wrote to Lair in early 1939, devastated by the news that WLW would be forced to return to 50 kilowatts: "It means that reception will probably be impossible for most of us and it certainly is a disappointment to realize that we can't enjoy the 'old time get to-gethers' any more on Sat. nights after the power change goes into effect."[79]

Money was a constant source of conflict between John Lair and his performers. If Lair thought he would escape such problems with the youngest female performers he was mistaken. While Lily May Ledford chafed under the Coon Creeks' countrified image, Daisy Lange and Violet Koehler found things to complain about other than gingham dresses and high-top boots. With road shows as well as performances on both WLW and WCVK, they felt they were badly overworked. Lange remembered feeling so exhausted that even the White House was "just another place to play." Furthermore, their "fairly decent salary" did not go far once they paid for hotels, costumes, and other expenses. Although the Ledford sisters resisted, all four asked Lair for better pay. In response, he gave them "such a sad story" about his expenses that Rosie Ledford offered to give up her salary.[80]

Lair may have wiggled out of responding to the Coon Creeks' legitimate complaints, but he did not lie about his financial situation. He held far less control over finances than the performers realized. Freeman Keyes wrote on June 8, 1938, "Now as for the talent situation and money, I am whole-heartedly in agreement with you that we should get money for our talent, and the Lord knows we are trying to get money for it, and are going to get good money for it this fall." Keyes promised that additional money would be coming in from the sponsors, Keystone, Pinex, Brown and Williamson, and Allis-Chalmers. "Now John," Keyes insisted, "I have tried to take the financial end of the worries off your shoulders. I have tried to use my best judgment."[81] In his next letter Keyes suggested that Lair himself might have been cheated: "Are you absolutely certain that no one can go south with any of that money? I tell you it looks like we are doing more business than you are getting paid for." Keyes also urged keeping good records of payment to the "talent" for tax purposes. "Otherwise," he warned, "we are all subject to jail. I don't think I'd look good in stripes."[82]

In the initial years of the Renfro Valley Barn Dance, developing a saleable product took precedence over making money. As Lair recalled, "We weren't making too much on the appearances of the radio people, on the radio shows, although we had some network shows. But we were taking them on spec and we weren't getting much money out of them. We were just proving we could do them."[83] Competition came from both within WLW and from a former colleague at WLS. In a September 1, 1938, letter, Keyes warned that WLW and WLS were planning a double booking unit.[84] Furthermore, George Biggar had left WLS to start a competing barn dance show in the Cincinnati area. Biggar's show, the Boone County Jamboree, played Emery Auditorium on Friday nights, while Renfro Valley played on Saturdays at the Cincinnati Music Hall. On September 29 a Cincinnati newspaper columnist, Paul Kennedy, described the war waged along the "hillbilly front." Both shows initially drew good audiences, Kennedy reported, but "there was and still is the ticklish question of whether Cincinnati is large enough to support bigtime hillbilly shows. Until that's settled you'd best git the houn' dawgs in and put the chilluns under the woodbox because the Lairs and the Biggars are a feudin' like all tarnation."[85] Although he continued to broadcast from WLW and kept his family in Covington, Lair moved the live show to Dayton for his final year in Ohio.

In the meantime, Keyes counseled Lair to be patient. "I honestly believe," he advised, "that we have one more year [at WLW] and that's all, but don't forget, Johnny, that we have the clients, and we can move into Detroit or maybe New York City. Who knows but what a Barn Dance would knock them cold in New York?" Keyes concluded by urging, "We might as well try to get along with them as easily as we can. Milk the territory we have built up, and start our other business as quickly as possible. For that reason, John, I am not inclined to worry too much about the details on the PLANTATION PARTY, such an [sic] Beherens and Foley and the rest of them. I am not inclined to crab too much whether Mr. Biggers [sic] goes to WLW or doesn't go. Let's take our minds off these details and concentrate on the big purpose we now have in mind. Look at the big side of it, forget the petty side. That's for both of us."[86] Although Lair did move his operation to Kentucky the following year, his relationship with WLW continued for a few more troubled years.

The construction of Renfro Valley the tourist site kept pace with Lair's construction of Renfro Valley the on-air presence. In a prospectus written shortly before he moved to Kentucky he stated, "A pioneer settlement has been re-created at the expense of approximately Forty-five Thousand ($45,000.00) Dollars, featuring the log cabin homes of early settlers in the Valley, the old log school-church house which has served as a community center in Renfro Valley for a hundred (100) years, and a new barn with a seating capacity of one thousand (1,000)." Despite his later claims that he wished to preserve the Valley, Lair suggested that the site promote a message of progress and that the collection of antiquated machinery might be used as a contrast to "the latest developments which the sponsor has to offer to make life easier and a little more enjoyable for the farmer-and-worker, the two greatest divisions of the American buying public."[87]

To accommodate visitors to Renfro, Lair built a lodge and restaurant as well as tourist cabins. These modern conveniences, constructed from logs by local builders, again signaled both tradition and modernity. As Lair would note in the 1940 *Renfro Valley Keepsake*, "It was all very well for the exterior of the cabin to look like the boyhood home of a Senator or a President, but the interior had to make some concession to modern living."[88] Cabins had pine or chestnut paneling and stone hearths in addition to steam heat and shower baths with hot and cold running water.

Given his mixed messages of tradition and modernity, Lair seemed most to want to sell sincerity and authenticity. The prospectus for his program read, "This will be the only program on the air actually originating in the setting it describes and enacts on the radio, and actually living the parts they play on the program. People listening to this program on the air or attending the broadcast in person will be convinced of the sincerity and truthfulness of the entire performance, and will be apt to give additional credit to any statement made in behalf of the sponsor." Lair appealed primarily to sponsors' profit motive but did not stop short of outright lying to make the case for his community's authenticity: "The talent on this show, most of which came from Renfro Valley originally, is moving back to that section of the country and will become a part of this re-created community doing their Saturday night broadcast from the barn built for that purpose."[89] Of the Cincinnati cast, only Lair himself and his nephew Harry Mullins (Little Clifford) were Rockcastle County natives.

Several members of the on-air Renfro Valley "community" balked at actually moving to Kentucky. Daisy Lange and Violet Koehler quit to work with the Callahan Brothers in Texas. To make up for the loss Lair added another Ledford sister, Minnie (Black Eyed Susie), to the line-up. Two other popular cast members of the Barn Dance also did not make the initial move to Renfro Valley. On September 23, 1940, ten months after the first broadcast from Renfro Valley, Lair told Keyes, "That stretch imagination you accuse me of having comes in might handy when you expect me to add Idy and Foley to the cast at no additional cost."[90]

No longer the shy Kentucky boy Lair had discovered in Berea, Red Foley aspired to greater fame. Although he had been one of Lair's original business partners in the Renfro enterprise, Foley and his wife expressed reservations about moving to Kentucky. "Eva hit here proclaiming loud and long she'd never have any part of this damn country," Lair reported to Keyes, later adding that Red was "fully sold on the big white hat stuff and I don't believe we could tempt him to come down." Lair advised, "You might do something with Red in Chicago—and he's still the best there is—but he'd never stoop this low after the visions he's had of Hollywood and Chicago greatness." Both Foley and Whitey Ford would eventually sell their interest in Renfro Valley.

Margaret Lillie also proved to be a tough customer. Lair did not want to pay "Idy" what she demanded nor give her the rights to the act's name: "I can't see where we'd gain anything by that. She'd be here about five weeks, then walk out with the name and go back to WLS or WLW for spite." Lair, it seems, already had a substitute "Idy," Ricca Hughes. In the September 23 letter he also referred to "either one of the Idys." The 1940 *Keepsake* noted that Hughes "pinch hits for A'nt Idy," but customers disliked the substitution. In January 1941 Harry Vannoy of the Paramount Theater in Anderson, Indiana, complained that several people had noticed that the advertising provided for a live performance did not picture the original Idy.[91] Despite the ill-feelings between Lair and Lillie, the original Idy, Lillie performed at Renfro Valley for a short period, but her act failed to achieve the popularity it once had in Cincinnati.

Lair's business sense apparently failed him when he decided to move his show during the month of November. The tourist trade felt off dramatically during the winter months; performances took place in a cold, unheated barn; and Lair had a large stack of bills to pay. Still, John Lair tried to keep his hopes up. That winter he observed to Keyes, "Freeman, it may look a little dark right now but I'm certain this thing will make money for all concerned. One week of fair weather will swamp us with visitors."[92] Whether or not that was Lair's true belief, his optimism was not misplaced. He soon found out how many people wanted to come to the country and see a barn dance in a "real barn." "Heck, I was surprised as anybody was. I built this barn to seat seven or eight hundred people. If I had known what I found out two years later, I'd of made it seat five thousand people," he reminisced.[93] Money would continue to be a concern for both Lair and Keyes, but the Renfro Valley Barn Dance was on the threshold of becoming the most popular barn dance in the United States, eventually pulling in a live audience that exceeded that of the Grand Ole Opry in Nashville.

4 Tooting the Horn: The Heyday of the National Folk Festival and Renfro Valley Barn Dance

> If a man tooteth not his own horn, the same is tooted not.
> —Masthead, *Renfro Valley Bugle*

During the mid-1930s, lifetime goals came into clear focus for John Lair and Sarah Gertrude Knott. The plans they laid then would occupy the rest of their lives. Certainly, many of their ambitious schemes failed, but the ability to dream large and risk failure is the mark of a successful person. From the late 1930s through the mid-1940s Lair and Knott began to reap the harvest of their hard work. As the world plunged headfirst into war, they found themselves at the top of their games.

While John Lair began to create the Renfro Valley Barn Dance in Cincinnati, Sarah Gertrude Knott set up shop in Washington, D.C. The move in 1938 brought the National Folk Festival into an era of visibility that Knott never again achieved. "From the beginning," she reported, "we have dreamed of a festival in the nation's capitol. This dream came true on the sixth, seventh and eighth days of May, of this year, when people from twenty-nine states laid aside the ordinary work of the day, declared a 'people's holiday,' and followed the winding roads that led to Washington."[1]

Knott found a Washington benefactor through the intercession of Homer T. Rainey, who "said, 'I believe Mr. and Mrs. Eugene Meyer of the Washington Post should sponsor this, . . . Let's call them up.' And he called them and we went right down there and it was a sale right away."[2] In 1933 Meyer, a former chair of the board of governors of the Federal Reserve System, had purchased the *Washington Post*, a debt-ridden newspaper with four major competitors in the city, and during the mid-1930s he dramatically increased its readership and political clout. Meyer took a five-year option on sponsoring the National Folk Festival and offered it secure if not lavish support and an almost unlimited supply of publicity.

Although the festival did not receive direct federal backing, affiliation with the *Post* allowed Knott to build an impressive cadre of supporters. In 1941 the newspaper reported that leaders in "official, social and educational life" had accepted membership on the festival's general committee. The publisher's socialite wife Agnes Meyer chaired the committee, with Eleanor Roosevelt as the honorary chair. The committee included a number of cabinet members' wives as well as Secretary of Labor Frances Perkins, Speaker of the House Sam Rayburn, General George C. Marshall, and future president and vice president Harry Truman and Alben Barkley.[3] Under Meyer's sponsorship planners tightened the festival's format from the sprawling, week-long programs of Dallas and Chicago into a three-day event at Constitution Hall, then Washington's only major concert hall. According to Knott, Meyer also formalized the policy of not paying participants with the exception of Native Americans, who did receive some support from the federal government.

The use of Constitution Hall was problematic because of the Knott's practice of prominently featuring African American performers. It is still not altogether clear how she navigated this particular Charybdis of racial relations. Decades later, after interviewing her about retirement, a *Post* reporter wrote that Knott "refused to sign a lease with the Daughters of the American Revolution, owners of the festival's Constitution Hall site, until they agreed to admit blacks to the event."[4] That account neglects the main issue. The unusual aspect of the DAR's policy, even for segregated Washington, D.C., was the "white artists only" clause in its contracts. Constitution Hall excluded African American performers; African American audiences were segregated through the hall's seating. The year following the National's first festival held at Constitution Hall, the DAR barred the renowned contralto Marion Anderson from performing there on racial grounds, an incident that received nation attention when Eleanor Roosevelt resigned from the organization in protest.[5]

A critical history of the DAR's policy states that, beginning in 1931, no black artists performed on the stage of Constitution Hall for more than a decade.[6] From 1938 to 1942, however, the National Folk Festival did feature African American performers, including such notables as W. C. Handy and Zora Neale Hurston. It may be that the National Folk Festival Association applied for an exception to the rule. The Daughters would later claim that Anderson's manager had failed to properly apply for the exception.[7] It would also have been characteristic for Knott to make promises to the DAR that she had no intention of keeping. It seems unlikely, however, that the DAR would have allowed the festival to continue for five years had Knott taken that route. Whatever the case, less than three weeks after Anderson held her legendary protest concert at the Lincoln Memorial on Easter morning of 1939 African Americans performed on the stage of Constitution Hall as part of the National Folk Festival.

The *Washington Post* years brought a radical change in Knott's policy on which cultural groups she featured at the festival. In 1939 she justified the "middle ground" course that neither included the folklore of recent immigrants nor limited the program exclusively to Anglo-Saxon performers but focused on the "most distinctively American expressions," including "the contributions of the Negro, lumberjack, sailor, miner and cowboy." After spending three pages on the importance of Native and Hispanic traditions, Knott stated, "Of course, no one doubts that the Anglo-Saxon expressions should predominate at the National Folk Festival."[8]

Although scholars may now take this as evidence of Knott's conservatism, the statement seems anomalous in a broader look at Knott's career.[9] The National Folk Festival always had a fundamental commitment to multiculturalism, and Knott seemed personally more interested in Native and Hispanic folklore than Anglo-American. She may have been compelled to make the point to appease what she believed to be the conservatism of the readership of the *Southern Folklore Quarterly*. Nevertheless, the policy of excluding recent immigrants came to an end during the *Washington Post* years as the festival became more inclusive. In 1938 two of the barrier-breaking groups that had performed in Chicago, the Wisconsin lumberjacks and Beliajus's Lithuanian American folk dancers, returned to the National. The program also included a tamburitza orchestra as well as a Swedish American hardanger player. The floodgates were open, and Scandinavian and East European groups became especially popular at the festival.

The National Folk Festival also took on a more international perspective in Washington, incorporating performers from other countries in the Americas as well as the American territories. Knott and M. J. Pickering, the festival's business manager, worked diplomatic as well as other Washington contacts to secure participation and sent letters to government officials in Haiti, Peru, and Panama as well as Canada and Mexico. In 1940, with contacts established through folklorist Martha Beckwith, Hawaiians performed at the festival for the first time.

Knott's perception of changing interests among the audience inspired the shift toward a more inclusive festival. During the depression years America's concerns had turned inward, something Knott perceived would change with war on the horizon. When she first moved to Washington Knott still touted the need for recreational outlets for underemployed Americans, but over the next few years she began to emphasize the need for mutual understanding across cultural differences. "Almost overnight we changed from a nation of isolationists to champions of international cooperation. All at once the need for understanding the peoples of the world, with whom our destiny must be intertwined, dawned upon us," she recalled.[10]

In moving to the nation's capitol, however, Knott did not neglect her commitment to the regional folklore of the festival's venue. In March of 1938 she held a meeting at the University of Maryland to explore the state's representation at the fifth annual National Folk Festival. The advisory committee, which included the university's dean of agriculture and the assistant director of the extension service, made a county-by-county, mapped survey to locate various contacts. The *Washington Post* quoted Knott as emphasizing the state's "rich and varied racial heritage and its unusual geography."[11]

The local regional focus covered other states in the Mid-Atlantic as well. The same month as the Maryland meeting, a representative from the Delaware Department of Public Instruction informed Christian Sanderson that Knott wanted help locating people "who play old fiddle tunes, sing ballads, and groups who can do square dances or singing games and would be willing to participate in the Festival."[12] Sanderson, an eccentric antiquarian from Chadds Ford, Pennsylvania, performed as a fiddler and square dance caller and would play a significant role in the National Folk Festival for years to come. He eventually took the role of the "town crier" who opened the event. When Eleanor Roosevelt attended the National Folk Festival in 1942, Knott arranged for Sanderson to perform.[13]

Regional festivals continued to play a significant role in Knott's general scheme, their goals changing gradually from a means of identifying talent for the National Folk Festival to a way of extending the organization's outreach effort. The "community plan" could reach audiences the festival did not.[14] Moreover, larger regional festivals provided a means of support for Knott during the eight months she received nothing from the National Folk Festival payroll. Knott also continued to dream of simultaneously having both eastern and western National Folk Festivals. She mentioned to Clinton P. Anderson of the Coronado Quarto Centennial that although the *Post* had a five-year option perhaps there could simultaneously be another festival, also called "National," as part of the Quarto Centennial.[15]

Along with the newly identified groups, the National Folk Festival continued to feature many old favorites during its Washington years, including the Kiowa dancers, anthracite miners, and Sailor Dad Hunt. Demonstrating Knott's embrace of individuals and groups of various ideologies, the 1942 National Folk Festival included performers from the Highlander Folk School. Established in 1932 in central Tennessee, this leftist organization was deeply committed to the labor movement. Under the direction of Zilphia Horton it also included a cultural program that featured folk music and dance as expressions of the struggle of working people.[16]

Not content to settle for the ample free publicity provided by the *Post*, Pickering and Knott concerned themselves as well with other forms of exposure in the mass media. In 1940 Knott wrote, "We are working on plans for a national broadcasting program over Columbia and NBC during the festival."[17] At the same time, Pickering had his eye on a nascent form of mass media and told Paul Green that officials from NBC felt that "folk presentations are particularly adaptable to television."[18] Knott did achieve some radio exposure for her festival, but in the end it was Alan Lomax who brought regular folklore programming to the air with the network program *Back Where I Come From*.[19]

During the early years of the festival, sound recordings captured the performances of many participants. Some initiative for making the recordings came from federal agencies, as when the Archive of Folk Song sent Lomax to record the Ohio Valley festival in 1938. The previous year the Works Progress Administration (WPA) Music Project had recorded the complete program of the National Folk Festival in Chicago.[20] During the 1939 festival the Kiowa performers made recordings of songs at the Bureau of Indian Affairs. During the *Post* years Knott and Pickering also contracted first with the Electreporter Company and then the U.S. Recording Company to record performers at the festival.[21]

Of course, the festival's sponsor provided the best media documentation of the event. The *Post* not only printed the schedule itself as well as special school editions of the program but also closely covered the planning stages. In contrast to the superficial treatment of previous press coverage, the newspaper took folk tradition seriously. As a preliminary to each festival it ran a series of relatively long articles, written by academics and collectors, to feature various traditions. Among those articles in 1939 was Ben Botkin's "The Function of a Folk Festival." While noting the contributions of scholars and federal agencies, Botkin stated, "It has remained to the folk festivals to foster the presentation of folk materials and the participation of folk groups as a living expression. As a national clearing house for State and regional festivals the National Folk Festival Association is in a strategic position to direct and co-ordinate this non-academic, non-professional activity."[22]

During the Washington years Knott continued to try to build academic support for the National Folk Festival. She added a number of new, academically trained members to the roster of board members, including Ralph Steele Boggs, a Latin Americanist who was developing Chapel Hill's curriculum in folklore; Africanist Melville Herskovits from Northwestern University; and the novelist and folklorist Zora Neale Hurston. She used Paul Green as an intermediary in communicating with Hurston, asking him in 1940, "Won't you try to pin Zora down and get her to let me know what she plans to do on the program?"[23]

Although not a member of the American Folklore Society (AFS) at the time, Knott did attend several of their meetings. In 1939 she reported to Green, "I was in New York Christmas and attended the Modern Language, Anthropology and American Folklore Society meetings. I met many of the people on our National Committee and discussed plans with them all—and with other authorities not on our committees. I found that practically all thought we were on the right trail. Miss Burchenal was the only one who took the opposite stand with the criticism that the people at our festival were 'snatched from their locale,' to which Miss Pound replied that it was true, but so had she snatched from the Hawaiian scene the lovely quilt she had on exhibit."[24] Whatever her objection, Elizabeth Burchenal, president of the American Folk Dance Society, served as a member of the national committee for the following two decades.

Academic conferences also continued as a part of the National Folk Festival program. In 1938 the conference was held at the American University and in the following years at area hotels. Reporting on the conference in 1941, the *Post* declared, "Folk Festival Hailed as Spur to Scholars." Hitting a cautionary note in his presentation, ethnomusicologist Charles Seeger spoke on "The Hazards of Exploitation of Folk Material."[25] Knott continued to struggle with the relationship between festival organizers and academic folklorists. In a memo entitled "Some Questions which Pester Me!" she asked, "Do you think it is wise to have a dividing line between the 'festival people' and 'folklorists'? Should festival leaders not do everything possible to become authorities in folklore by research from books as well as studying the traditional heritages in their living forms from their neighbors and friends in home communities? Of course, folklorists everywhere should be behind the festival movement."[26]

Although Knott continued to build bridges with academics, programming for school children stands as one of her greatest achievements of the *Washington Post* years. The National's premiere in St. Louis had involved special matinees for school children, but the limited planning periods of the Chattanooga and Chicago festivals and the June date of the Dallas National made school cooperation impossible. Finally, Knott had the right structure to rebuild school support. Attempting to reach all schools, public and private, in the District of Columbia area, she created a general school committee that had sectional chairs for senior high, junior high, and elementary levels. A 1941 *Post* article quoted Principal Elizabeth Andrews, the chair of the school committee, as saying, "The study of the indigenous and vernacular music of our country enlivens and enriches the social studies in the school."[27]

The committee provided educational materials on folklore to all schools in the District, many of which included folk music in classes and assemblies. Some even sponsored small festivals themselves. By special ruling, boards of education in the District and nearby communities authorized school absences on festival days, and the *Post* printed special permission forms for early school excusals. School children's tickets, which sold for 25 cents, could be purchased through PTAs. Always pragmatic, Knott realized that school programming helped promote adult attendance. Near the end of her active career she observed that "school children's attendance, in addition to its value to students, has served a definite purpose in helping to make the budget by bringing in school children and especially by advertising it to adults. Wherever there has been a large school attendance there has been a large adult attendance."[28]

As the National Folk Festival's five-year contract with the *Washington Post* approached its end the country prepared for war. The first wartime festival would be the newspaper's last. In March 1942 Knott announced that the festival would be devoted to "upbuilding of national morale in wartime America," and the program included choruses from the U.S. Army, Navy, and Marine Corps.[29] The emphasis on cultural understanding became even more pronounced and pointed. A large contingent of "Palestinian" singers and dancers, mostly American students representing various Zionist youth organizations, represented the culture of Jewish pioneers in what would become the state of Israel.[30]

The year 1942 also brought the first and only double-sited festival. Immediately after the Washington event, the *New York Post* sponsored a smaller version of the ninth annual National Folk Festival in Madison Square Garden. Interviewed on network radio by Mary Margaret McBride, Knott directly connected the New York performance to the war effort, arguing that the festival could help win the war through promotion of cultural understanding of groups in the United States.[31] According to Knott's account, the total audience for the festival was more than twenty-two thousand, and the New York press gave the event a "splendid account" the following day.[32] The *New York Times*'s review was a glowing one: "If any doubt remained as to the great public interest in folk dance and music, the first New York session of the National Folk Festival at Madison Square Garden yesterday afternoon and evening must have dispelled them." The reviewer noted the inexhaustible enthusiasm of the more than nine thousand school children "seeking autographs from those most anonymous of all creatures, folk dancers, and [behaving] themselves generally just exactly as American folk would want their youngsters to behave." He added that the National Folk Festival was "late in making its New York bow, but the unquestionable success of its first venture here should assure its becoming an annual event in this sophisticated but folk-conscious metropolis."[33] Despite the rave review, New York City never again became the venue for the festival while Knott was director.

Whether or not the *Washington Post* would have chosen to continue its association with the festival, wartime conditions precluded that option as Washington became increasingly crowded. A surprising wartime ally came in the form of the Order of the Sons of Italy in Philadelphia, with Judge Eugene V. Alessandroni spearheading the effort to move the festival to his city. In January 1943 Alessandroni responded to a letter from Chris Sanderson: "I thoroughly agree with your sentiments and if the plans that are now under way succeed, Philadelphia will have the honor of holding it this year."[34] The choice of Philadelphia also allowed Pickering, who graduated from the University of Pennsylvania and had been directly involved in the opening of Philadelphia's Coliseum, to further exploit his contacts in the city.

The tenth annual National Folk Festival opened at the Academy of Music in Philadelphia in May 1943. The *Philadelphia Bulletin*, describing the forty-eight-year-old festival director as "blonde, blue-eyed and pretty," quoted Knott as saying, "We decided on Philadelphia because it was the first capitol of our Nation and because of its great historical importance."[35] The major theme, however, was unity within diversity. Writing of the Philadelphia festival several years later, Knott stated, "The older folk expressions still predominated on every program, but there were many new groups. Among them were: Scandinavians, Italians, Jews,

Bulgarians, Chinese, Finns, Rumanians, Filipinos, Portuguese, Russians, Czechoslovakians, Poles, Spaniards, and Lithuanians. Many of the native lands of the participants were in the camp of the allied nations; others were not. No line was drawn. The festival reflected the broadened attitude of our people and symbolized the democracy we claim and were fighting to protect and make more real."[36]

As much as Knott felt that the country needed the festival more than ever, it was difficult to compete with wartime production. In late 1943 Botkin, by now assistant in charge of the Archive of American Folk Song, grew concerned about the fate of the recordings of the Washington National Folk Festivals. An inquiry revealed that the U.S. Recording Company had scrapped its collection of recordings of the festival and been ordered by the War Production Board to salvage the aluminum in the disks. Botkin requested that the disks be located and copied: "Our immediate interest in the collection, however, arises from the fact that minority folk music, of which we have a minimum collection in the archive, is especially well represented in these recordings. This factor is of special importance at the present time when the demand for such material is great, as evidenced by a recent request from the Office of War Information."[37]

As it turned out, Pickering and Knott had difficulty locating the recordings, and a number of those finally shipped arrived broken. Once he heard them for himself, Botkin must have had reservations about either their quality or content. "I suggest," he said in an internal Library of Congress memo, "that you hear samples of Miss Knott's records before proceeding." Eventually, Botkin returned the recordings to Knott and Pickering, explaining that duplication could not be made "on account of budgetary limitations."[38]

Although the National Folk Festival always remained foremost in her mind, it did not occupy Knott full-time. The *Philadelphia Bulletin* reported that during her months off from planning the National she directed smaller regional festivals, taught an "American Folk extension course" at Washington University in St. Louis, and "in between times" was writing a book, "giving a cross section of the folk life of years gone by and that of the new American groups."[39] Despite attending some of its conferences, Knott had yet to join the AFS. In 1944 Pickering contacted Botkin, now president of society, to ask for information about the upcoming conference scheduled to be held in Philadelphia. Knott, he said, had returned to Kentucky following the sudden death of her brother-in-law and would not return in time for the meeting, but Pickering added that he hoped to attend AFS sessions that would be of relevance to the festival. Pickering also invited Botkin to stop by the *Bulletin* offices so he could see a display of their work of the past eleven years.[40] Two months later Knott mentioned to Botkin that she would like to become a member of the society: "I have been asked, of course, to do this, but somehow I have neglected doing it. Would it be possible? I have attended a number of meetings in New York from time to time and know it would be worth my while." She also included a copy of an unfinished article and asked for suggestions to improve it.[41]

After the 1943 National Folk Festival the *Philadelphia Evening Bulletin* had taken over sponsorship from the Sons of Italy, although Judge Alessandroni continued as a key player. In her "Chart of NFFs" Knott notes that "money was no object" for the festival and lists a budget of $18,000.[42] That figure, if accurate, indicates that the *Bulletin* spent twice as much money as that allocated by the *Post* per festival. Despite the level of support from the *Bulletin*, the war created a large attrition rate among regular performers. Knott devoted a sizable portion of a newsletter sent out before the eleventh festival, relaying news of the many who were serving in the armed forces. She particularly felt the absence of Arthur Campa, then a lieutenant in the army, and tried to compensate for his lost expertise by contacting the director of the Hispanic Institute at Columbia University. She also added another western academic folklorist, Wayland Hand of UCLA, to the national committee.[43]

The war also brought performers. In the newsletter Knott mentions hope that some English sailors currently in the United States would play a hornpipe for the festival. The 1944 festival also included a contingent of Chinese officers then living in Swarthmore, who would perform "songs that have grown up during the last eight years of China's great struggle for liberty."[44] Despite the problems she encountered in keeping a full slate of performers, the need for wartime entertainment brought audiences that filled the concert hall; in 1944 three thousand school children attended each of the four matinees.

The festival in Philadelphia also brought Knott a new assistant from the ranks of the recreation movement. She met Priscilla Urner through Urner's work with the New England Folk Festival, and Knott asked her to escort some performers down to Philadelphia. Trained in languages and involved with developing recreational activities, Urner viewed folk activities as a means toward world peace. Her responsibilities at the National Folk Festival, however, were often more mundane and included escorting an old sea-chanteyist to the event. "He was almost always drunk," she recalled, "and the mike would be here and he'd be going this way and part of my job was to try to keep him less drunk before he went on to sing his song, so the mike would be in front of him." Another of Urner's jobs involved keeping the Native American dancers from jingling the bells on their clothing too much backstage.

Priscilla Urner felt that Knott had a special touch in working with performers. On the one hand, "She could get down to the level of being with them so that they would open up to her with all this and share with her. Information that they never shared with anybody else, you know. Because she could make them realize that what they had—that's the important thing; she could make them realize that what they had was a valuable contribution." On the other hand, "She could be a Tartar. To work with, too. I mean, things had to be exactly her way." Although Urner admired Knott, she felt that her greatest failing was the way that she "drained" people and did not always give volunteers proper acknowl-edgement. Seldom was Urner's name on the program. "I did an awful lot in bringing people down and escorting them and taking care of them backstage. . . . A lot of people paid their own expenses to come and help with this and names wouldn't be there [on the program]. . . . And I, I don't think I ever brought it up to her because somehow—even though I loved her and worked with her—I was a little scared of her. I think everybody was a little scared of Sarah . . . she could be so snappy about something and you, if you were in the middle of working with her, you didn't want that attitude there, . . . So you kept things on a quieter level."[45] Still, Urner, like many other loyal friends, continued to give active support to the National Folk Festival over several decades.

During the war years, with Knott touting ideological justifications for her festival more than ever, even she may have had doubts about whether she actually believed her words. Typically, however, she even gave her doubts a positive spin. She wrote of the 1944 festival, "One day just before the Festival opened when I was passing through the 'slough of despond' which preceded every Festival when we know definitely what the pro-gram is to be, I said to my secretary, 'I wonder if I have just formed the habit of saying these things or if I really mean it.' She said, 'Well you have dictated those words many times but somehow each time you say the words you seem to give them fresh emphasis. I think you believe it.'"[46]

Whatever her doubts, the 1944 festival must have been enough of a success that the *Bulletin* invited Knott to continue activities throughout the next several months. The first activity, "Elfreth Alley Day," included strolling folk musicians and dancers, folk songs from the Order of the Sons of Italy, the A. C. Bilbrew Negro Chorus, street criers, and Chris Sanderson and the Pocopson Valley Boys. For the next four weeks, as part of the Fifth War Loan Drive, Wednesday evening performances by various national and ethnic groups were held at Snellenburg's Department Store. In July the Evening Bulletin Folk Festival Association and the Park Commission began a square dancing program in the parks, attracting, according to Knott, thousands weekly. There were also square dances for patients at the State Hospital in Trenton, New Jersey, and for service men and women at the Labor Plaza USO in Philadelphia.[47]

Perhaps the most significant *Bulletin*-sponsored activity, aside from the festival itself, was publication in 1945 of the *Folk Festival Handbook*, a sixty-page manual for preparing and presenting a community folk festival. The war had not yet ended, but the handbook was intended to instruct communities on how to organize folk festivals as "part of America's postwar planning." Knott's previous festival guidelines usually were brief and mimeographed, although in 1940 the *Washington Post* had printed a small booklet. The *Handbook* provided far more extensive guidelines in three parts: a practical planning section, a brief introduction to the lore of various folk groups, and an extensive bibliography. The planning section gave many specific suggestions, for example, "If yours happens to be an industrial town, don't overlook participant possibilities among the workers." And, "If your town happens to have settlements of one or more foreign-born groups, it is important that each nationality be represented." Towns that once but no longer had a Native American population were instructed, "Do not make the mistake of dressing up town citizens as braves and squaws to do an Indian dance on festival night. That is pageantry not in folk festival tradition." Finally, the *Handbook* cautioned against using a festival for fund-raising: "Money making is not the objective of a folk festival—nor should it be."[48]

The language of the *Handbook*'s introduction clearly suggests that the *Bulletin* planned to continue to sponsor the National Folk Festival: "It seems entirely fitting that The Philadelphia Evening Bulletin should undertake to be of some aid in this work and that Philadelphia should become the permanent home of the National Folk Festival." Philadelphia did not become the permanent home of the National Folk Festival, however, and no more festivals would be held in that city. War-imposed travel restrictions forced the cancellation of the twelfth Annual National Folk Festival, scheduled for May 9–12, 1945. For the first time in a dozen years there was no National Folk Festival.

By the end of summer, peace was at hand, and Knott was preparing to retool. Undoubtedly using her new connection to Wayland Hand, she published "The National Folk Festival after Twelve Years" in the *California Folklore Quarterly*.[49] In it, Knott traced the development of the festival, especially the transition toward including recent immigrant cultures and international perspectives, and touched briefly on an issue that would soon become central to the National Folk Festival: the role of revivalism. In 1939 she had stated in *Southern Folklore Quarterly* that the "revival of folksongs, music and dances, without traditional transmission lacks the original spontaneity and joy which is their chief charm."[50] Seven years later she noted that in original plans for the festival "provision was made for the inclusion of revivals and arrangements based on folk themes, which, as the years have passed, have been admitted more and more."

Knott always preferred those revival folk arts still anchored in ethnic or regional identity. During the Washington and Philadelphia years the increase in revival groups resulted largely from including the cultures of more recent immigrants to the United States. Most of those displays of culture came in the form of formally organized dance troupes. The issue of revivalism touched on in the *California Folklore Quarterly* article presaged concerns for the negotiation of authenticity that would be a critical issue for Knott in coming decades. The 1945 article also outlined Knott's new purpose for her festival after the war. As much as she promoted the positive aspects of ethnic and racial identity, she foresaw that ethnic enclaves and segregation would no longer be acceptable:

> Returning veterans will not be content to revert again to the status of "Indian," "Negro," "Spanish-American," "Polish," "Italian." Our service men and women are returning with their ideas of democracy stronger, more definite, and more insistent for realization; they cannot reconcile the idea of fighting for democracy abroad with the practice of discrimination at home. We must somehow find a common ground of mutual respect, measuring up to the nation's twentieth-century idea of our fathers' belief that "all men are created equal." Just how to do this is recognized by many as one of the most serious postwar problems. Folk activities cannot solve it but democratic use of them can help.[51]

As Knott enjoyed her seven-year stint presenting folk traditions in Washington and Philadelphia out in Kentucky the first radio barn dance held in a "real" barn became a reality. With the barn, tourist lodge, cabins and trading post ready to go, Lair began broadcasting by remote from Rockcastle County, Kentucky. On November 4, 1939, he came on the air with "Howdy, folks, this is the Renfro Valley Barn Dance coming to you from its new home down in Renfro Valley." Having spent two years finding a loyal audience on WLW, Lair's challenge was to make the radio audience truly care that they were now listening to a show emanating from a real rather than imaginary rural setting.

Even in its opening weeks, WLW touted Renfro Valley as the "Shrine of American folk music." Shrines suggest pilgrimages, and part of the allure of Renfro Valley was the possibility that one day listeners could make their way to the site. Even those who had no reasonable expectation of ever actually getting there expressed their longing to visit. Not only could visitors have firsthand experience with the good times of the "boys and girls" who performed at Renfro Valley, but an array of log buildings built by "neighbors" also greeted them, providing both the allure of tradition and the comfort of modern facilities for travelers.

One could also purchase a piece of tradition as a souvenir in the trading post, which was run by Virginia Lair and the Lair daughters and included local crafts. The 1940 *Renfro Valley Keepsake* pictured Ann Lair, the eldest, tending a display of carved hound dogs, ceramic flowerpots, and old-fashioned brooms. Visitors could also view local women turning out rag rugs on ancient looms and a woodworking shop run by Lair's nephews. Undoubtedly, the "Fireside Industry" of Berea College just twenty miles north of Renfro inspired Lair's promotion of local crafts. Berea's primary aims, however, were philanthropic and educational. Lair, although engaged in some philanthropic acts, was more interested in promoting the local economy. Had the concept of "heritage tourism" been invented, Lair would have led the bandwagon.

The local business interests seemed to welcome the opening of Renfro Valley. Just weeks after the attraction opened, the *Mt. Vernon Signal* ran a special supplement to commemorate the event and celebrate the advances of progress brought by the automobile. As one advertisement read, "But of great value still is the service the automobile has rendered in making us a more educated, progressive and enlightened people. . . . Our vision is no longer limited to a few square miles."[52] On the surface, that message would seem directly in opposition to Renfro Valley's theme of the good old days when life was slower and everyone knew their neighbors, but Lair was well aware that his business was built on the advances of technology, specifically the radio and the automobile, and progress fueled nostalgia.

Ultimately, Renfro Valley would become more successful as a tourist site and live show than as a media empire. In the early years Renfro Valley was well equipped to outstrip competitors in the barn dance field. If enough people showed up, Lair put on shows all night. Still, he never forgot his radio audience (or the sponsors that paid for the shows), nor did he confine himself only to the barn dance format. Perhaps Lair's most experimental radio show was *Monday Night in Renfro Valley*, which ran during the 1940–41 season. The show, set in the relocated Redbud

Schoolhouse, featured the "good old customs of plain American ways of livin'." Lair did not keep listeners within the confines of the schoolhouse but took them by remote to an actual hayride, possum hunt, and fish fry. Broadcast both on WLW and the NBC Red Network, the Monday night show, although short-lived, hit a chord with listeners.

Lair continued his early practice of attending carefully to listeners' mail, and in many instances he responded personally. A man from Indiana wrote, "I heard the possom hunt it sounded Real. Could hear the dogs. I am in the market for a good night dog." Lair responded within a couple of days that he knew of just the dog. The *Keepsake* also gave the reader visual images to associate with memories of aural events. After receiving her copy, a woman from Ohio wrote, "Especially did we enjoy the 'Possom Hunt' pictures, since we heard the cracking of the fire (—as you held the 'mike' down over it) the barking of the dogs and the hearty laugh of 'Freezy' [Hershell Nelson] when he had Mr. Possom in hand."[53]

Listeners responded to the Monday night show and the Renfro Valley Barn Dance with reminiscences and longings for the past, requests for songs, and stories of hardship. They even congratulated Lair on the fine products he promoted. A listener from Texas noted, "Incidentally I am now smoking Big Ben—no joke, to prove it I enclose a coupon to prove it." The letter that best shows that Lair hit his mark was from John Martin of Greensburg, Indiana, who thanked him "for taking your radio broadcast from the land of make believe and making it a thing of reality—not a thing or place only in imagination, as most broadcasts are, but a place to be seen and admired." Martin concluded, "I have a fond hope, that I may some day be able—have the means—to come to your big barn, meet each of you personally and spend at least a day or two with all you folks, in lovely Renfro Valley."[54]

If Lair successfully attracted visitors to Renfro Valley, he had more trouble recruiting and keeping good performers. Renfro lacked the allure of big-city markets, and its relatively remote location made it difficult for performers to make a living wage there. Radio performers generally supplemented their salaries by live appearances and various forms of self-promotion, and Renfro provided less opportunity for such activity. Furthermore, Lair could not, or would not, support a star system. For him, the Valley itself should be the star of the show, and in any case he could not afford to compete with the salaries that big radio stations offered to top performers. Lair had a knack for spotting and developing young talent, and despite his reputation for being tight with money he typically offered attractive enough initial salaries. Many performers, however, soon came to believe they could make more elsewhere, or they chafed

under the control Lair had on the production. Some left and then, real-
izing the grass was not necessarily greener, returned. In most cases Lair
welcomed them back.

Performers at Renfro Valley can largely be divided into two groups:
those who came, made a name for themselves, and quickly moved on, and
those who chose to stay for decades. The latter group included women
with family commitments and performers who liked the lifestyle Renfro
Valley offered. The performers' views of Lair as a person, and the relationships they developed with the boss, also shaped their choices. Two
who joined Renfro Valley in its early days when they were only teenagers
had radically different perceptions of Lair. Not surprisingly, one chose to
stay on and the other left. In 1938 Jerry Byrd, a high school student who
played the electric steel guitar, found his first big break on the Renfro
Valley Barn Dance, then broadcast by WLW from Memorial Hall in Dayton. After graduation from high school, Byrd rejoined the show, which
had moved south to Kentucky. He did not consider Lair either warm
or accessible. "He was a reserved person," Byrd said, ". . . never felt a
warm feeling. . . . He kind of kept a distance between . . . himself and
the talent. I think that was for, more for business purposes than, than it
was actually his personality, because he liked to be around entertainers
and players of country music, the *real* country music. He was a kind of
a purist, you know. So he was kind of hard to get to know, personally."
Byrd felt that even Lair's favorites, the Coon Creeks, Slim Miller, and
others, would have said of Lair, "Well, I worked for him for years, but I
never really knew him."[55]

Although Byrd respected Lair and appreciated the big break he
offered, the men quickly came into conflict over money. After moving
to Kentucky, Byrd settled into one of the log tourist cabins and initially
worked only for room and board. Eventually, Red Foley interceded, and
Byrd was paid $13.50 a week, from which he had to pay for his hotel bills
and meals when the troupe traveled. "John was tight with his money,"
he recalled. "I had to run him down every week to get him to sign that
check. I'd get the check, but nobody's signature would be on it. And
I guess everybody else had to do the same thing pretty much. And he
would stop; I'd catch him running up the lane from the Lodge going over
to the Barn or somewhere. . . . And he always walked like he was carrying a load of books in his arm or something, he had a, a shuffle walk
. . . they called him 'Buffalo' because he had that big head and always
looking down toward, he looked like a buffalo walking along. And I'd
chase him and run him down and he wouldn't say a thing, he'd sign the
check and keep right on."

Performing at Renfro could definitely be a mixed blessing. If Lair sometimes did not pay a living wage, he did allow each performer to have a moment in the spotlight. "He never was unfair about his treatment," Byrd observed, "giving each person a chance to do his thing. He was smart that way, he got a lot out of his people for very little money because they felt like they were at least doing something on their own that could possibly bode well in the future. Whereas the Grand Ole Opry wasn't that way at all, it was, in fact, just the opposite." For young and ambitious performers, however, the opportunities were not great enough, especially for those who wanted to make records. "Well," Byrd said, "people like Homer and Jethro and myself and Ernie Lee could see that if we stayed there, you'd dry rot."[56]

During the early 1940s, before Jerry Byrd moved on to greater success in country and Hawaiian music, Lair hired another young performer who also began her career while still in high school. Virginia Sutton grew up in Brown County, Indiana, and was performing on radio with her cousin in Indianapolis. After Lair extended an invitation for them to join the Barn Dance the extremely nervous girls took the bus down to Renfro Valley. As Virginia Sutton Bray recalled, "I thought it would be a man in a suit and a tie. In he came with an old pair of riding breeches on, they were torn in the knee and he was eating an ice cream cone. So he put it at ease right now." At Lair's request Sutton shed her cowgirl attire and began a career at Renfro Valley that stretched over forty years. During that time, Virginia Sutton, who married her husband, Phyllis Bray, in 1946, had her own show, filled in for the Coon Creek Girls and Farmer Sisters, and eventually managed the Renfro Valley radio station. "We all loved Mr. Lair and we admired him," she said.[57]

Similar to Byrd, Sutton initially moved into one of the little log cabins and took part in the grueling weekday schedule that began at 5 A.M. Unlike Byrd, Lair paid her $50 a week, and she felt that she "was really in the money." Another offer briefly tempted her to return to Indianapolis: "This person up there wanted us to come back, and offered us quite a bit more money . . . and we did go back for a little while, but we weren't happy. You're never happy after you've been to Renfro Valley."[58]

Bray loved the informality of Lair's programs and the family feeling in the Valley: "We would, we would do our programs, then we'd go up to the Lodge and eat breakfast. And lots of time someone would play instruments and some of us would get up and jitterbug and just, it was just a fun thing. But we would go and have breakfast together almost every morning over at the Lodge. And it was just a fun thing, we just enjoyed each other. And we would go, Lily May'd cook big meals and we'd go to their homes and eat, and you know, and it was just a lot of fun, it was a family affair, it really was."[59]

Eventually, Lair came to rely more and more on individuals like Bray who happily settled into the homey atmosphere of Renfro Valley. But in the early 1940s his major task was to rebuild the show, which fell into disarray following the move to Kentucky. The Coon Creek Girls, minus two of the original performers, seemed "to have gone to hell generally as far as their work goes" he complained to Freeman Keyes in September of 1940. Lair also urged Keyes to "keep your eye open for a good voice we can convert to hillbilly." He hoped that, ultimately, sponsors would "raise the ante" but in an uncharacteristically pessimistic mood noted, "I'm not asking for more money until I get the talent I feel is worth more and right now I don't know where to find it."[60]

By the time the *Keepsake* came out a few months later the Coon Creek line-up included only one of the original performers, Lily May Ledford. Despite the reconfiguration of the group Lair continued to tout the Coon Creeks' famous performance at the White House, never noting the change of performers. The Coon Creek Girls continued to perform for almost another two decades with a shifting line-up that included various Ledford sisters, the Amburgey sisters (including Martha Carson), Virginia Sutton, and, for a time, another of the original Coon Creeks, the once rebellious Esther Koehler (Violet), who had subsequently married Lily May's brother, Custer.

By the time Lair wrote to Keyes he had already added what would become one of his most popular acts of the early 1940s, Homer and Jethro. The guitar and mandolin duo of Henry Haynes and Kenneth Burns began in their native east Tennessee. They played in a jazzy style, and despite his traditionalist predilections Lair hired them when they tried out at Renfro Valley. He also helped them perfect their comedy act. Part of their on-air comedy routine, however, was to mock Lair's musical preferences and poke fun at "them old wore-out, old-time songs."[61] Cast as two rubes who "come frum the hills but refuse to sing hill country music," they offered instead to play "swingeroo" or "jitterbuggy music."[62] As with Lair's framing of cowboy songs and blackface comedy, Homer and Jethro's act provided an acceptable way to include songs such as "Deep Purple" on the show.

Years later the duo provided a sense of the fun they had at Lair's expense on the Monday night show: "Each show was a brainstorm from the agile mind of Mr. Lair. One night it was a live possum hunt, direct from the woods. For weeks we got fan mail from possums, coons, and a couple of unemployed hunting dogs who were trying to pickup some club dates. We never knew if any people heard the show or not. We doubt it."[63]

Haynes and Burns were pleased with the $50 a week they each received at Renfro Valley and the network exposure that made them household names. They referred to Lair as a "wonderful man" who knew "more about folk music than any living human." Life in the tiny (and dry) Mt. Vernon, Kentucky, however, proved mighty slow for two young men, and they, like many other performers, began to believe that Lair did not pay them what they were worth. The armed services laid claim to Burns, however, before other radio shows could lure away the act. When he returned to Renfro, Lair made Homer and Jethro "an offer they could refuse." They were off to seek their fortune elsewhere.

Whether Lair could have prevented the talent drain from Renfro Valley is questionable. Despite its popular success Renfro Valley did not achieve financial stability during its early years. Furthermore, larger radio stations notoriously poached talent, and the more ambitious radio performers tended to be a peripatetic lot, moving frequently at the lure of better offers. In order to appear fully in charge Lair may have tried to disguise the lack of financial control he had over his business, a situation that would account for the notorious practice of handing out unsigned checks. He asked Freeman Keyes in February 1941 whether the payroll check might be sent earlier so he could pay acts on Monday before they left for the week's booking tour: "Our present schedule of receiving the check some time Wednesday, makes it hard for us to get it to them and of course none of them ever have money enough ahead to get by if they don't get their checks right on time."[64]

Lair was more obsessive than greedy. His dream was not to amass wealth but build up Renfro Valley, a vision he often pursued with a singularity sometimes in disregard of others' needs or his own best interests. His obsession often led him to live up to his reputation as being pettily tight with the money, a fact that even his youngest daughter, Barbara Smith, acknowledged. "One time there at the Barn," she remembered, "they had over-ordered on some colas of some kind . . . and they weren't going to be able to sell them or what. And Daddy said, told the guy there, the emcee, says, 'Close the windows in the barn tonight, and tell them in the back to salt the popcorn. We'll sell them before the night's over.' And they did [laughed]. But, you know, I thought, gee, that doesn't sound too nice Daddy." Smith expressed concern, however, about stories that Lair did not get along with performers or treat them well. In her view, her father got along with everyone. "Maybe he did have a temper," she added, "maybe he was too tight with the penny . . . or maybe that was just the businessman. . . . But when I hear something like that, it strikes me as very foreign, and very strange."[65]

John Lair was under many pressures in the early 1940s. Although he could pack the barn many times over during the summer, there were few visitors in the winter. "If the bad weather runs us out of our barn, as it is very likely to do," he advised M. L. Stover, "chances are we will want to come to Dayton for the Saturday night broadcast until the weather opens up. What is the story on Memorial Hall?"[66] For the next decade Lair continued to flirt with the idea of moving the show to another site for the winter, although for most of that time he settled for the smaller, and warmer, lodge for the broadcasts.

Keeping sponsors happy was another major headache. The advertising manager of Keystone Steel and Wire Company, a major sponsor, informed Keyes that he was unhappy with the number of announcements made by Lair. He suggested that visitors' announcements could be cut down to a sentence, although listeners' mail clearly suggested that Lair's personal attention to visitors and listeners was a successful strategy. The advertising manager also commented, "I also think you have plenty of entertainment more impressive than Homer and Jethro steadily."[67] Yet Bill McCluskey, the booking agent for WLW, had praised Lair two months earlier: "Homer and Jethro did a terrific job at Columbus and our part of the show was really the highlight."[68] Another advertiser seemed to view Renfro Valley as his personal game preserve. In December 1940, E. G. Bentley from Brown and Williamson, Renfro's other major sponsor of the time, announced: "Freeman Keyes has been good enough to write you explaining that if at all possible I would like to come down there some weekend during hunting season and perhaps knock down a quail or two."[69]

Lair aspired to better the standard of living for himself and his family, and in early 1941 he told Keyes that he needed to build a new home: "The one I am in is just too cramped for us and too danged hard to heat in the winter time." After the completion of the Renfro Valley complex, the Lair family had moved first to the upstairs of the lodge, then to the tourist cabins, and finally to an old house owned by Renfro Valley Enterprises. Lair wanted the company to sell him the land to build a new house near the other facilities, "as I don't want to get too far away from camp." His object was "to build the kind of home I would like to settle down to bring the kids up in and of course I wouldn't want to do that unless I owned the property on which the house stood."[70] Another three years passed before he reached that goal.

Meanwhile, Lair chased down every dream. Although he derided Red Foley's Hollywood aspirations, Lair, too, flirted with the opportunity to make films. In 1939 and 1940 he corresponded with two acquaintances from his WLS days, Earl and Larry Kurtze of Artists Bureau in Hollywood. Writing shortly before Lair's move back to Kentucky, Earl Kurtze suggested that Republic Studios might be interested in making two-reel shorts of songs Lair had dramatized. In response, Lair offered to furnish "all factual material as well as copyright clearance on any numbers used and from my extensive music and Americana library take care of all research work necessary, even down to costuming etc." He expressed concern, however, that everything be "correct and authentic," and added, "I can't afford to have anything out that would hurt my standing as an authority on American Folk Music."[71]

The Kurtzes continued to pitch titles, but Lair did not want to give the studio too much control. He could be persuaded, however, if they granted him some supervisory power, "especially if a part of it at least could be filmed here."[72] Earlier negotiations for the shorts involved bringing a film crew to Renfro Valley, but Earl Kurtze responded that he now thought doing so would be too expensive a proposition. Still, he believed that a deal could be struck using Lair's story idea and talent. Lair stalled, however, and negotiations fell apart.[73]

Lair also kept a keen eye on Henry Ford's doings in Michigan. Since the 1920s Ford had been sponsoring old-time fiddle contests and building a museum of American artifacts. Both the barn dance and the folk festival producers watched with interest. A number of radio performers, including several from WSM's Grand Ole Opry, competed in fiddling competitions sponsored by Ford.[74] On September 8, 1939, John Kettlewell of the Russell M. Seeds Company wrote to Lair that he had told "my personal sentry in Detroit to advise me the moment that Henry Ford returns to the city." One of Ford's secretaries thought an appointment could be arranged, and Kettlewell wished Lair a speedy recuperation from a short illness because he would need "to feel good when you and Henry start 'jawin' about those hillbilly tunes."[75]

An opportunity to jaw with Ford was not forthcoming, however. A year and a half later Lair advised Keyes that a man "who scours the country picking up old stuff for Ford" had made himself known after a visit to Renfro Valley. "He says that Mr. Ford knows something of what we're doing here and has shown considerable curiosity and interest," Lair wrote. Ironically, Ford was apparently concerned that Lair's work might be too commercial: "Says that he is still just a bit wiry [sic] of the set-up and has a suspicion that it might be just some clever scheme for effective radio advertising, but that he has expressed himself a time or two believing possibly that I am really sincere in trying to do something for something leading toward deeper appreciation of Early American Institutions." The man invited Lair to Ford's Early American Village and promised to arrange time with Ford "provided I will promise not to try to sell him something right away." Ford might also have been willing to come to visit Renfro if he could be assured of privacy.[76] Lair responded by featuring one of Henry Ford's favorite songs, "I'll Take You Home Again Kathleen," on his broadcast, but the desired meeting apparently never materialized.

During the years immediately following his return to Renfro Valley, John Lair continued to refine his acts. Along with Homer and Jethro's popular song parodies and hillbilly humor, a number of other humor and novelty acts graced the stage during the early days of broadcasts from Kentucky. A native of Detroit, Beth Cremer (Little Eller), who stood several inches over six feet tall, made her debut at the National Barn Dance, and in 1940 she joined the Renfro Valley cast, paired with Walter "Shorty" Hobbs (who really was short). The four-foot-nine Flora Bell Williams (Granny Harper) joined the show about the same time. Already close to sixty, the jig-dancing, pipe-smoking Granny Harper continued performing for another twenty-five years. In addition to her, Lair added Danny Duncan (Uncle Juney) to the cast as part of the "Harper family," which had Little Clifford and A'nt Idy at the core.

During the early years of the Renfro Valley Barn Dance Lair also promoted at least two animal acts. By the end of 1939 the cast was joined by Si and Fannie Otis—"Si, Fannie and Abner, two people and a trained mule"—an act that had previously performed at the New York World's Fair. From the late 1930s, Lair also worked on and off with Billy Sheets, "the Singing Dog Trainer," and Rex, "the Wonder Dog." In October 1940 Lair suggested to Earl Kurtze that Republic Pictures might make use of the act: "If there is such a thing as a hillbilly dog, this is it."[77]

Lair also began to place a greater emphasis on religious music than in earlier programming. In 1939 the Crusaders Quartet that featured four-part southern harmony style rooted in rural shape-note singing joined the cast. Other gospel groups would soon follow.[78] In 1943, with the sponsorship of Ballard Flour, what would become Lair's most enduring radio show had its debut. His Sunday morning *Gatherin'* combined religion, inspiration, patriotism, and especially nostalgia. It also allowed a number of the elements of the innovative but short-lived Monday night show to be incorporated through a relatively subdued tone and an emphasis on Lair's storytelling.

John Lair helped pioneer the live-audience radio barn dance, and, not surprisingly, the Renfro Valley Barn Dance possessed similarities to many radio barn dances that sprang up throughout the country. The show from Renfro, however, was especially notable for its fast tempo. As Lair's daughter, Nancy Griffin, recalled, "My father really knew how to pace the shows. They would . . . start playing . . . 'Wait for the Wagon,' or something like that, a fast piece of music, and they would all come running out, all the performers. They were all required to stay on the stage for the entire performance, there was no going back and forth, they backed everybody up. There was square dancing going on one side, a comedian was acting silly on another side, it was very fast-paced."[79]

In contrast, the *Gatherin'* moved at a more deliberate pace and tended to be more scripted than spontaneous. Performer Linda Martin remembered: "[Lair] never did rehearse that barn dance, it never was rehearsed. He didn't want it rehearsed. But he rehearsed the heck out of that Sunday morning program, he used to drive me nuts. I mean everything was just right down to the minute, boy, and timed." Many listeners took the *Gatherin'* for a religious show and even believed that the broadcast emanated from a church. Martin said, "He didn't do anything that would make them think like that, but there was a lot of hymns, and a lot of songs that . . . and the church bell [actually a brake drum off a truck] at the end of the program."[80] Lair's daughters believe that of all his shows the *Gatherin'* lay closest to Lair's heart. It featured much of his own writing and allowed him to indulge his love of tradition and the past. The *Gatherin'* also proved popular with sponsors because it offered a more novel format than the Barn Dance.

An element of irony existed in Lair's promotion of his entertainment as a nostalgic return to good, clean, wholesome fun. As he well knew, many in the rural South still had religious objections to dancing and instrumental music. With the advent of the jazz age, however, some radio listeners became more disposed to see fiddle music and square dancing as good, clean fun, and radio barn dances, along with the recreation movement, promoted that idea. Yet moral conservatism ran deep in the South. Not a few of the Renfro performers, including Lair himself, came from families that disapproved of string-band music and dancing. Manuel "Old Joe" Clark, who joined the cast in the mid-1940s, grew up in a religiously conservative family from east Tennessee. "If you run around up and down the road with a banjo or a fiddle," he said, "you was Hell bound. And they told you, your home folks told you, that you was going straight to Hell for doing that, that was their belief."[81]

Class issues also motivated some disapproval of string-band music. Lily May Ledford's mother, keenly aware of the family's status as tenant farmers, did not initially approve of her daughters performing at dances, given that doing so ran counter to her dreams for their upward mobility. Class was a central issue in promoting the music of the barn dance as "folk music." Lair possessed genuine interest in folk music, but he, like many other radio professionals of the day, used the terms *folk* publicly and *hillbilly* privately. The term *hillbilly* had lower class connotations, and Lair knew that the label *folk* sold better to station owners and sponsors who hoped to reach more of the middle class. The promotion of Renfro as "folk" played a critical role in Lair's move in 1941 to WHAS in Louisville, where he successfully sold the executives on the idea that his show offered legitimate and authentic folk music.[82]

During the early 1940s, Lair's active participation in the folk festival world waned, and his concerns with building an empire at Renfro Valley dominated. He had not lost interest in featuring folk music, however, or with incorporating song histories into his shows. In 1941 a music teacher from Indiana commented, "May I commend your Monday evening programs and say I feel that you are making a great contribution to Folk Music . . . I am asking my music classes to listen to your program in connection with our study of folk music."[83] A couple from Ohio wrote, "Think your arrangement of old timers and negro songs are the best on any network."[84] During the early 1940s Lair also negotiated with John Jacob Niles, a folk collector and performer, about a series of appearances on Lair's CBS programs.[85]

Lair continued what would be a life-long habit of collecting and researching songs. As Barbara Smith recalled, "[H]e liked the ballads, the mountain songs. He liked any song that somebody had told him that their grandmother had sung to them, and he would immediately go to their home with pencil and paper, you know, 'Tell me what you remember,' and try to copy down the words. Most of our vacations and travelings always had a purpose, that we were going to somebody's home, or to somebody's state, because he had heard of something that this person could contribute to this library of knowledge in his head."[86] In the 1940s and early 1950s he sought advice about song research from the academic folklorist George Pullen Jackson, who in 1946 sent Lair an article from the Greyhound Bus Lines' magazine *Highway Traveler*. Presaging the coming folk revival, "Minstrels . . . in the Mountains" noted that an "enterprising group of musician-promoter-balladeers has yanked American folk music by its own bootstraps out of the secluded corners of the hinterland and boosted it to a place of national popularity it never had before." Among the featured entrepreneurs were Bascom Lamar Lunsford, Roy Acuff, and John Lair himself.[87]

During the mid-1940s, once again in cahoots with Lunsford, Lair made another stab at organizing a folk festival, this time at Renfro Valley. April 18 and 19, 1946, marked the debut of the Red Bud Folk Festival. According to coverage by the *Louisville Courier-Journal*, the event played four performances to near-capacity paid audiences. Most of Lair's regular musicians did not perform. Instead, the festival stage included amateurs who came "many at their own expense, either because they hope to become professional or, they said, just because they love to make music." The future darling of the folk revival, Jean Ritchie, then a senior at the University of Kentucky, was on the bill.[88]

Lunsford and Lair seem to have taken a page from Sarah Gertrude Knott's notebook, not only by not paying most of the performers but also in emphasizing diversity. In "Many Participants in Folk Festival of April 18–19," an article published on April 15, 1946, in the *Renfro Valley Bugle*, Lunsford announced that performers would come from an area that stretched from the red hills of Georgia to the Great Lakes. The show included a performance of dances by Chief Carl Standingdeer of the Eastern Band of Cherokee as well as a demonstration of the "influence of tribal dancing upon the traditional folk dances of the white people" through a performance by a square dance group from a region adjacent to the Eastern Cherokee Nation. Also featured were spirituals from the nearby, and all-black, Richmond High School. Lunsford described being moved to tears by their rendition of "I'm Standing in the Safety Zone."

Lair and Lunsford showcased plenty of Anglo-American performers, including old-time fiddlers Bill Hensley and Dock Roberts, dulcimer player Sherman Cooks, and any number of dance groups. Along with Lunsford's western North Carolina groups, performers from Tennessee under the direction of Fred Colby (also active for many years in the National Folk Festival), students from nearby Berea College, and a group of twenty from the Highlander Folk School danced at the festival. Considering that a few years earlier Renfro talent had performed for Republican rallies in east Tennessee, it was a significant sign of the times that Lair had no problem including a group from the distinctly leftist Highlander.

Lunsford ended his article with a statement about Lair's commitment to traditional culture: "Most of us know something about the contribution that John Lair is making through his means and untiring energy in establishing Renfro Valley as an outstanding recreational and folk music center, but I want to pass on to all those devoted workers in every sta-

tion in life, who are desirous of preserving for posterity the best and finest in our traditional culture, regardless of race, color or creed, that it is
inspirational to know how well he is equipped in mind, heart and spirit
for so worthy an undertaking."

Despite Lunsford's comments, Lair's programming at Renfro Valley
tended to be exclusively Anglo-American. In the early years of Renfro
Valley, African Americans held only menial roles. In the 1940 and 1947
Keepsakes, the only African Americans pictured are the kitchen staff.
There is also a picture of Freezy Nelson holding two possums by their
tails. Lair had a soft spot for minstrel shows and occasionally featured
blackface humor on the barn dance. In 1947 the *Bugle* ran an article on
the act Honey Gal and Sugarfoot, which featured two regular Renfro
entertainers who usually performed not in blackface. As Honey Gal, Gene
Cobb, manager and emcee of the Lair's touring "Big Show," revived a
character from earlier vaudeville and minstrel acts. When not playing Sugarfoot, Charles Elza performed as Kentucky Slim. The *Bugle* instructed
fans to picture Honey Gal as a "Negro servant in the Renfro Valley lodge
kitchen" and Sugarfoot as a "general roustabout Negro employed as an
all around barn and stable boy."[89]

Rockcastle County had a relatively small African American population, and Lair held opinions common to those of his time and place.
In most of his writings and interviews he seldom commented on race,
although later in life he took a stance against the civil rights movement.
If Lair was a southerner, however, he was also a Kentuckian, and Abraham Lincoln figured as a personal hero. He glorified Lincoln on the air
and in print. If he did not share Knott's commitment to the presentation
of African American traditions, neither did he embrace Jean Thomas's
and Annabel Morris Buchanan's purist representations of Appalachian
culture as a product solely of Elizabethan England. Much like Lunsford,
Lair largely presented only Anglo-American tradition, but he acknowledged the influences of African American and Native American culture.
His notion of the origins of the songs he presented was realistic, and if a
piece had an African American author or came from African American
tradition he would typically acknowledge that fact.

The complexities of Lair's racial attitudes were shared by some of
his performers, notably Clark, who performed a blackface routine early
in his career on the minstrel circuit and later railed against the fact that
blackface was no longer an acceptable form of entertainment. "They
wasn't against the black people, it was funny," he insisted.[90] He also
acknowledged, however, the influence of African American music on
his own music and that of others at Renfro Valley. Several musicians,

including himself, Claude Sweet, and Red Foley, made a point of going to black churches to listen to the music. "And we listened to those songs and we'd come back home and not remember a word of them," Clark recalled, "but we would do the same thing that the rest of them is guilty of, we would take that prettiest hymn, that pretty tune, and we would put words to them ourselves."[91]

In the 1947 *Renfro Valley Keepsake* Lair noted that in six years "more than a million and a half" visitors had come to the Valley, and many millions "in every state in the Union" had heard Renfro Valley on the air. Whether hyperbolic or not, the live audiences during the early 1940s far outstripped those of competing radio barn dances. Much like Sarah Gertrude Knott, Lair, during the late 1930s and early 1940s, found himself at the cutting edge of his field. Success, however, must not always have seemed close at hand. Building the Renfro Valley complex involved a huge financial outlay, which, despite the undertaking's success, burdened Lair financially. He also struggled with his relationship with WLW. The station broadcast his shows but aired others that directly competed. In 1941 that conflict came to a head, and Lair switched his affiliation to WHAS. The impending switch did not necessarily solve the problems. The week before Lair began broadcasting with WHAS, J. Richardson of Russell M. Seeds, furious with WLW attempting to hire away Lair's top talent, informed him: "Freeman and I have had a long discussion regarding it and feel that you must make every effort and sacrifice to keep your talent intact."[92]

Both Lair and Knott had the misfortune of hitting their strides just as America entered World War II. In 1942 Renfro Valley was in a fragile financial condition. Keyes wrote in March that the auditors insisted that some token payment be made to his advertising company. The alternative would be bankruptcy, "which, of course, is impossible." Keyes, however, expressed interest in a plan Lair proposed: rent the entire enterprise to the government for use as a training base.[93] Lair was "definitely certain that we should not attempt to go through another Winter here, especially in view of present day conditions." Still, he had his eye on the future. "Incidentally," he commented, "if we could make the proper deal with the Government on this site we could afford to put up a large barracks room to be later converted into a horse barn or use to seat a larger audience than our present barn will accommodate and have it paid for by the time we are ready to use it again."[94]

That particular scheme did not pan out. Renfro remained an entertainment site rather than a training base, and somehow Lair made it through another financial crisis. In any case his pessimism tended to be fleeting. Just the month before he had written to Si and Fannie Otis (correspondence apparently not being one of their mule Abner's many tricks), "Looks as if the booking business might be pretty good this Summer."[95]

Wartime presented many challenges for Lair, including restrictions on travel and some of his performers being drafted, yet he rode the crest of country music's "great wartime surge."[96] Similar to Knott, he tried to gauge public sentiment to best promote his shows, and the combination of nostalgia and patriotism effectively reached radio audiences. Many requested that songs be played in memory of lost loved ones or for those who sought solace. Some had better news. Signing her letter "Your Radio Pal and Listener/Your unseen friend," Virgie Grantham wrote to Lair from Alabama and enclosed a poem her sister had written after their brother had been injured in the Pacific. "He was overseas for eleven months and came back in a pretty bad condition," she said. "He was shell shocked and had malaria. But he is doing nicely now."[97]

Despite the war, John Lair succeeded in building his enterprise during the early 1940s. He sent two tent shows on tour for those who could not travel to Renfro but wanted to see live entertainment. One, the local unit, toured nearby so performers could come in for their Renfro Valley shows; performers in the other, the "Big Show," did not broadcast regularly and traveled considerably farther afield, from the Deep South in winter and then toward the north in summer.

Although tent shows brought additional money and sometimes critical success, they often failed to break even. In November 1943 Gene Cobb wrote from Georgia that the show consistently lost money. If grosses did not soon improve, he said, "I will be ebbed so ebby that I will need hospitalization." Cobb speculated that small-town and rural Georgians either could not afford tickets or could not get to town often on their gas rations. Still, he found that those who did attend responded enthusiastically: "The public's reaction on the show here is, that it's the best hillbilly show they ever saw . . . (NOT BARING ACUFF)."[98]

John Lair's inexplicable ability to obtain gas rations helped fuel the wartime success of Renfro Valley's tent shows. That not only gave him an advantage over the competition but also attracted performers such as Emory Martin, a one-armed banjo player. Martin, who earlier in his career booked through the Grand Ole Opry and toured with Uncle Dave Macon, had returned home to work for his father, a rock mason. When he heard from a friend that Lair still had touring shows, Martin auditioned, and early in 1943 Lair sent him out with the Big Show. Although he also became the musicians' driver, he never knew how Lair got ration stamps but was glad he did. "I'd already checked around and there wasn't nothing going on in the way of bookings," Martin recalled. About the same time, Lair invited the young female musician Linda Lou (Wanda Frances Arnold), who played the fiddle and steel guitar on the WSB Barn Dance, to join the tent show. In November of 1943 Martin and Linda Lou married. Both had fond memories of traveling with the tent show. The Ketros, a former circus family, took care of all setting-up. It was, Emory Martin claimed, "one of the easiest jobs that I had in my life." Linda Lou added, "Now when we played the theaters and auditoriums in the winter, that was hard, that's where we had the long jumps and everything. But on the tent show, we would, maybe we could sleep till nine o'clock, or something like that, and get up and eat breakfast." Being employed by Lair had another advantage, Emory Martin recalled, "Mr. Lair stuck his neck out by paying us people that put a show on, he paid us a salary." Many musicians, including Martin, resented the times Lair did not share profits from a big show, but Martin did recognize the advantage of having a set salary rather than a share in the profits. He also noted Lair's down-home appeal: "He was a well known man, well known man all over. And he went around Renfro out there, you know, that's what people liked about him, with a sweater on that had a hole in the elbow, or something, you know. Walking up and down Renfro Creek there, talking to the neighbors and everybody."[99]

In February 1943 Lair tried yet another means of reaching out to Renfro Valley fans by establishing a monthly newspaper, "published weakly," called the *Renfro Valley Bugle*. Under the direction of managing editor Minnie "Black Eyed Susie" Ledford, the *Bugle* grew in its first three years from six to fifteen thousand subscribers, growth fueled in part by a contest in which listeners sent in subscriptions to vote for their favorite radio show emcee. Subscriptions cost $1 a year or could be paid with coupons found in Ballard's Obelisk Flour. The *Bugle* contained information on Renfro Valley shows and events, stories on performers, historical pieces on the area, song lyrics and poems, and letters from listeners.

Perhaps nothing signaled that John Lair had finally achieved success more than the completion of his eleven-room home in 1944, a structure that aptly expressed the borderline identity of Rockcastle County. If Lair, in his on-air persona, clearly identified himself as a mountaineer, at home he seemed to yearn for the lifestyle of Bluegrass gentry. The first floor was of cut limestone, a material traditional to that part of Kentucky, and the second floor was constructed of hand-hewn logs, a building material more commonly associated with the eastern part of the state. Just as much of the music Lair loved could be properly categorized as a product of the popular music trends of the late nineteenth century, so, too, much of the detailing of the house, including its many gables decorated with vertical boards in a fish-scale motif, suggested the Victorian era. In the final analysis, as with his radio shows, the Lairs' house was more about tradition than of tradition.

As with the tourist cabins and lodge, Lair brought in "neighbors," local craftsmen, to do the labor on the house. He also employed a Lexington architect, Wayne W. Haffler, although Lair, with the help of his daughter, Ann, designed many of its elements. The house also reflected Lair's personal eccentricities. When he insisted on an outside fireplace on the porch on the dwelling's east side, a builder asked, "What are you going to do, John? Try to heat the entire outdoors?" Much as it spoke of tradition, the house also signaled upward mobility. It had more than 3,500 square feet of living space and sported such niceties as cedar-lined closets, a laundry chute, and tiled baths. Behind the house Lair built tennis courts and a swimming pool.[100]

With its proximity to his commercial enterprise, the Lair home provided a public statement as well as a private dwelling.[101] Despite its relative grandeur the house did not intimidate tourists, and interruptions to family life were constant. As Ann Henderson recalled, "Mother always said everybody took him very literally when he said, 'you all come see us.' Because they did. They'd knock on the door, 'here we are!'"[102] The intrusions bothered the more retiring Virginia Lair, but, according to Barbara Smith, her father, who seldom took a day off, relished them: "I don't remember ever sitting through a meal without somebody coming to the door, wanting to shake his hand, or say something, or the phone ringing, you know for him. And he always got up and talked or went to the door. He enjoyed it. It wasn't a chore for him, it wasn't."[103]

The year after completing his house, Lair built a massive limestone and vertical-board stable, with six dormers, a cupola, and a center-gabled wing. The stable contained twelve stalls, a tack room, and buggy storage area. The three youngest Lair daughters showed horses as well as ponies in harness class. His enthusiasm for the horses, much like his enthusiasm for music, was as a facilitator not a participant. Barbara Smith remembers him riding only once or twice although his interest in showing horses lasted for a long time. Lair's other enthusiasms for family hobbies were often short-lived. One year it would be archery, the other, tennis. He "liked to try new things," Smith said, "and I think he liked to have it as something to talk about, as much as anything."[104]

Just months after the war ended Lair laid the cornerstone for another massive building, the Renfro Valley Museum and Studios. He again used the combination of limestone and logs, but the building evoked a more traditional plan than the Lairs' home. With an open-air central passage and end chimneys the building took the form of a gigantic dogtrot house. The structure, which took two and a half years to complete, housed a museum on its second floor that contained regional artifacts and memorabilia from listeners. New offices and broadcasting studios were on the first floor.

In 1947 John Lair published his second *Renfro Valley Keepsake*. In the seven intervening years from the first *Keepsake* both the physical complex and the programming had grown substantially. Indicating a busy year-round schedule, the calendar of Renfro Valley events included a horse show, a gospel quartet contest, an all-day gospel sing, a Thanksgiving shooting match, a New Year's Eve square dance, and a Christmas party that included a tree for "underprivileged mountain children" and baskets for the needy. In 1947, Lair split the Redbud Festival and the Folk Festival into two separate events, with the latter moved to August. The entry for the folk festival does not emphasize cultural diversity but does note, "No professional entertainers or radio artists are invited to participate." Lunsford once again presided.

The *Keepsake* promoted the images John Lair chose for Renfro Valley and for himself, usually as a man of the people, sporting the same plaid shirt that he prescribed as the standard uniform of most of his male performers. Page 31 presents a more scholarly Lair, wearing glasses and closely studying an ancient book. The accompanying text on the Music Library notes, "Historians, writers and scholars have come from all over the country and from England, Canada and the Bahama Islands to do research on musical subjects." The final pages of the *Keepsake* present a prosperous Lair family. The two middle daughters, Nancy and Virginia, pose astride their prize-winning ponies, while the youngest, Barbara, drives a pony cart. At the bottom of the page John and Virginia Lair are shown standing alongside "their favorite saddle horses," Lair dressed not in his favorite plaid shirt but in a coat, hat, and tie. This was no struggling young man trying to make a buck nor a hick from the hills but a prosperous, middle-aged Kentucky gentleman who oversaw a large business enterprise.

With the publication of Knott's "The National Folk Festival after Twelve Years" in 1946 and Lair's *Keepsake* in 1947, each must have looked back over the past decade with satisfaction. Despite economic depression and world war, Knott and Lair had created innovative institutions that would survive them, albeit in vastly changed forms. The years had been rocky, especially financially, but the popularity of the National Folk Festival and the Renfro Valley Barn Dance had reached their heights. From similar beginnings Lair and Knott had chosen differ-ent paths. Lair pursued the life of the country gentleman, whereas Knott became cosmopolitan and well-traveled. By the late 1940s the paths of country music and the folk festival also began to diverge as country music grew more commercial and new audiences discovered folk music and dance. These trends would seem to augur smooth sailing for Knott and Lair in the future. No one, however, remains on the cutting edge for long, and the growing popularity of country music and the folk revival would pose new and difficult challenges in the decades ahead.

5 The Changing Scene

Standardization has been consciously encouraged
by many groups; records of music have pushed "live"
musicians farther into the background; country music
floods television and radio.
—Sarah Gertrude Knott, 1961

The stubbornness and tunnel vision that propelled John Lair
and Sarah Gertrude Knott to center stage in their forties served them less
well as they each entered their second half century. During the depression
and war years they seemed in tune with the pulse of America, and, having
found winning formulas, they stuck to them. The postwar era brought
seismic shifts in the politics and culture of the United States, however,
as well as colossal changes in mass media. Lair and Knott would both
be challenged to keep their shows from becoming anachronisms during
the 1950s and 1960s.

With the war over, the National Folk Festival moved from the eastern seaboard. In 1946 Cleveland was its host, and then in 1947 it went
"home" to St. Louis, where it would stay through 1955, the longest period
of stability the festival enjoyed under Knott's directorship. She, however,
maintained an apartment in Philadelphia for several years and moved
back to St. Louis only for the four months immediately preceding the
festival.[1] During most her adult life the peripatetic Knott moved from
whatever city apartment she chose as home base, to the National Folk
Festival, to the various regional festivals, and then to sojourns with her
sisters in western Kentucky. Later in life she joked, "I've been on so many
buses that I don't even like to look in the face of a bus." But she also knew
how to adapt to the constant moving: "I'd stay a little while and I'd get

to feeling at home . . . I had a few things I'd take around, a picture or two and different little things I'd put out that were mine and would kind of make me feel at home."[2] Priscilla Urner recalled that Knott "lived on a shoestring" in a "one room apartment type thing." Knott loved beautiful things, however: "She used to have in her apartment beautiful, you know, things that people of these different folk groups all, would always give her some token of something."[3]

Knott's younger sister, Gladys, often aided her in attending to the various details of home life. As Yvonne Dodge, Gladys's friend, observed, "[Miss Gladys] would teach school during the year, always go to the festival in the summer and look at her clothes, her closets, her apartments and see what she thought she needed." Sarah Knott might have had a "way with a place," but she did not have the same standards as her sister. "Miss Gladys," Dodge said, "would always look into how big the closets were, how the view was . . . how big the rooms were. She liked comfort, you know. Not cramped conditions. But now Sarah probably would not object to those things, she didn't really care that much about that. She was more into . . . her own appearance, her work and getting her festival going, than into where she was living at the time."[4]

The 1946 festival took place as part of the Cleveland Sesquicentennial Celebration. Thirty years later Knott reflected, "It was right after the end of the war and people had just come home that year in Cleveland. That was the important time."[5] Although the event lacked understanding of being "national," Cleveland, she said, provided "the best opportunity we ever had of being on the home ground of a city where a large part of the population was made up of people who had recently come to this country." Local ethnic, social, and benevolent societies sponsored a number of performers.[6] Still, the Cleveland program also featured many regulars, including the Kiowa dancers, Bascom Lamar Lunsford, the anthracite miners, and W. C. Handy. As always, Knott sought new regional talent, and Fred Evans, winner of many Ohio fiddlers' contests, performed with his Ramblin' Hencacklers. Fellow Kentuckian Jean Ritchie, who had sung the month before at Lair's Redbud Festival, shared the stage with other members of her family, and the Early American Dance Orchestra sponsored by Henry Ford was squeezed, improbably, between a plethora of ethnic groups that included a performance of the "songs and dances of New Palestine."[7] Knott later crowed that the Cleveland festival included many war veterans and that men who "had not been enthusiastic about folk dances when they went away needed no persuasion to dance when they returned."[8]

Unfortunately, postwar justifications could not serve Knott forever.

As the nation moved to a new status quo, so did she and the festival. The move to St. Louis provided a safe choice. In retrospect Knott felt that only in Washington, D.C., had her festival met with as friendly and favorable response as in its city of birth. Once again the "local merchant commerce" paid the bills; from 1947 to 1951 the Associated Realtors of St. Louis sponsored the National Folk Festival. As postwar prosperity and complacency grew the event became harder to sell as an antidote to national problems, but immediately after the war it still provided a vehicle for national propaganda. In 1949 the U.S. Army Office of Civilian Affairs made a thirty-minute motion picture about the festival for use in occupied countries, and the following year the Voice of America recorded portions for use in international broadcasts.[9]

The return to St. Louis provided Knott with the opportunity to reflect on the changes that thirteen years had brought. Under the banner "The Past Is Prologue" the program of the 1947 festival noted the changes that had taken place: "The thirteenth annual program consists of survivals, revivals and songs and dances consciously taught. New Americans play their parts throughout the festival. The attitude of our people toward folk expression has changed; so has the National Folk Festival."[10] The festival always grew as a matter of accretion and with relatively little plan behind its growth. After more than a dozen years it was incredibly diverse but no longer particularly innovative. The number of academics with direct involvement noticeably declined although an impressive roster still graced the advisory board. Participants in the morning conference sessions consisted largely of local collectors and "practitioners." A notable exception was Don Yoder, later dean of the American folklife studies movement, who spoke in 1951 on Pennsylvania Dutch spirituals.

In 1952 the *St. Louis Globe-Democrat* assumed sponsorship of the festival, and the reorganization precipitated the resignation of Knott's long-time business manager, Major M. J. Pickering. Her records do not reveal the exact cause of the break, but she would later say that they did not quarrel but rather "came to a parting of the ways." As she recalled, "he got sick and my relation with him and the whole thing just ended there and the *Globe* went on with it. He didn't." Knott suggested that the newspaper had insisted that Pickering resign "because he was ill and he was hard to get along with."[11]

Despite her protestations it is clear that considerable acrimony existed between Knott and Pickering at the time. As she reported to Paul Green, who had amicably resigned as president of the National Folk Festival Association the previous year, "I've been through a battle in this reorganization business. MJP wouldn't work with an Ex. Com. Everything was done according to Hoyle. He was elected Bis. Mgr. As always. Finally, he suggested he be paid to get out. To my amazement, he was. So for 2½ yrs of festivals, I'll be doing the work and he'll be getting paid same as yours truly. That's okay though! My conscience is crystal clear. It was either reorganize or give everything up."[12] A couple of years later, and in his own letter to Green, Pickering stated that after two decades of "steering the National Folk Festival through the shoals" he sold out to the "so-called" National Folk Festival Association.[13] Pickering died shortly thereafter, and by that time Knott seems to have overcome any anger she may have felt.[14]

In later years Knott always insisted that Pickering receive due credit for keeping the festival afloat. "If it hadn't been for Mr. Pickering," she asserted, "I don't think the National Folk Festival would have made it because those were real hard years." The *Globe-Democrat* took over the business management, but Knott knew that the business and program could not be kept separate: "[T]he people at the *Globe-Democrat*—they were good on the business angle. I didn't have to do anything about the business. But it was never as good, even with all those people that we had working on it."[15]

Reorganization did bring one positive change: a closer tie with Washington University, whose support Knott had long courted. In 1951 she approached the university again, and as a result John Francis McDermott, an associate professor of English, became "entangled" in the affairs of the National Folk Festival. As he recalled to Roy Mackenzie, former head of the English department, several years later, "A small group of us reorganized the Executive Committee, secured the *Globe-Democrat* as sponsor, and struggled with the affairs of the Association. Our second year with the *Globe* was quite successful—we cleared our debts. And could look forward to new life. The *Globe* of course could and did give splendid promotion to the Festival."[16] Unlike Paul Green, McDermott aspired to be more than a figurehead president. He dreamed especially of boosting the festival's acceptance among academics. To that end, in 1953 he expanded the morning conference, always a part of the event, to a longer conference co-sponsored by the festival and the university.

The *Globe-Democrat*'s coverage of the two-day Washington University–National Folk Festival Association Folklore Conference included a photograph of four academic folklorists, one of whom was Richard M. Dorson of Michigan State University. By 1953 Dorson had begun his campaign against the popularization of folklore, coining the term *fakelore*. In the early 1950s, however, he apparently approved of the academic credentials of the National Folk Festival and participated enthusiastically. In March 1954 William Bascom, first vice president of the American Folklore Society (AFS), informed McDermott, "I would like very much to accept your kind invitation to address the National Folk Festival Association, and to participate in its general sessions which I have heard from Dick Dorson are very interesting." Gertrude Kurath of the Michigan Folklore Society also said, "Dick Dorson reported favorably on last year's meetings." About the same time, Dorson himself wrote, regretting that he could not attend the next conference but requesting a copy of the program literature for his write-up of folklore meetings in Franklin Meine's *Yearbook*. "I gave a good plug to the National Folk Festival in the 1953 round-up," he concluded.[17]

The successful 1953 conference came at a critical juncture in the development of folklore as a discipline. During the 1940s an active interest in its applied uses existed among many academic folklorists, and the American Folklore Society formed the Committee on the Utilization of Folklore. In 1950 the Mid-Century International Folklore Conference, held at Indiana University, addressed "Making Folklore Available" during one of its four symposia. During the same time period, however, folklorists also began turning toward issues of professionalization within the discipline. Up until 1953 all American-trained academic folklorists held degrees in other fields, typically literature or anthropology. During the late 1940s, Indiana University developed the first doctoral program in folklore in the United States and in 1953 awarded its first Ph.D. As folklore began to emerge as an autonomous discipline the lines between those who held academic degrees and those who did not grew more rigid, as did those between the scholars and the popularizers ("practitioners" as Knott labeled them).[18]

Although positive word circulated in academic circles about the WU-NFF conference, McDermott failed to adequately build on its success the following year. In November 1953 the AFS's secretary-treasurer, MacEdward Leach, informed McDermott of his interest in the next such event, "I have heard from various people that the last conference was a great success. Do you plan to publish any of the papers?" Leach also mentioned that plans to have a folklore conference at the University of Pennsylvania had fallen through. "Evidently in the east we're not as folklore minded," he added wistfully.[19] McDermott's files for the proposed 1954 conference indicate that he planned an ambitious program, unfortunately, however, events in his personal life worked against following through on those plans. During the summer of 1953 his father died of cancer, and McDermott's mother-in-law suffered a heart attack on New

Year's Eve. Consequently, he did not send invitations to the April conference until late February.

By the time McDermott sent invitations for the 1954 event, potential participants either had other commitments or no more funds for travel. Stith Thompson of Indiana University pleaded overcommitment: "I am interested to hear about your Folklore conference in April. I wish we could be represented, but I have spoken to several of our men here, and am afraid we will not be able to get over this year." Also from Indiana, Erminie Voegelin commented on the "queer fatality in conflict of dates that is happening each year in connection with my attending the National Folk Festival Association meeting." Tristram Coffin of the University of Pennsylvania did not have time because he was completing the index to the *Journal of American Folklore,* and McEdward Leach reported, "I'm tied up with too many things. I had thought this year would be easier." Arthur Campa's travel budget was "tapped out," words Herbert Halpert of Murray State in western Kentucky used as well when he noted his commitment to the state's folklore society meeting the same month. Richard Dorson had also committed to the folklore conference in Kentucky and could not get additional leave. William Bascom felt "an especial obligation to accept as an officer of the American Folklore Society," but, unfortunately, "the dates of [the] meetings conflict with prior commitments, and I must beg to be excused."

Along with the more traditional subjects of academic folklore of the time, McDermott hoped to include papers on folk art and folk museums. Louis Jones of the Farmers' Museum at Cooperstown commented that the problem of the folk museum was "one that interests me tremendously and one that I believe is an important aspect of the over-all picture of folk culture in America" but regretted he would not be able to attend due to a limited travel budget. Jean Lipman, asked to speak on folk art, also declined because of a number of commitments in New York. One of the few positive respondents, D. K. Wilgus of Western Kentucky State College, committed to give a paper entitled "Hillbilly Broadsides." When he heard that the conference had been canceled he replied that he had looked forward to attending. "I will try to have something for you next spring," he added.[20]

Wilgus did not make it to the 1955 conference and neither did many others prominent in the academic folklore world. McDermott did, however, pull off another two-day event that included a session on "Folklore in Use" and Knott's dinner presentation on "The Utilization of Folklore." Earlier in the day, Erminie Voegelin, having finally overcome the "queer fatality" of dates, spoke on "The Emergence Myth in Native North America." The final session of the conference featured "American Folk Heroes: History, Legend, or Fiction?" Participants included Warren Roberts of Indiana University, William H. Jansen of the University of Kentucky, and John W. Ball of Miami University. Richard M. Dorson chaired the session.[21]

By the time of the 1955 conference Dorson had joined the executive committee of the National Folk Festival Association. He continued to serve in that capacity through the rest of the decade, although there is little record of his active participation after 1955. Knott became more wary in the 1960s as Dorson's attacks on popularization and his promotion of professionalization of the discipline became more vociferous. Early in the decade she reported on the meeting of the AFS: "I know now that we shall have the cooperation of practically every individual member of the American Folklore Society, with exception of Richard Dorson, he is not against, but he has a way of not exactly cooperating."[22] Still, one might speculate whether Dorson might have remained more actively involved had Knott succeeded in maintaining an academic base at Washington University.

Even in 1953 Knott's relationship with the *Globe-Democrat* had grown rocky. Although she subsequently blamed the end of the newspaper's support on its purchase by New York interests in 1955 and the subsequent death of long-time editor E. Lansing Ray, Knott had long struggled with the *Globe* for control of the festival. In February 1954 McDermott reported to Mackenzie: "SGK grew afraid that the *Globe* wanted too much control: the *Globe* became so interested that it wanted a very large voice in matters. Last summer the Executive Board was in general in favor of continuing with the *Globe* but negotiations hung fire through most of the fall. Finally before Christmas I managed to reconcile Sarah and the *Globe* and now she is down there working quietly and everybody is happy (but for how long?)." McDermott hoped that Washington University might be persuaded to take a larger role in the festival. Although Knott had failed to arouse interest on campus, he wrote, "Last fall, when it seemed likely that we might not go back to the *Globe,* I had a series of talks with Reals and Hopkins and Blackwell and others about university sponsorship: and found a real interest (certainly the fact that we had had a very successful season downtown impressed them). It is quite possible that we shall develop a program at the university in addition to the Festival downtown." Despite his optimism about university support and the fact he found it "rather fun, bustling about as a promoter of folklore activities," McDermott fretted about what lay ahead in keeping peace between the sponsors and Knott. Mackenzie was sympathetic. "The whole business of Gertrude and her activities and ambitions continues, I see, to unload the troubles on your doorstep," he replied, "and lucky she is to have a man so good to assume so many responsibilities for her."[23]

St. Louis hosted its last National Folk Festival in 1955. The decision to leave the city appears to have been made in response to changes at the *Globe-Democrat*. Several months after the event Knott exclaimed to a friend, "I think we should move from St. Louis Chris! The road is hard! The G.D. had problems this year—change you know and it knocked them for a loop. It effects [sic] their promotion."[24] In 1956, for the first time, Knott failed to produce the National for reasons internal to the festival itself. Without Pickering at her side, and distrustful of organizations that would take too much interest in and control of her festival, she floundered. Along with the internal conflicts, she and her organization could not fully comprehend the changes in the political climate of America and the shifting audiences for folk music and dance.

The St. Louis years brought Knott one ally who would connect her with the growing folk revival as well as its attendant political problems. Pete Seeger, son of the ethnomusicologist Charles Seeger, had dropped out of Harvard University in the late 1930s and become associated with the emerging leftist folk revival. About the same time, he attended his first National Folk Festival. Although he and Knott did not meet until more than a decade later, he held a favorable impression of the show at Constitution Hall. Charles Seeger did not. "I'll have to say my father, the musicologist, just didn't really approve of her [Knott]," the younger Seeger observed. "He felt that her introductions were—looking down from above." However, "She wasn't long-winded," Seeger recalled, "she managed to say in a few sentences what needed to be said." Although his father felt that Lunsford, unlike Knott, was "one of the people," Pete did not like the limited format that Lunsford employed: "He had an all-white festival playing mountain music." On the other hand, "Sarah was trying to present a wide spectrum. And did a pretty good job of it, especially when you consider . . . those days." Pete Seeger also noted that Knott, like Lunsford, believed in fast-paced staging: "I was very impressed by the way she would have a soloist work in front of a big curtain, but while the soloist was entertaining the audience in front of the curtain, she was lining up a group of square dancers in the back. So the moment the curtain opened, they started. . . . So she managed to make a fast-moving show by alternating soloists and groups. . . . And I've often thought that this should be . . . used more often nowadays."[25]

In the late 1940s Pete Seeger, with the singing group the Weavers, began to transform folk music into pop hits. Their version of Leadbelly's "Goodnight, Irene" became the most popular song of 1950. At the peak of their popularity Seeger received an invitation to sing at the National en route to an appearance the Weavers had at a Denver nightclub.[26] Knott was hardly ready to transform her festival, but she found the new folk revival intriguing. The fact that Seeger was willing to play for little, if any, payment, probably further encouraged her enthusiasm for him as a performer. Throughout the early 1950s Pete Seeger was a regular at the National Folk Festival, and in 1955 the *Globe-Democrat* reported that his popularity in the children's programs earned him the title of "honorary uncle."[27]

Behind the scenes, however, the avuncular Seeger faced serious political problems. Given the growing anticommunist political climate of the era, the Weavers' politics were under increasing scrutiny even as the group brought songs to the hit parade. Not a few of the early folk revivalists, including Seeger, had been members of or sympathizers with the Communist Party in the vastly different political climate of the 1930s and 1940s, and in the 1950s they came to the attention of the House Un-American Activities Committee (HUAC). Seemingly, Knott and the *Globe-Democrat* preferred to remain oblivious to these developments. A few months after the newspaper ran a story touting the return of the "folk festival balladeer" to St. Louis, a subcommittee of HUAC called Seeger to testify.[28]

Less than two months after his August testimony, in which he refused to answer questions about former activities and affiliations or take the Fifth Amendment, Seeger traveled at Knott's invitation to the Acadian Bicentennial Festival in St. Martinville, Louisiana. Decades later he could find humor in events that ensued:

> I arrived there a few days early because she said, "You ought to come down . . . you can hear more of the local music then." . . . But, on the second day I was there, Sarah Gertrude said, "This evening we're going to the home of somebody . . . you'll get a chance to hear more Cajun music." And we went to a nice ranch house on the outskirts of town. And the door was opened and Sarah Gertrude said, "Pete Seeger, meet Congressman Willis." . . . Congressman Willis had been one of the people questioning me only a month before. Well, he did a slight double take and so did I, but he didn't say anything and we all went in the house. And pretty soon others arrived; pretty soon a party got started. [Sarah Gertrude] said, "Pete, get your banjo out." So I was leading some singing. I glanced out of the corner of my eye and there was Willis, sitting

in the corner just glowering. And finally when he caught my eye, he beckoned with his finger . . . told me to come towards him. So I put my banjo down and followed. He went into the kitchen. Said, "Well, Mr. Seeger, this is a small world. How did you get here?" I said, "Well, I was invited." "Who invited you?" He was sure there were communists in his hometown. Well, it was the Chamber of Commerce.[29]

The next day the head of the Chamber of Commerce assured Seeger, "This festival doesn't have anything to do with politics; we're in music. I'm going to try and bump heads with Willis." Later that day, however, he admitted, "I'm afraid Willis has a harder head than I had." "The upshot was," Seeger recalled, "that I bid farewell to Sarah Gertrude and the rest and said, 'No hard feelings.'" Knott and Seeger stayed on good terms "ever after."[30]

The authenticity of Knott's apparent obliviousness to Seeger's political problems until that point remains impossible to judge. Perhaps the invitation to Willis's home was an act of defiance or a demonstration that she could invite whomever she pleased to the festival. She may, however, have genuinely, if naively, believed that political differences could be overcome if people sat down and enjoyed folk music together. It was inevitable that the new political climate of the country during the 1950s was a challenge for her broad coalition of individuals and groups of vastly different ideological persuasions.

Two years later Knott could no longer avoid dealing with Seeger's problems along with those of another long-time participant, Jenny Vincent of New Mexico. Knott had accepted the Oklahoma Semi-Centennial Commission's invitation to hold the National as part of the state's celebration, themed "Arrows to Atoms." With the final program planning almost complete, she asked McDermott:

> Did you see in paper today piece about Pete Seeger and contempt of court? That will mean we can't have him and we agreed I'd write today— They were disturbed. You know Jenny Vincent was questioned too. I know nothing about this—except I heard it in New Mexico—and no one believed it. The same is true of Pete: but I've talked to him about why he just didn't come out and tell the committee what he told me—but this has us at a spot, where we can't have him. Don't you think so? I know from Oklahoma's standpoint, we can't. Now since this has come up, I just wonder if we'll run into trouble with Jenny?
>
> I told Mr. Burge [director of the Oklahoma Semi-Centennial] that I had known this charge about Pete—and had talked to him—exactly as I did—I didn't believe it and thought it was settled. I didn't mention Jenny—I'm wondering if I should. I'm not F.B.I.—and I don't believe a

thing but the best about her. I was going to have her come and sing to school children—now I just wonder? Advice?

McDermott responded:

> It is indeed unfortunate that Pete and Jenny have been having trouble. I have seen nothing about it in the papers. What happened? Is it one of those too frequent cases of good people being led into unwise acts by misplaced sympathies?
> Both Jenny and Pete are attractive. However, I agree with you that the Folk Festival must be very careful not to have any Communist connections of any kind. Anyone of proven Communist sympathy, no matter how desirable otherwise, must be excluded. I know that the Oklahoma sponsors feel the same way.[31]

The Oklahoma program did not include Seeger's name, although he recalls having attended.[32] Knott's concern always lay in what served her festival best, not political ideology. Both Seeger and Vincent again performed at the festival in the 1960s, and although the era of McCarthyism may have waned they would again bring political problems to the festival.

Ironically, while the National Folk Festival floundered, folk-inspired music found a new audience as a new and nonpolitical wing of the folk revival began to grow in the mid to late 1950s. Knott could not figure out how to capitalize on the new interest, nor could she afford to pay many of the revival performers even had she wanted to. A different type of revival, the square dance revival, had more immediate impact on the festival. Even during the 1930s and 1940s many dance groups that Knott featured were essentially revivalist in nature, although dancers came mostly from the ethnic or regional background presented in their performances. In 1949 Vyts Beliajus, the Lithuanian dance leader, commented on what he viewed as an alarming new trend at the festival, the predominance of Western-type dance "regardless of the region the dancers hail from." He also expressed concern about square dance groups performing numbers not native to dancers' regions or ethnicities. "Personally I felt extremely hurt by the fact that the Denverites performed Chiapenecas when a Mexican group was present," Beliajus wrote, "but this crime was committed throughout the whole festival, as it never occurred before."[33]

Knott had already benefited from the growing enthusiasm for square dance, keeping Philadelphians dancing through the final years of World War II. Dance groups became a mainstay of her festival throughout the next two decades. She knew, however, that the dance revival created problems for her festival. In 1951 Knott mentioned the "state of confusion throughout the country in folk activities now, due to the sudden and widespread interest." She also urged performers to "stay in the folk tradition" and not learn dances, songs, or tales especially for the festival, fearing that the festival might otherwise become "nothing but a poor amateur show."[34] Knott also grew increasingly adamant about one purist policy: Dance groups could not perform to recorded music. Repeatedly, she fielded letters from groups that insisted they always danced to recorded music. Knott countered that if they could not bring their own musicians, performers at the festival would play for them.

Even as Knott entered her sixties her thoughts did not begin to turn to retirement. Rather, she fixed on how to keep her festival afloat in quickly changing times. The year 1956 must have been a particularly bleak one for her. In correspondence with the *Farm Journal* about potential articles, Knott scribbled on her copy, "I want to make the money."[35] With the *Globe-Democrat* ending its sponsorship, she lost not only financial backing but also the support of Washington University, her last, best chance for an academic base for the National Folk Festival. In January 1956, Maud Karpeles of the International Folk Music Council wrote sympathetically from London, agreeing with Knott about the importance of bringing academics and popularizers together. Karpeles wished she could offer practical help. "It would be wonderful," she said, "if you could get a university, and I would say preferably Indiana, to sponsor the festival." She added, "I do so hope that you will be able to keep on with the festival. There is so much bogus folk dancing everywhere now that yours stands out like a shining beacon."[36]

Throughout the 1950s Knott continued to organize smaller regional festivals, generally earning $100 per week plus expenses for doing so. These included the American Indian Pageant in Anadarko, Oklahoma, in 1951, the Southwest Folk Festival in Albuquerque in 1952, and the Southern Illinois Folk Festival in Carbondale in 1954. The two events that probably had the greatest impact, however, were the All Florida Folk Festival, which Knott directed in 1953 and 1954, and the Acadian Bicentennial Folk Festival in 1955 in St. Martinville, Louisiana. The All Florida Folk Festival, notable especially for its longevity, still survives. Both of the Florida festivals organized by Knott emphasized the "multicultural background of today's Floridians" and included Seminole, Hispanic, Jewish, and African American participants.[37]

A single-year event, the Acadian Bicentennial Folk Festival played a significant role in reviving interest in Cajun culture, which the 1936 Dallas National Folk Festival had given national exposure. Knott featured

Cajun music at a number of subsequent Nationals. Pete Seeger credits her festival with his own exposure to, and fascination with, Cajun music.[38] The Acadian Bicentennial Festival, from which Seeger found himself excluded, culminated Knott's work with Cajun culture. Twenty-two years later Paul Tate told her that the St. Martinville festival marked the beginning of a cultural revival as the "first event to my knowledge recognizing in a grand way our Acadian heritage." Knott also brought a new audience to Cajun music. Tate wrote, "Through the exposure of Cajun music at the National Folk Festival, Pete and Mike Seeger, John Cohen, Ralph Rinzler, Theo Bikel, George Wein and others became interested and in 1963 and 1964 and two or three years thereafter, Cajun music was presented at the Newport Folk Festival."[39]

After leaving St. Louis, Knott produced only two more National Folk Festivals during the 1950s. The lack of a state appropriation delayed the planning process, but the Oklahoma Semi-Centennial Commission and the University of Oklahoma agreed to co-sponsor the twenty-second National Folk Festival in 1957. Knott's experience coordinating regional activities in Oklahoma must have helped immensely as she sprang into action to organize a number of preliminary activities, including folk festivals in various counties, a Tulsa festival, a fiddlers' contest, a miners' gathering, a "Negro festival," a tale-telling gathering, and an arts and crafts exhibit at the main library in Oklahoma City. In early May she observed to John and Mary McDermott in her usual telegraphic style: "Oklahoma is just ready for this—as I thought—but getting out over state takes time of which there hasn't been enough. This is a square dance state. Few other kinds of dances. There are still a lot of fiddlers, and I think ballad singers and singing-games. In other words, the things that predominate everywhere—still exist in greater numbers than in most places; but they are fading here, as elsewhere. The Okla. Sq. Dance Federation is most active. They usually use live music—but there's no, or little connection with the survival forms." Knott was concerned that Oklahoma lacked a place nearby "where there's a center of newer American activities." The festival would be more "old American," but she asked McDermott to try and secure the participation of an Israeli dance group from the YMHA in St. Louis. "This has been a mix up deal," she concluded. "It is an inexperienced group—The Grandstand Show is still not definite—but I like all the people. They are fine."[40]

A few months earlier Knott had consulted with McDermott about the letterhead and the issue of who to add to the executive board. She suggested two new academic members to join the three academic folklorists already appointed: Richard Dorson, Arthur Campa, and Louise

Pound. Knott suggested that they invite W. Edson Richmond of Indiana University, who fell, she believed, "between the two ideas festival and scholarly," and William Hugh Jansen from the "univ. and state which has one of best folk activity programs."[41] Jansen, of the University of Kentucky, subsequently became one of Knott's academic mentors in the final decade of her active career. Although she continued to be concerned about maintaining an academic base, the absence of academic folklorists in the morning conferences that accompanied the Oklahoma National Folk Festival was notable.

As Knott predicted, the Oklahoma festival did include a noticeably smaller percentage of "new Americans." A major Lithuanian dance gathering kept Beliajus from attending. Had he been present he might have commented on an Oklahoma City group dancing an Austrian dance that was a "new version of an old dance learned by the Snyders at Comp Oglebay, West Va., from Dave Rosenberg." Although the Oklahoma Square Dance Federation took part in the National, Knott took pains to ensure that they did not predominate among the dance performances.

While Knott worried about the preponderance of square dance enthusiasts in Oklahoma, there were also concerns about other faux folk. Longtime participant Leonard Austin said, "I do hope that you watch carefully that you keep out the hillbilly singers. Oklahoma is full of imitation Elivs [sic] Presleys who fancy themselves folk singers."[42] The Oklahoma festival featured few performers who could be considered country or hillbilly, but for the first time the program included Jimmie Morris, soon better known as Jimmie Driftwood. He performed his song "Eighth of January," which the following year as "The Battle of New Orleans" became a hit record for singer Johnny Horton and won a Grammy Award for song of the year.

In planning the Oklahoma festival Knott had also been in contact with another country music star, John Lair's former partner Red Foley. In February of 1957, Robert "Fiddler" Beers contacted Knott about lining up paying engagements for him in Oklahoma. Beers indicated that he heard Knott had talked with Foley, and he hoped she might do so again on his behalf. Red Foley's program did not deal with authentic folk material, but Beers had "ideas which would allow the presentation of our material without injuring it's effectiveness from the folk standpoint, and at the same time, not lacking entertainment value . . . Also, it would be a wonderful way to plug the National Folk Festival."[43] Knott scribbled "can do" next to this section of Beers's letter, but she did not leave of record of whether she successfully persuaded Foley to plug her show.

In 1958 the National Folk Festival again failed to find a home. The following year, however, it moved to the Nashville Coliseum and was sponsored by the *Tennessean* and the Maxwell House Hotel. Although located at ground zero of the country music industry, Knott found few native singers in Nashville. The program once again included Jimmie "Driftwood" Morris from Arkansas and several imports from Kentucky, including two academic folklorists. Leonard Roberts spoke on "The Folk Tale—Its Use Today," and D. K. Wilgus addressed "Country Western and Folk Music." Knott split the Nashville conference into two sections. The first, held at the Coliseum, focused on folk music and dance and featured practitioners. The second, at George Peabody College, was billed as a "Conference for Leaders" and featured more academics.

Just as in the immediate postwar confusion of the late 1940s Knott had retreated to the comfort of the festival's birthplace, St. Louis, in 1960 she set her sights on her other favorite venue, Washington, D.C. There she hoped to catch the attention of the growing urban folk revival and "campaign for national recognition of the importance of folk expression in the life of our people, and to attempt to enlist the aid of government and private sources in welding together our varied cultural groups though a common understanding and appreciation of our rich folk heritage."[44]

In 1961, twenty-two years after she first published in *Southern Folklore Quarterly*, Knott contributed another article, "Folksongs and Dances, U.S.A.: The Changing Scene," a reflection on the postwar years. Until the end of World War II, she noted, the development of folk festivals grew gradually and objectives seemed clear, but "when peace came and the long tension was lifted, widespread enthusiasm and popularization burst into unparalleled activity in many states." As Knott saw it, this revival proved a mixed blessing, for it was difficult to avoid having folk festivals "become hodge-podge." Standardization and the mass media became a threat as "records of music . . . pushed 'live' musicians farther into the background; country music [flooded] television and radio, often replacing the traditional." Although, Knott noted, many country musicians knew and liked traditional music they found "so little general encouragement that it would be almost an innovation which they hesitate to venture."[45]

In the folklore journal Knott blamed the mass media for the death of folk traditions, but behind the scenes she continued to search out any form of media that would bring attention to her festival. Two months after her article appeared an acquaintance in Hollywood told her, "I have the same faith that you do concerning a film or spectacular . . . but one has to find a sponsor first . . . for TV, or the right opening for a film. . . . I am keeping the Folk Festival much in mind—and will contact you as soon as I develop an interest."[46] That interest apparently never developed. The National Folk Festival would never become a "spectacular" on either television or in the movies. In 1961 Sarah Gertrude Knott had just begun to see the damage the folk revival would inflict on her career.

John Lair and Sarah Gertrude Knott had little if any contact with each other after the war. Still, they both faced many of the same problems and challenges. Changes in mass media became even more critical for Lair as radio began to change beyond his control, although the years immediately after the war must have been optimistic ones for him. He built his new house and stables, expanded other amenities around his home, and broke ground on the new administration building and museum. Two disastrous business enterprises, however, were among the larger problems he soon encountered.

Lair's first attempt at factory production addressed what would be an ongoing problem for him—lack of access to recording companies for his talent. The radio barn dance and recording and commercial marketing of hillbilly music had developed simultaneously in the 1920s. Lair, who entered the business about 1930, made a smart business choice by putting all his eggs in the radio basket; record sales dwindled during the years of the Great Depression. In the 1940s, however, the balance began to shift in favor of the recording industry. The more ambitious Renfro Valley performers had little access to the industry in rural Kentucky, and many, as Jerry Byrd put it, realized that they would "dry rot" if they chose to stay. It is typical of John Lair's thinking that when he came to terms with this problem he decided to cut out the middleman and build a record company himself.

On December 15, 1946, the *Renfro Valley Bugle* announced that a new corporation, the Ekko Recording Company, had been organized in the Valley "for the purpose of making phonograph records and electrical transcriptions." As always, Lair developed ambitious plans. The *Bugle* announced that the plant, once finished, would be capable of producing about 120,000 records each month and employ thirty to fifty people in three shifts. A separate article in the same issue noted that several Renfro Valley performers had traveled to Cincinnati to make recordings that would soon be on sale through Renfro Valley.[47] In August of 1947 Lair reported to W. M. Ellsworth, "I am sending you twelve pressings of Doc Hopkins' record 'The Blue Tailed Fly.' For some reason, the Duke of Paducah's records are being held up in transit."[48] Although Lair had signed a number of contracts with current Renfro talent as well as old friends such as Hopkins and Ford, his record business never got off the ground. The new equipment, defective, was never installed, and Lair sued. The legal wrangling continued for several years.

The second venture came right on the heels of the first and may have been an attempt to find an alternative use for the record factory building. In 1947 Lair and Freeman Keyes began a black walnut cracking and packing plant under the name Renfro Valley Products, with Keyes investing more than $100,000 in the project. The enterprise proved an unmitigated disaster. Supply, delivery, and grading problems caused numerous delays, and the stored walnuts began to sprout.[49] Bad public relations also ensued when the local bank found out that financial transactions would not be processed through it. In November 1948 Lair observed to Keyes, disgust thinly veiled, "If you think I'm speaking out of turn for the small part I have in the whole setup I'd be perfectly satisfied to see you take over the whole job in Chicago. . . . I don't feel that we are doing the Renfro Valley name any good and certainly it hasn't been worth anything to Products so far."[50] The lingering problems came to a spectacular end a week later when the walnut factory went up in a blaze that could be seen for miles. Two weeks later a desperate Lair commented that the fire "marked the termination of a very disastrous venture for both of us." He added, "Writing it off as a loss on my personal income tax this year will not help me a dime's worth, as I probably will not have to pay a tax anyway, or at least a negligible amount."[51] Although Lair's investment in the walnut factory was small compared to Keyes's, he could ill afford the setback.

Lair overextended himself in the late 1940s and also experienced difficulties with his bread-and-butter operations. During 1948 and 1949, highway construction drastically cut back on the number of automobile visitors to Renfro Valley and rerouted buses so that they no longer stopped at the lodge. Lair, always one to try and make something positive out of hard luck, took the opportunity to build a new ballpark and grandstand for Renfro Valley. He had to face the fact, however, that he could not continue to carry as many musicians, and in June 1948 he tried to interest Chick Kimball of WSB in Atlanta in a number of Renfro acts: "I have more than twenty people on the programs here when ten or twelve would really be enough. . . . My only interest would be in seeing that they were taken care of. I have no strings on any of them and do not want any part of their salary."[52]

During the same period Lair began to experience difficulties with his major sponsor, Ballard and Ballard. The flour company, having also overextended itself, began to pull back from its commitments to Renfro Valley. In September 1948, Lair told a former employee who wished to be re-hired, "We have had a very tough summer. The Ballard week-day programs have left the air and conditions generally are not good."[53] Similarly, a month earlier Lair had written to politician-musician Pleaz Mobley, who had also inquired about employment at Renfro, "We have lost the early morning Ballard shows, except Sunday, which has cut out [*sic*] income down to such an extent that I am letting several staff members go."[54]

The surviving business correspondence does not indicate what precipitated Ballard and Ballard's final pullout from Renfro Valley. Much of the reasoning behind the decision probably had to do with the changing priorities of mass-media advertising. Some former employees believed Lair's stubborn insistence on moving his enterprise to Florida during the winter of 1948–49 predicated Ballard and Ballard's final withdrawal of sponsorship. There is no correspondence between Lair and the flour company, however, that specifically mentions Florida as a point of contention. Lair did tell the Loan Agency of the Reconstruction Finance Corporation on November 13, 1948, incorrectly, that the contract with Ballard and Ballard had just been renewed for another fifty-two weeks and he needed the planned three-month trip to Florida in order to make up on revenues lost from highway construction and the dwindling success of the tent shows. "It is my personal opinion," he said, "that the Florida trip will be successful and will be in a position to go ahead with our general building campaign next year."[55]

Lair remained confident that something would work out until the very end. On December 16, 1948, he contacted both Vic Englehard of Ballard and Ballard and Bill Jones, the radio director for the public relations firm that handled the account. Lair expressed excitement that his old friend Doc Hopkins was thinking about leaving WLS and joining the Renfro Valley cast and that he had finally found a singer who sounded like Linda Parker. To Jones, Lair urged, "If you would give me the benefit of your actual opinion on what the chances are for Ballard to continue, it would help me a lot in making some decisions."[56]

Lair found out shortly thereafter that the account had been canceled, and he then arranged to move most of his show to Florida for the winter of 1949.[57] Pete Stamper, in a memoir of Renfro Valley, recalled that some felt that the move was the "biggest blunder in Renfro Valley's history" and speculated that Lair might have deliberately set out to alienate his sponsor in order to rid himself of the partnership of Freeman Keyes.[58] Keyes did become less involved with Lair's enterprises after 1950, but that explanation seems unlikely because he seemed willing to invest in Lair's Florida schemes. Writing to Lair in Orlando in March 1949, Keyes regretted not being able to come down to Florida because of his work but gave Lair the go-ahead on a pending deal. Despite the walnut fiasco, Keyes concluded optimistically, "We never have failed to come out on any deal we went into, so let's go again."[59] The deal, however, was never struck.

The 1949 Florida sojourn was not a complete disaster. Winter always created financial difficulties in Renfro Valley, and Virginia Lair far preferred the Florida climate. The Lairs' daughter Virginia (Ginalee) thought her father made a mistake not because he took the troupe to Florida but because he did not stay. She recalled that the show was an overwhelming success, and people offered to buy Lair land if he would move the barn dance to Florida in the winter. Despite Virginia Lair's pleading, Lair responded that he had made a commitment to his community and that was where he would keep his shows.[60]

Some entertainers had fond memories of the trip. Emory and Linda Martin remembered the ranch house where the entertainers lived outside Orlando and taking road trips throughout the state from January to April. "We really enjoyed that," Linda Martin said. "We stayed there in Orlando, lived there, but we went up and down one side of, the Atlantic side, clear down to Miami. . . . And then come up back through the Gulf and we didn't miss any in-between. We played every town in Florida."[61]

Within months of returning from Florida, Lair found Renfro Valley in crisis. "I will have to get a little outside help or disband my present talent group," he reported to Keyes in May 1949, adding, "I believe you can sell the show in such a way as to make this help with the payroll a good investment."[62] Keyes did try to help, and there seemed some chance that a deal with television could be struck. By December, however, Keyes, who still had made no progress on the deal, told Lair, "All I know to tell you is to cut down your staff to a minimum; try to keep the nucleus around which you can rebuild if and when radio and television break."[63] Two months later Keyes reported that the television deal had been held up because of costs, and he was "sorry as the very dickens" that he was not in a position to sell Renfro Valley on the radio at the present time.[64]

Lair was savvy enough to recognize the competition that television might pose to radio and eager to talk business when WAVE in Louisville contacted him about supplying talent for its television station. Inviting the program manager down to see Renfro Valley, Lair admitted, "All my plans and developments for the past eight years have been toward television and I believe we have here the best setup for it anywhere in the country."[65]

Lair's willingness to engage in discussions with WAVE came also from his dissatisfaction with WHAS. The station continued to develop shows that competed directly with those broadcast from Renfro, and Lair now felt that little effort was being made to help him find a new sponsor. He complained to Bill Jones of WHAS's inaction: "It is up to me to plan a move and not be caught with my pants down."[66] Among other schemes, Lair investigated the possibility of a remote broadcast for WLS in Chicago, arguing that the station could save money on talent by having a program from Renfro Valley.[67]

In trying to break into either television or the movies, Lair fortunately had some Hollywood contacts. In 1950, Pat Buttram, an acquaintance from the WLS days, contacted Lair on Gene Autry's behalf to ask for some good songs. "As you know," added Buttram, "these Hollywood writers just don't have the touch or the naturalness for our type of songs."[68] A few months earlier Lair heard from an old friend, Tom Hargis, in Hollywood. Hargis, who worked for Roy Rogers, inquired whether Lair had plans for television and added, "If you can get on the cable it should be wonderful for people to see the Renfro Valley Folks." He concluded, "Television is very active here but still no money to be made from it."[69]

During the lean years of the late 1940s Lair also worked with a Los Angeles publicist, Frances Lynne. In late 1949 she informed him that although she was making good progress on the synopsis for a projected movie story it would be highly advantageous to get a magazine story lined up as well. Lynne, who clearly thought big, was considering *Life,* the *New York Times,* or the *Saturday Evening Post.* "Now is the time for your story to break, while the square dance craze and general vogue for 'hillbilly' music is at its height," she said. "It might not last indefinitely."[70]

As if television alone did not pose a big enough threat, John Lair was also coping with rapid changes within the country music business. By the late 1940s the recorded music played on jukeboxes and the radio seriously eroded the market for live musical performances. Honky-tonk, which had explicit lyrics about drinking and cheating, began to take center stage in country music. The new style did not much impress Lair and neither did Hank Williams, the musician who became its central star. Still, he was willing to give a "jukebox act" a try if doing so would boost audiences. In the spring of 1950 Lair asked M. D. Howe of F. and M. Stage Shows, "Are you finding anything in the way of a name jukebox act for our prospective show? A number of people have suggested that Hank Williams who is not so hot but rates very high in record sales, would be a good draw the country over. Personally, I doubt if he is of the character and type we would want to build too much on."[71]

Although dubious about trends in country music, Lair hoped to cash in on the developing folk revival. A few months earlier he had explored

the idea of staging a "genuine American Folk Music show," something he
had always wanted to do. "This could be made up from the Renfro Valley
cast or could include groups from all parts of the country," he commented
to Howe. "This, too, would require considerable scenery and staging and
would have to be absolutely authentic if I put my name on it." Lair went
on to mention the possibilities of bringing in Lunsford to arrange square
dancing and inviting Romaine Lowdermilk "or some other genuine cowboy singer to do the westerns." He added, "With the upper bracket interest in Folk Music prevalent, especially in the Eastern cities, and with the
present trend toward square dancing, I believe I could assemble a show of
this kind which would be the talk of the country."[72]

The year 1950 saw the worst of times and the best of times for Renfro Valley. At the beginning of the year it must have seemed as if the
enterprise was in danger of collapsing. Just at its bleakest hour, however,
a new financial savior for Renfro Valley appeared on the horizon. Unlike
Freeman Keyes, Tom Wood, a young graduate of Harvard University Business School, did not bring his own money to the rescue but rather his
youthful energy and expertise in advertising. An assistant advertising
manager for General Foods, Wood had been home visiting his family in
Kentucky when his father, a life-long friend of Lair, convinced him that
he could sell Renfro Valley to national sponsors. Decades later Wood
wrote that for reasons he "still did not understand" he quit his job and
took the assignment. As he recounted, it would be a "long, hard, selling job—that would take nine months, all of my savings, and test every
ability I could muster."[73]

Wood planned initially to sell the sponsors on the idea that Renfro
Valley programs could reach a rural market that television had not pen-
etrated, but he had little success other than with old friends at General
Foods and the Benton and Bowles Advertising Agency. The breakthrough
came at dinner one night when Wood and his friend Oakley Bidwell, a
vice president at Benton and Bowles, decided to join together and sell
a rural advertising plan directly to General Foods. "Here we were," he
remembered, "thoroughly familiar with the largest food company in the
world—with tens of products needing supplementary rural coverage.
Lets pretend it is our assignment and lets put all of these products into
a Renfro Valley plan." Woods decided not to try to sell the barn dance
because "every big city had one." Instead, he asked Lair to develop a new,
fifteen- or thirty-minute, five-day-a-week "strip" show to sell along with
the *Sunday Gatherin'*.

Time was of the essence. Word had gotten out that General Foods
was considering sponsoring rural programs, and the "sharks"—WLW and

the Nashville radio stations—were circling. Having already sent copies of General Foods commercials ahead to Lair, Wood rushed to Renfro Valley to put in some hard work developing the new show. When he arrived, however, Lair merely instructed him to listen to a tape. "To my complete surprise," Wood wrote in his scrapbook, "a fifteen minute 'Country Store Program' began—complete with an opening theme song which John had composed, jokes, sound effects, songs . . . and, complete commercials rewritten in John's style, delivered by him from the scripts I had just sent him. Not only did he have one fifteen minute country store tape—he had two of them—each with different product commercials and they were good . . . so good they were later run on the air unchanged." Wood told Lair that he was a genius. "So I've been told" was the reply.

The clincher for selling Renfro Valley emanated from Wood's chance discovery of a portable tape-recorder in a shop window in New York. He had never seen one, and he counted on its novel effect in his presentation to General Foods. Dramatically uncovering the tape-recorder, Wood played the *Country Store* tape complete with General Food's current commercial as rewritten by John Lair. "So enthusiastic was the response," he said, "that within two weeks contracts were signed for over a $ million (a lot of money then)—for all three programs, a total of some 120 CBS stations in fourteen states covering half of America." He added, "This was the biggest rural radio sale of the year and certainly one of the most complex of all time."[74]

In pitching Renfro Valley to the New York advertising agency Lair attempted to again dignify the type of music he featured. According to one presentation developed during 1950, Renfro Valley appealed especially to southerners: "To these people old-time music is not 'hillbilly.' It is folk music, a definite part of their heritage." A list of suggested program titles in the presentation materials included "John Lair's Notebook on American Music," "Tune Tracer," "Song Searcher," and "History in Song."[75] In the General Foods proposal Lair suggested that Renfro Valley could even sponsor "a National Folk Festival." In advertising the new shows a CBS promotion in December 1950 spoke of "new programs of authentic American folk music, homespun humor and a grassroots, down-to-earth feeling about life in general."[76]

The new, General Foods–sponsored *Sunday Gatherin'* premiered on January 7, 1951. WHAS arranged for Kentucky's governor to attend, and Lair was made a Kentucky colonel. The most commercially successful years of Renfro Valley were off and running. The General Foods contract allowed Lair to bring back a number of performers who had either been let go or left Renfro, among them Jerry Behrens, who left acrimoniously.

In August 1949, however, he wrote to Lair to apologize. "A man can be such a fool sometimes," he admitted. "The only decent break I ever got in radio, was with you, Mr. Lair, and from the looks of things the only one I'll ever have."[77] A year later, in November, Lair informed Behrens that he had signed the General Foods contract. Moreover, "The unions are setting up my talent scale right now and I do not know exactly what it will be but I do know that it will be considerably better than anything we have had before."[78]

The new regime demanded some adjustment in Lair's standard practices. The sponsor insisted on increased emphasis on rehearsals and instructed Lair to slow his quick-paced delivery. Although General Foods had bought the idea of Lair rewriting and delivering its commercials, the advertising agencies restricted what could be said about the products. In March 1951, for example, instead of saying Post Toasties were "the best thing that's happened to corn since the Indians discovered it," Lair ad-libbed, "Some of the boys up in the hills may not believe that Post Toasties is the best thing that's happened to corn, but we here do." The agency that handled the account was prompt to respond, "This probably would refer to corn liquor distilled by some of the neighboring hill people. While we personally have no serious objection to this, we do think that it would be better to eliminate any such product tie-up with liquor even if in a joking way."[79]

Lair could no longer take listener correspondence and read it on-air. Instead, he forwarded the letters to the advertising agencies, which selected ones for broadcast, rewrote the letters, and obtained releases from the authors. The advertisers also devised six form letters to respond to fan mail. Lair, remarkably, remained relatively compliant. In one instance he complained that he had formerly been told to "give the product my personal endorsement, rather than try to make a plug commercial of them." He added, however, "I will try to conform if you can tell me just what is wanted."[80]

Four months after setting up an office at Renfro, Wood compiled a summary report for the Benton and Bowles office. Lair had, he reported, worked seven days a week and was "most cooperative" in complying with the requests of advertising agencies. Lair had expressed concern about too much commercialization threatening the character of the *Sunday Gatherin'*. An understanding had been reached, however, and Lair felt that he enjoyed "more freedom of expression."[81]

Wood did not mention another objection that Lair launched during the first month of the General Foods campaign. On January 30, 1951, he notified Benton and Bowles in no uncertain terms that he liked nothing about the cartoon *Renfro Valley Folks,* which the agency had produced: "Over a period of years, we have built up in the minds of the plain common people, reached and affected by our radio programs, that the Renfro Valley Folks are people just like they themselves are. They will certainly not appreciate your artist's conception of us and consequently of themselves."[82] An amateur cartoonist himself, Lair had strong feelings about the dividing line between "funny" and "smart alec," and he possessed a keen sense of his audience and what would be seen as insider humor and what would be interpreted as ridicule.

Sponsorship by General Foods allowed Lair to continue to put his radio fictions into a tangible form. He not only created a *Country Store* radio show but also built an operating country store and stocked it, of course, with General Foods products. Arrangements were also made with Gulf Oil to build a service station constructed from logs and "in keeping with the valley."[83] Lair's tourist enterprises obviously held less interest for General Foods, but the live shows prospered with the greater network exposure and by April 1952 he could report a rush business. The second barn dance show sold out by 10 A.M. one Saturday, and Lair asked permission to move the *Sunday Gatherin'* to the barn to accommodate the crowd that came to see it.[84] Tom McDonnell of the advertising firm Foote, Cone and Belding agreed that it would be bad public relations not to try to accommodate visitors and encouraged Lair to see whether he could approximate the studio sound in the barn.[85] Business and public relations people also seemed eager to see Renfro Valley. No less than fifteen visitors from Benton and Bowles, Foote, Cone and Belding, and General Foods arrived during the first four months of General Foods sponsorship.

In 1951 Benton and Bowles pursued the promotion of Renfro talent. In his 1951 report Wood observed, "Undoubtedly one of the finest vehicles for publicity and national interest is the record production of our talent. . . . We have already issued an invitation to Victor to visit Renfro Valley this June and review our talent and songs."[86] In a memo a few months later Wood noted that he was in touch with representatives from Decca Records, with the help of Red Foley, and Columbia.[87] Apparently, little came of those contacts, and the following year Foote, Cone and Belding arranged for Golden Records to record a Renfro Valley album as part of a premium offer. Although many of his performers believed Lair did little to promote their careers with the recording industry, that was clearly not the case during the early 1950s. Responding to plans for a premium offer he wrote, "I could not make any money on this but I think I see possibilities of building up a demand for records which might lead to national recognition of some of our talent."[88]

Throughout the late 1940s and early 1950s Lair continued to flirt with the idea of a Renfro Valley movie but could never find the right deal. "We always bog down in our negotiations when I will not allow them to make a Western film under the title of Renfro Valley," he wrote in 1948.[89] Tom Wood observed in his 1951 report that for the fourth time in ten years Hollywood had approached John Lair. This time it was an independent producer who wanted to make a full-length film at Renfro Valley with Judy Garland as the star. Wood commented that a first-rate movie would provide fine publicity, but it was "equally true that a cheap, out-of-character production could prove disastrous" and therefore Lair remained "extremely cautious."[90] Foote, Cone and Belding also pursued plans to have Lair appear either on Arthur Godfrey's television show or do "some of the old original Kentucky Folklore numbers" on a guest shot with Bing Crosby.[91]

Meanwhile, Lair tried again to create shows that featured his song research. In 1951 he wrote to Benton and Bowles to propose a show on "Darling Nellie Gray," suggesting that the sponsor might ante up for the reinternment of the actual Nellie Gray alongside her sweetheart, Joe Shelby.[92] Two years later he developed a television pilot script of the same story for "farm TV."[93] When Benton and Bowles requested information on hillbilly songwriters Lair responded that he preferred the label *homefolks* and provided information on Lunsford, Scott Wiseman, and himself. He was ashamed, he admitted, to put his name on his own biggest song-writing hit, a somewhat risqué song entitled "The Man Who Comes Around," "because it was so foreign from my type of work."[94]

In the late 1940s Lair planned to write a book on "some of the phases of American Folk Music" for "the general reading public as well as the folk music enthusiast."[95] Then, during the General Foods years, he focused on songs reputedly known by Abraham Lincoln. In conducting his research Lair corresponded with folk music scholar George Pullen Jackson at Vanderbilt University and invited him to come up to Renfro for a "discussion over the air of Folk Music" along with Francis Lee Utley of the Ohio State University, whom Jackson had recommended.[96] Of all of Lair's publications, *Songs Lincoln Loved* (1954) best represented his life-long passion for research in folk and popular songs. As with most of his other books, however, Lair offered the volume as a premium for a commercial product.

From the time he took his job, Tom Wood must have wondered how long it would all last. In September 1951 he informed his bank, "I am being very honest with you when I state that I look upon my present assignment at Renfro Valley as temporary. I am currently an agent for a very risky radio property which may be cancelled by the sponsor at any time. It is most probable that I will not be here for the remainder of the year. As a matter of fact, at the present time I am living in a tourist cabin and am making no plans of establishing a permanent residence in this area."[97]

Perhaps it served Wood's best financial interest to be as negative as possible; still, he could not have helped but fear the challenges ahead. For two years advertising agencies and promotions flooded Renfro Valley, and then, one by one, the General Foods brands started canceling sponsorship. Post held onto the *Sunday Gatherin'* through 1954, but in February 1955 the product manager for Postum, a coffee-like beverage, notified Lair that Postum's sponsorship would discontinue as of April.[98] Wood went back out again to sell Renfro, but major advertisers no longer retained much interest in investing in radio programming, given the inroads that television was making.

In his 1951 report Tom Wood had discussed the possibility that a successor for John Lair would need to be found, although he assured sponsors that Lair remained in good health. Clearly, Wood pointed out, a single person probably could not fill Lair's shoes. Lair himself had suggested that they might first find a writer and then later a "voice."[99] He did not mention the need for a successor to run the business, but with prospects once again looking bleak for Renfro Valley he saw in Wood the male heir he never had. The still-youthful Wood, however, knew his future lay elsewhere. "Much as I would appreciate Renfro Valley," he observed, "it was not my dream and there is no way my limited talents could ever replace him."[100]

The mid-1950s found John Lair in much the same boat as Sarah Gertrude Knott. After surviving the uncertainties of the postwar years, both found generous sponsors and the promise of stability in the early 1950s. Then, through circumstances largely beyond their control, they were once again forced to go begging. Neither seemed inclined to retire at the age of sixty. Even had they financial means to do so, they had grown used to being in control. Neither was willing to sit idle.

In the winter of 1955 Lair was as much disgusted as downhearted. General Foods had praised his efforts and told him that the *Gatherin'* rated third on the Neilson list for all Sunday network radio shows. On March 3 he informed Freeman Keyes, "If the above is the usual pattern of sponsorship, and we have found that it is, then I am ready to agree with you 'to hell with the sponsor. Let's sell our own product.'" Their last venture into a food product had been a disaster, but, Lair wrote, "If you want to go into the country ham business, let's get started. I will sell or give away all these dam ponies, clean my barn down to the clay floors and hang the whole thing full of hams." Keyes would own the business, to make or lose money "as you chose," while Lair would be paid a salary equal to 25 percent of profits after taxes. Lair had two more ideas. He had made and sold several hundred gallons of sorghum molasses the previous year and now proposed that he and Keyes get into that business in a much larger way. Lair also mentioned that he hoped to begin a mail order business, building on his current mailing lists of those who had purchased items from Renfro or subscribed to the *Bugle.* "Even if we never see a microphone again," he told Keyes, "we have built up a name and have a sales outlet that we should be able to cash in on."[101]

On the same day he wrote to Keyes, Lair also contacted Tom Wood in Chicago, "If a rating and sales like this does not produce a radio program, what in the heck does?" he asked. Lair briefly described his plans for marketing ham and molasses and then told Wood of an even more ambitious plan he did not mention to Keyes. Lair had contacted a lending agency with a plan to finance a shirt and overall manufacturer to move to the Valley and produce items under the Renfro Valley name. The plan would include "converting Renfro Valley into a fairly good-sized village, still with the original and present center." Lair assured Wood that he did not intend "to do entirely away with radio," and he hoped Wood would come back to Renfro, as "I feel you could do yourself more good with me in a setup like this and I certainly need a younger man on whom to put a big part of the load." Wood could purchase up to 49 percent of the stock with the provision that he could have controlling interest after Lair's death. "Frankly," Lair said, "I can not look forward to more than five or six years of active management and participation, but I do want to get something like this rolling and under way so that my family would have a source of income and a chance to participate in the work."[102]

The "valley where time stood still" did not become a textile-manufacturing town, however, and neither did Keyes and Lair go into big-time marketing of food products. Ultimately, Lair decided that if radio could not compete with television then he would have to accommodate the changing times. In May of 1955 he informed William McBride of WDBO in Orlando that it looked "like we have to go TV if we go at all." Breaking into television presented problems, however. Louisville stations and WLW had their own talent and Lair could not interest them in a Renfro show. Moreover, a deal with ABC in Columbus, Ohio, had fallen through. Finally, Lair got to the point. Could his show come to McBride's station to "keep the ball rolling until we could lay into a network deal"?[103]

A few weeks later Lair chided Keyes for being skeptical about the possibilities of a hillbilly television show and pointed to a recent spate of them, including Red Foley's Ozark Jubilee, the Grand Ole Opry films, and a new show by Pee Wee King. "Without station backing or money for a pilot film," Lair stated, "I sit here twiddling my thumbs, when you and I both know I could put on a better TV show than any of this bunch mentioned." Lair wrote that he found himself "in a desperate situation" and would willingly leave Renfro Valley to go to any station.[104]

Throughout 1955 Lair tried to get his enterprise back on firm ground. As he told someone from the advertising agency, "A man sitting in the middle of Renfro Valley where time stands still with a vengeance has a chance to hatch up a lot of ideas."[105] Lair contacted a number of former associates as well as prominent media people. He suggested to Tom Hargis, for example, that it would be a particularly good time to break into television and added, "Wish to heck we could get Gene [Autry] to peel off a small bankroll for a big piece of a show he himself would love to appear in, if possible."[106]

Despite the sudden boom in "hillbilly TV," however, no one seemed interested in pursuing a deal with Lair. CBS, which had carried his shows on its radio network, responded, "If we were planning, at this time, a television hillbilly show, you would be one of the people, I am sure, we would want to talk to," but, CBS added, "for the time being we do not have such plans."[107] In efforts to secure a deal, Lair sent letters and copies of his Lincoln book to notables in the entertainment world, including the Washington, D.C.–based country music entrepreneur Connie B. Gay and Dave Garroway, Ed Sullivan, and Arthur Godfrey.

He finally hit pay dirt when he contacted his old friend Oakley Bidwell, who had moved from Benton and Bowles to Campbell-Mithun, an advertising agency that represented Pillsbury Mills. Bidwell responded, "I've got tremendous faith in your setup as a television film possibility. The very authenticity that sets you apart from anything even remotely similar could never have come off as well on radio as it could on television." Although he could not promise anything, Bidwell thought Pillsbury might be interested in sponsoring a Renfro Valley television show.[108]

A half year later, in July 1956, Lair taped a short commercial at Bidwell's request for Ballard Flour, now a subsidiary of Pillsbury. Lair himself was more interested in Pillsbury than renewing the association with Ballard. Pillsbury had broader distribution, and Renfro Valley's audience was stronger north of the Ohio River.[109] Bidwell complied with Lair's request to pursue Pillsbury and encouraged Lair to start roughing out ideas for fifteen-minute programs.[110] "Looks like we are on our way again," Lair informed Tom Hargis on July 13. "We have sold Pillsbury

Flour a fifteen minute TV show, once a week, and five minute transcriptions five times a week. Not much, but it gets our foot in the TV door and takes us off the hook financially. . . . We are assured by Pillsbury that if the TV thing is successful they'll expand to half hour, throw Grand Ole Opry off and put us coast to coast next year."[111] By the beginning of October 1956 the Pillsbury radio show went on the air, and production began on the television show.

Surprisingly, Lair, a natural on radio and on the stage, was less comfortable in front of a camera. On October 2 Bidwell urged him to try and look a bit more pleasant: "When you were handling your live audience in the barn the night I saw that show, your facial expression was exactly what I think you should do on television. And never once that night did you look as if your were 'fixin' to bite someone'!"[112]

"I seriously believe I am the dam [sic] meanest looking character I ever saw on a TV screen," Lair replied. He added, "Standing on a marked spot, or sitting in an unfamiliar position, not allowed to make a move on account of eyeglass reflection and reciting unfamiliar words is not conducive to the exudation of much personality." He also complained that the copy girl not only put words in his mouth but also tried to think for him. He was "crammed so full of plug copy there is not time or room for atmosphere or to gently lead the listener into the train of thought to make him most receptive." Lair had other complaints as well. The musical director, he felt, edited the country out of country music: "Songs are a little too smooth, voice too sugary and accompaniment too light." In addition, he resented that the costume woman had taken the Coon Creek Girls out of gingham dresses and high-button shoes and put them into ballet slippers and swing skirts. Although sharply critical in some of his comments, Lair added, "Having seen so many temperamental hillbillies I am anxious to do nothing that might cause me to be included in that category, so I have passed over many things that I should perhaps have fought for."[113]

Bidwell agreed on some points. If Lair felt that over-refinement diluted the country flavor, then his views must be respected. He was less sympathetic about the costume issue, informing Lair that the "swing skirts" were homespun skirts from Berea College, and the Coon Creek Girls had asked to wear their flat-heeled shoes in a scene in which they had to dance. Most important, Bidwell agreed with Lair's complaint about commercial plugs: "You are probably correct in saying that your biggest personal asset, to this or any show, is probably your ability to paint a word picture with your own words, and make people want the end product. The tape you sent us on biscuits before we ever decided to buy the show was to me an excellent example of what you can do. And it's just criminal if we don't get all we can of that gift into the show."[114] Now half-way through filming, Bidwell assured Lair that he appeared "relaxed and pleasant-looking" and that the product supervisor for Pillsbury was enthusiastic and had been particularly enthralled with the outdoor shots that lent the program "an authenticity that certainly sets it apart from anything now on the air."

Lair, however, fretted about the success of the show. In January he asked Bidwell, "Do you have any sort of a rating on our TV shows as yet? Most important of all, are we selling any flour?"[115] What concerned Lair was failure to come up with a successful booking campaign to compete with that of the Grand Ole Opry. Regional focus posed one problem. Pillsbury broadcast the Renfro television show exclusively in the South, whereas Lair's live shows had more success further north. And, as Lair complained to Luther Dodd in Florida, the "Grand Old Opry has had to deliver such big casts of big names to do business that they've almost ruined it for the rest of us." He added, however, "There is a lot of territory they're worn out in where we have never been booked."[116]

Increasingly, Nashville assumed the role of capital of the country music industry empire, which the recording industry ruled. Lair hated unfavorable comparisons to the Grand Ole Opry and continued to worry about the ascendancy of recorded music. As he explained to Bidwell, "It seems that nowadays records are the builders. More talent by far is built up by recordings than any other medium—and we have more or less neglected that end of it. There's nothing wrong with any phase of the Renfro operation that money can't remedy. There are plenty of good recording names available outside of Nashville and there is plenty good talent to be discovered and promoted."[117]

Almost across the board Lair received praise from advertising personnel who handled the Pillsbury account although filming had run over budget. In early 1957 the head of the film company informed him, "We hope that the series will prove successful as we hear something about the remote possibility of making more. This we would like to do as it will give us an opportunity to recover some of the rather heavy costs not contemplated when we compiled our figures for the agency."[118] Lair found that he liked the new recognition that the show brought him. After a trip south, Lair reported to Bidwell, "I was very well pleased with the reception our TV shows seem to be getting. . . . I was recognized on the streets, in restaurants, stores, ect. [sic] by people who introduced themselves to tell me they and their neighbors watched the shows on the Atlanta station."[119] As it turned out, however, Pillsbury did not continue the television show past its original fourteen-show contract, and by the spring of 1957 Renfro Valley's association with Pillsbury had ended. It was the last national sponsor Lair would have.

Despite all his talents Lair could not successfully buck the tide in country music or the mass media. Although he tried to accommodate to change, television and recording did not comfortably fit his natural skills as a showman. Lair's eldest daughter, Ann Henderson, although proud of the television show, believed her father's true skills were in radio: "I do think that he was the master of radio. I don't believe he would have ever done as well with television as he did with radio. Because radio, like he said, it calls for the reader to supply half the script . . . what you're talking about, they have to imagine. And I think that was his real strong point, he could do that."[120]

Even as his association with Pillsbury wound down Lair had one more ace up his sleeve. In April 1957, Renfro Valley's own little radio station, WRVK, went on the air. Although he hoped to create an originating station for his own network programs, with a lack of major sponsors, WRVK only served the local community. Much as Lair railed against disk jockey shows, he frequently used that format at WRVK, and a few Renfro performers such as Manuel "Old Joe" Clark became popular deejays. More important, the station also provided jobs for a handful of long-time Renfro performers in the lean period following the Pillsbury shows.[121] A number of other performers began to retire. Emory and Linda Lou Martin had already bought a service station and settled nearby, and in 1958, after more than twenty years under Lair's management, Lily May Ledford called it quits.

After the end of the Pillsbury contract CBS continued to carry the *Sunday Morning Gatherin'* unsponsored for another two years, until April 1959. In desperation, Lair contacted many of the larger 50,000-watt stations and offered them the *Gatherin'* on a taped basis for $38 a show with the station providing commercial sponsors or $8 a show if the station wished to broadcast the show without commercials. Although that represented an enormous step down from the General Foods days, it kept the show alive. The *Gatherin'* continued to be carried by WHAS, several southern stations, and even more in the Midwest, including WLBK in DeKalb, Illinois, owned by Lair's old friend and former rival George Biggar. If Lair hoped that distributing taped shows would be only a stopgap measure, that was not the case. As the bad times of the late 1950s became the bad times of the early 1960s he finally prepared to make a pact with the devil, the Nashville country music establishment.

Although Lair and Knott did not cross paths much if at all in the 1950s, during that decade country and folk music intersected and diverged in new ways. Lair had hardly been the only person in the country music industry to promote the genre as "folk music." The Opry's George Hay, publisher Fred Rose, and many others recognized that labeling their products as "folk" provided a way to sell them to audiences and sponsors otherwise put off by the negative connotations of the term *hillbilly*. When the Weavers' hit "Goodnight Irene" in 1950 spawned a number of pop and country covers, including one recorded by Red Foley, the label *folk* seemed even more desirable. As various members of the Weavers ran afoul of the House Un-American Activities Committee, however, many in the country music industry became unwilling to be associated with folk music. By the mid-1950s the term *country* finally became fully institutionalized within the industry.[122]

Both country and folk revival musicians did achieve some crossover success into popular music during the 1950s, but audiences began to separate into two distinctly different groups. The one for folk music became more predominantly urban, East Coast, liberal, and youthful, whereas listeners to mainstream country were apt to be more conservative and rural and from the South or mid-America. Curiously, however, the folk revival spawned new interest in the roots of country music. Harry Smith's six-record *Anthology of American Folk Music*, first released in 1953, featured a spectrum of early commercial recordings of blues and hillbilly tunes and eventually became the touchstone for a new generation of folk revivalists.[123]

By the 1960s a number of the early country radio and recording stars found second careers on the folk revival circuit. Ultimately, many folk revivalists also embraced bluegrass music, which they saw as the legitimate heir to earlier, "old time" music. Bluegrass, having been increasingly excluded from mainstream commercial country music, found its hard-core audience in a curious coalition of conservative, rural people and members of an emerging youth culture.

To some degree Lair and Knott held exceptional attitudes in their fields. Although many early folk festival organizers condemned hillbilly music, Knott, occasionally critical of commercial radio, maintained an open mind. Academic folklore itself slowly came around to exploring the connections between hillbilly and folk music. The path for doing so was blazed by D. K. Wilgus, who presented papers on the subject at National

Folk Festival conferences. For his part, Lair did not back away from the folk label as many of his compatriots did during the 1950s. His use of the term was calculated, but he had a genuine interest in folk music.

By the early 1960s Lair and Knott should have been well positioned to take advantage of the folk revival. Lair, now a traditionalist within country music, might have been able to sell his product to a young audience newly appreciative of the older forms. Knott, as director of the largest folk festival in the country, might have moved her event into a central position in the world of the folk revival. Neither thing happened, however. Both Knott and Lair, past their sixty-fifth birthdays, had difficulty understanding the new audience. Nor, for various reasons, did folk revivalists embrace them. During the last decades of their active careers, neither rode the crest of a wave brought by a new and youthful audience for folk and traditional country music. Instead, they would be forced to fight for the survival of the institutions they had created.

Through the magic of photography Lair transported his Chicago cast to Kentucky in the early 1930s. Lulu Belle and Red Foley are pictured at far left, Lair stands at the center with Linda Parker. Several of the Cumberland Ridge Runners appear more than once. (Southern Appalachian Archives, Berea College)

The original Coon Creek Girls with Margaret Lilly as A'nt Idy (seated). Left to right: Rosie Ledford, Esther "Violet" Koehler, Lily May Ledford, and Evelyn "Daisy" Lange. (Southern Appalachian Archives, Berea College)

Renfro Valley Barn Dance, Cincinnati cast, late 1930s. The front row includes Whitey Ford (the Duke of Paducah), Girls of the Golden West, Slim Miller, A'nt Idy and Little Clifford, and the Coon Creek Girls. Lair is standing in the middle of the back row with Lunsford. (Southern Appalachian Archives, Berea College)

Remote broad-cast of coon hunt, circa 1940. (Southern Appalachian Archives, Berea College)

The cast of the tent show, 1944. (Southern Appalachian Archives, Berea College)

Texas dance group at the 1946 National Folk Festival. The post-war years brought a boom in the popularity of western square dance. (Department of Library Special Collections, Folklife Archives, Western Kentucky University, Bowling Green, Kentucky)

Sarah Gertrude Knott dressed in a Kiowa outfit. (Department of Library Special Collections, Folklife Archives, Western Kentucky University, Bowling Green, Kentucky)

Part of a panorama photograph of the 1949 National Folk Festival, with Knott, as usual, center-stage. (Department of Library Special Collections, Folklife Archives, Western Kentucky University, Bowling Green, Kentucky)

John Lair, Tom Wood peering over his shoulder, early 1950s. (Southern Appalachian Archives, Berea College)

Lair during the General
Foods days, early 1950s.
(Southern Appalachian
Archives, Berea College)

Knott at her desk, probably in the 1960s. (Yvonne Dodge Collection)

Melville Hussey passing the gavel to Lawrence Derthick as Knott looks on, early 1960s. (Department of Library Special Collections, Folklife Archives, Western Kentucky University, Bowling Green, Kentucky)

Cover of the program for thirty-third National Folk Festival, the first held without Knott as director. (Department of Library Special Collections, Folklife Archives, Western Kentucky University, Bowling Green, Kentucky)

John and Virginia Lair later in life. (Southern Appalachian Archives, Berea College)

6 The Prima Donna of Folk

She wanted to be the prima donna of folk.
—Loyal Jones, 1995

Sarah Gertrude Knott could hardly consider her return to Washington, D.C., as triumphant. Usually, she endeavored to put a positive spin on all her festivals no matter what happened, but Knott expressed little pleasure with the 1960 National Folk Festival at Carter Barron Amphitheater. Always most comfortable with theatrical conventions, she found the audience hard to control in an outside venue. With unusually hot weather for early June, the four thousand school children attending each matinee "chattered and squirmed under the blazing sun," and she "decided right then and there that it is a mistake to think that folk festivals should be held outdoors." More significant was that Knott found the same concerns "as those facing folk festival leaders everywhere in these days of sudden popularization." Even the old guard expressed interest in change. "One special friend," she wrote, "wondered why we were not more 'up to date.' 'Same old format!' she exclaimed in evident disappointment. 'Same old country!' I replied." Knott was proud of the fact that she held to the same basic pattern of presentation for more than twenty-five years, but others began to see her festival as antiquated. Most crushing to Knott, the festival received critical reviews in the press. She had returned to Washington with memories of the glory days when the *Washington Post* paid the bills. To receive critical reviews from her former sponsor floored her.[1]

Although Knott may have hoped to return to the success of her previous Washington days, she also dreamed of establishing a folk festival center on a year-round basis. Recognizing that Congress had begun to consider federal support for the arts in 1960, she felt she had made a "real dent in some of the governmental agencies and private educational-cultural organizations" in Washington.[2]

Even as Knott lobbied for support in Washington she came close to running afoul of governmental remnants of McCarthyism. She had long been aware of rumors about the political affiliations of folk singer Jenny Vincent but continually invited her back because she "came first and helped most." In 1960 Vincent arrived early to fill a date for a television show. Then a very different form of publicity ensued—the Senate Internal Security Subcommittee called Vincent to appear the Thursday of the festival. Knott immediately moved to pull strings to have the hearing postponed until the Monday following the event, and Vincent voluntarily withdrew from the program.

Not satisfied with simply avoiding negative publicity, Knott decided to pay a personal visit to J. Edgar Hoover's offices. As she informed one of Hoover's assistants, "I could not go along in NFFA [the National Folk Festival Association] and do the job that cries to be done in the United States and forever be looking over my shoulder for communists. I had no weakness whatever for that form—and that I did not belong in the clan—the ones who believe it was okay to include communists (or Nazis) in NFFA."[3] The incident seems to have come to nothing, but it does demonstrate Knott's generally pragmatic politics. She maintained that she had no time, nor should she be expected, to investigate the political backgrounds of participants. If J. Edgar wanted to send his agents to do the job, however, that was fine with her. Luckily, the age of the anticommunist witch hunts was rapidly waning, and no one called Knott's bluff.

Knott's developing friendship with an attorney who lived in the same hotel provided one bright light in her first year back in Washington. S. Melville Hussey, who worked for the Civil Aeronautics Board, soon found himself deeply involved with the folk festival scene. For the next few years, as part of the National Folk Festival Association, he complemented Knott's missionary zeal with considerable business and legal acumen. By 1961 he held the position of executive vice president.

Following the 1960 program at Carter Barron, the National Folk Festival Association reincorporated and made Washington, D.C., rather than St. Louis its official home. In 1961 the festival moved back to Constitution Hall, where it had previously enjoyed so much success. If the school audience had been squirmy in the hot sun at the 1960 festival, it was nonexistent in 1961, an absence Knott attributed to the fact that new National Folk Festival Association staffers who worked on the festival's business aspects did not consult her. Moreover, her suggestions for the "handling of the schools were rejected, and our school-child attendance was practically nil."[4] Knott never again staged a festival at the hall owned by the Daughters of the American Revolution.

The 1961 "Silver Anniversary" festival started conventionally enough with Chris Sanderson acting as town crier, followed by a performance of the Kiowa dancers. There were, however, some harbingers of change. A few urban folk revival musicians performed, most part of the locally based folk scene, and a Washington-area bluegrass group also took part. Knott saw the challenge of the urban folk revival but did not necessarily hold antagonistic views, particularly if it meant the survival of her own festival.

In January 1963 Irwin Silber, editor of *Sing Out!* magazine, responded to an inquiry from Knott about young urban folk revival singers. Silber suggested Bob Dylan, Judy Collins, and others but noted that "the big-pitch these days in our folk festivals is to get the real country singers. Perhaps that is the way it ought to be."[5] Rather than getting big-name revivalists, however, Knott mostly tried to emphasize the different, more authentic, nature of her festival. She was not hostile to the emerging folk craze on college campuses but tried to stick to "diamonds in the rough."[6]

The large festivals that catered to the growing and youthful audiences of the folk revival posed an enormous challenge to the National Folk Festival. The premier urban revival venue, the Newport Folk Festival, began in 1959 under the direction of George Wein. Many performers at the first Newport Folk Festivals were professionals, and the event succeeded in attracting large numbers of college students. Under the influence of Pete and Toshi Seeger among others, the festival moved toward inclusion of more authentic performers. As Pete Seeger recalled, "My wife and I and Ewan MacColl and my sister criticized George Wein. Said this is, was, not a real folk festival. Where are the folks? There are a lot of great folk singers in America and you didn't have 'em—you had the Kingston Trio there; you had the Brothers Four on there; and you had Peter, Paul, and Mary on there. But where are the people they learned from?" When Wein asked how they would pay the performers the Seegers suggested a small token gratuity. As Seeger reflected, "And it's a nice tradition . . . it was carrying on, I guess, Sarah's tradition of not, not trying to pay star salaries."[7]

Although Seeger acknowledged some direct influence of the National on Newport the newer festival set a different standard of audience expectation. Some performers such as Jimmie Driftwood and Jean Ritchie appeared at both, and the inclusion of certain genres at Newport, such as Cajun music, was directly attributable to the National Folk Festival.

Newport, however, catered more directly to the emerging youth culture put off by the patriotism and pageantry of the National. It was a youthful audience that revered elderly blues musicians or ballad singers but responded less generously to an evening-gown-clad emcee rapidly approaching her seventieth year.

Newport also featured a genre that Knott largely neglected, the blues. Harry Smith's *Anthology of American Folk Music* helped create an audience for African American vernacular music, and by the early 1960s a blues revival blossomed. Although Knott always included African American folklore and had several times featured W. C. Handy on the program of the National, she often relied on recommendations of African American church leaders and educators, who frequently viewed the blues as less than respectable. Instead, African American offerings at the National tended toward religious forms of expression as well as work songs and games.

Soon enough it became clear that Newport could attract both audiences and performers away from the National. Following the 1963 National Folk Festival, Helen Sommer, assistant director of the NFFA, observed to Knott, "I guess now we know why some of the old regulars were not in Covington, Ky., for our festival—that is, you do if you heard about the Folk Festival they had in Newport."[8] If Seeger viewed the payment of a mere $50 as carrying on Knott's tradition, Sommer saw it as stealing the National's performers. It was Newport's large and youthful audiences, however, rather than its token payment that likely attracted many artists.

As Knott pondered how to capture the new audience for folk music she also worried about keeping academic folklorists interested in her endeavor. In 1961 she presented a paper on "The Problem of Utilization of Folklore" at the annual meeting of the American Folklore Society (AFS), one of only twenty-one papers given. A few months earlier she had written to MacEdward Leach, who now held the role of the president of AFS, asking for his advice: "I do think that as Edson Richman [*sic*] said, either the scholars should advise us and help make the National Folk Festival Association serve the best possible way, or as he said 'they should do nothing.' However, I have felt and do now feel that by far the majority do believe in what we have done. They believe in it because folklorists have helped make the plans."[9]

Leach failed to rally the AFS firmly behind Knott's plans, but she continued to work on the society's officials. Two years later Tristram Coffin, secretary-treasurer of the AFS, told Knott, "I think that your idea of having the American Folklore Society appoint a committee to work closely with your Board is excellent and I will bring the subject up to

Mel Jacobs [then president of AFS].[10] The tiny discipline of folklore grew exponentially during the 1960s, and Knott had difficulty keeping up with its vast changes. Although academic folklorists and revivalists often kept each other at arm's length, the folk revival fed the academic programs. Keeping both groups happy, however, as Knott discovered, proved a difficult task. In 1966 Leach firmly stated that the NFFA must try and decide whether to try for "folk authenticity" or "to emulate Newport."[11]

Knott's hopes of boosting her credentials with the academic community received a crushing blow in 1962. For more than two decades she had labored over her history of the folk festival movement, which she then sent to academic folklorists she trusted for review. In the spring, Arthur Campa mailed Knott's manuscript to MacEdward Leach in Philadelphia. The package never reached its destination. After a year's investigation the post office concluded that it had been destroyed by a fire in the St. Louis post office. No other copy existed. A decade later, after retirement, Knott attempted to reconstruct the book, but it would never be published.

In 1962, for the third time in seven years, the National Folk Festival skipped a year. The board hoped to gain greater financial stability and work on governmental or foundation support. Although NFFA offices remained in Washington, D.C., the dream of the city as the permanent site for the festival began to fade. Exciting developments emerged in Knott's home state of Kentucky, however, as Governor Bert T. Combs moved to create the Kentucky Council of Performing Arts and within it a Division of Folklore. In an effort to "stimulate the state's cultural wealth and spur its economy" the council initiated a survey of folk arts, to be directed by Knott.[12]

For the first time, Knott saw the potential of Kentucky becoming the permanent home of the National Folk Festival, and she began to make plans to hold the 1963 event in the commonwealth. She had high hopes that William Jansen, who served as one of the directors of the newly formed council, would facilitate support from the University of Kentucky. Much to her disappointment the council chose Covington in northern Kentucky as the site of the 1963 festival. As Knott recalled many years later, "I was put in a low-down place in Covington, Kentucky, where I didn't want to be—and in a park instead of at the University of Kentucky."[13]

In planning the Covington festival Sarah Gertrude Knott struggled to make the best of a site she disliked. In March she wrote to the group that she felt "should form the very backbone of the 1963 NFF." Despite her continued ties with western Kentucky, the "backbone" group—Raymond "Bun" McLain, Edith James, Edna and Jean Ritchie, Jean Thomas, and John Lair—all came from the eastern half of the state. With the pressure of the new folk festivals, Knott also pondered novel ways to stage her event. In a collective letter to the Kentucky advisors she mused, "One way I was thinking of doing part of the program (overall) is to have almost everybody grouped around—like theatre in the round—and just get up from where you are and get going—those who need entrances can have them though." In experimenting with new theatrical forms Knott conceived of staged vignettes that would come into action. "What would be characteristic of you? And yours?" she asked Lair. "At one time could it be a religious sing, with audience joining in? At sometime, I had thought of benches (if we can get them) like a church—turn on spots just on that and let it be a church—Amazing Grace, Wondous [sic] Love. What else, John, could it be like your radio show, presenting some of your singers?"[14]

Knott counted on Lair to do more than just appear at the festival. She enlisted his help with the program, exhibits, and especially the awards committee. Burl Ives had offered prize money for outstanding performers, and Knott appointed an awards committee that included Lair, academic folklorists D. K. Wilgus and Kenny Goldstein, and fiddler Robert Beers. In one of her collective letters she urged, "Whatever suggestions any committee member has, please send to John Lair immediately. John will pick up the ball from here on." If she thought this group of strong-minded men would come to any easy agreement she was mistaken. The committee became highly contentious, and the split did not necessarily fall between academics and "popularizers." Jansen and Lair supported the idea of contests; Beers and Goldstein opposed it; and Wilgus's opinion, although always emphatic, shifted. Early on, Wilgus suggested to Knott that they stick to traditional genres, perhaps adding blues and finger-picking guitar to the singing, banjo picking, and fiddling she had suggested. "Let's try to keep 'new folk' songs out of it," he added. "Let them get their prizes from the recording industry."[15] When sharp disagreements arose among committee members, Lair wrote:

> See the contest idea has stirred up quite a bit of commotion. I fail to see wherein the danger lies, but if it's going to cause controversy among those with whom you work maybe it would be better to leave it off. To me it seems a very simple matter of having judges who know what they're about and having the courage of their convictions. After all, anybody who knows anything about folk and traditional music should be able to tell the genuine thing from the spurious. . . . Since, however, some of your principal people seem to be set against it you might do your cause a lot of overall damage by going ahead with the contest. I'm going to have our

festival here before the end of the year and if Ives wants to promote a contest he is welcome to present it here and there'll be no difficulty.[16]

Knott had also asked Lair to arrange to bring musician-politician Pleaz Mobley as well as Bradley Kincaid to the festival. Requesting a "squib about you & Renfro Valley," she ended her scrawled letter, "Don't be silent! I need your help."[17] Lair responded that Mobley was out campaigning but had agreed to come, but he had yet to hear back from Kincaid. He added, "Give me what leeway you can on the program announcement—in other words let's not tie it down to my first sugges-tion 'American Ballads.' Make the subject something like 'Radio's Effect on Folk Music' and I can drag Bradley in as the first folk singer on radio. That will please him and maybe get his cooperation."[18]

At first the Kentucky festival seemed promising. Knott had returned to her home state, Governor Combs officially endorsed the festival, and Kentucky appropriated state funds for the event. Unfortunately for Knott, however, it turned out to be a bitter time. Not only did she not have control over the site of the festival but she also, ultimately, lost control over the festival itself. Her elder sister, Lannie Ransdell, fell ill, and Knott needed to spend time in western Kentucky. According to her ver-sion of events, distraction made it possible for an NFFA newcomer to attempt a coup. In a subsequent draft of a letter to members of the board and National Advisory Council, Knott charged that "a very small, but very aggressive group of NFFA personnel from Washington took it upon themselves to interfere with my work, to misrepresent my relationship with the NFFA and to impair the confidence of the Kentucky group."[19] She was a bit more pointed in a letter to friends:

> I have had a battle royal—with a Judas Iscarout [*sic*] or two who wanted to oust me and gave me a stab in the back here in Kentucky—my own state last year . . . but at rehearsal last Festival they succeeded in taking over and putting program in hand of unknown. I have no knowledge—and went along for the reason that 'the show must go on.' But when the Festival was over—(and my dear Big Sis died a few weeks later) when that was over, I faced the NFF—Dr. Derthick—and all of the Kentucky gang—Result I got em. . . . They are on their knees to me and only one person at the bottom.[20]

Knott subsequently found out that several weeks before the 1963 festival NFFA staffers had sent a letter to all participants, informing them that her work in connection with the festival had ended and they should no longer communicate directly with her about the event.[21] Many years later she recalled that after the 1963 festival Melville Hussey had valiantly come to her aid and asked Lawrence Derthick to resign the presidency of the NFFA even though he was not directly responsible for what happened in Covington.[22]

After the first Kentucky festival Hussey took a far more active role in the activities of the NFFA, probably out of personal concern for Knott. "All is well," he told a friend, "but I am so concerned about SGK and the fix she finds hereself [sic] in as a result of her selfless devotion to an idea. The time, effort and sacrifice she has put into it would have made her well off if devoted to some commercial pursuit. No use talking about it, however, because this thing is her whole life. All we can do is to try to hold up her hand and back her up."[23]

At about the same period Knott became aware of rumors that she had a problem with alcohol. Although she may have been raised a Baptist in rural Kentucky, her personal habits, particularly the fact that she chain-smoked and would "take a highball whenever I got ready," were more in keeping with those of an urban sophisticate. Knott attributed one rumor to an incident with Jimmie Driftwood: "I had this festival at Mobile, Alabama and I worked my head off for the three or four days. . . . And Jimmie was there and so we went to a place to have lunch. And so I said, 'Let's have a drink.' And he didn't take any, and I took three or four." Later Knott got word that another friend had told May Kennedy McCord that Sarah had become a very heavy drinker. "And I picked up the telephone and called her and said, 'What in the world do you mean by saying that I've become a heavy drinker?'"[24]

Despite the difficulties that 1963 posed, the year ended with an accomplishment that would make a lasting contribution to the emerging profession of public folklore. Knott moved to Washington just as an administration more sympathetic to the notion of federal support for the arts came into power. With the emerging legislation for support of the arts in the Senate, and with Melville Hussey, a lawyer long in government service, by her side, she was well positioned to be heard. Under the leadership of Senator Claiborne Pell, the Senate held hearings on the pending arts legislation. Livingston Biddle, who worked for Pell on the bill and later chaired the National Endowment for the Arts, recalled the strong impression Knott made: "She reminded me then, and as I see her again in memory, of a great square-rigged ship making for home, all ropes taut, sails billowed, pennants flying in a stiff following breeze. Her white hair was fixed in an old-fashioned bun; her wide-set eyes were both shrewd and all-seeing. In her the folk arts had a passionate advocate. No doubt she had instructed the more reticent Melville Hussey to prepare the legislative language now presented to elevate the folk arts to a position of unquestionable and lasting importance." Biddle, who had drafted much of the legislation himself, stated, "it was beyond dispute" that Sarah Gertrude Knott was responsible for the inclusion of the folk arts in the legislation.[25]

Although Covington wanted the National Folk Festival to return in 1964, Knott thought that doing so was not "logical."[26] Lacking other strong choices, however, she subsequently agreed. In early spring the planners moved the site nine miles away, to the new grandstand at the Latonia Race Course in Florence, Kentucky. Knott found the venue a considerable improvement even though Covington officials threatened to withdraw financial support. This time around Knott attempted to include more representation from the western part of the state. In the "search" letter that she sent to "Kentucky Friends," she asked about river songs from Paducah and songs from the western coalfields "around Central City and Greenville where Merle Travis came from?" She added, "What about a Festival over about Central City or Greenville to round up singers? What about the guitar picker and banjoist who taught Merle Travis?"[27] Although Knott remained open to exploring the roots of country music, the 1964 Kentucky program does not suggest that she met with much success.

Even before the 1964 festival, negotiations began for the site of the next event. Knott expressed interest in a western location but soon settled on St. Petersburg, Florida. After the struggles of the Kentucky festivals Hussey was taking a more hands-on approach and oversaw most of the business affairs of the festival in Florida. In Florida especially, he and Knott had to deal with popular misconceptions of folk musicians. On October 29, 1964, the *St. Petersburg Independent* ran an even-handed story about the possibility of the National Folk Festival coming to the city but then personified the event in a cartoon as a guitar-toting, bearded beatnik. Hussey advised the editor that the cartoon "gave us a chill" and admonished, "As we prepare to bring our 'folk' to St. Petersburg, do not demean them by cartooning them in advance as beatnicks. They are you. They are me. . . . You will learn to feel a great affection for our National Folk Festival participants. Above all, you will acquire a great respect for them."[28]

Even Knott, typically generous in her attitudes toward the folk revival, followed Hussey's harder line. She was quoted in the *St. Petersburg Times* as saying, "A brand of pseudo folk singer has sprung up, usually a poor counterpart and often a burlesque of the real thing. These commercial products are altogether worthy entertainment, but they often create an entirely false image of genuine folklore in the minds of the uninitiated."[29] If the newspaper stereotyped the National Folk Festival Association as beatniks, others believed that communists could be found within its ranks. A story entitled "Folk Festival Communist Tie Held Untrue" noted that a small group was "seeking to peg the coming National Folk Festival as a Communist Propaganda front."[30]

Dismissing the "radical far rights," Jim Gray, the tourist and convention director who acted as business manager for the Florida National Folk Festival, hoped to attract some big name "folk performers." In early November he asked Hussey's opinion on trying to invite the folk group Peter, Paul, and Mary in order to assure heavy attendance and financial success.[31] Hussey replied by reminding Gray that Knott held total control of programming and then labeled the group as "pseudo folk entertainers, and not folk singers within our terms."[32] A month later the topic of inviting Pete Seeger came up. Hussey still feared harassment from the "far rights," but Gray assured him that he would welcome Seeger with "open arms."[33] A few months later Gray inquired about whether a "headliner" like Burl Ives might appear for free.[34]

Throughout his correspondence with Gray, Hussey's affection for Knott was evident. In negotiating the contract, he tried to arrange for a private office for her. "Personally, I'd rather share an office with Hurricane 'Hilda' than with Miss Knott, once she gets under full steam," he added. In early February 1965 Hussey observed that tempers might flare as the early April festival date drew closer even though Knott spoke in glowing terms of Gray's "unfailing courtesy, kindness and cooperation." He added, "In the tensions which build as the date of the festival draws closer and closer, nerves sometimes become ragged (as I, being short tempered, know only too well). It is apparent that you and she continue to work well together, and you will find that it will pay off." Hussey closed the letter, "Continue to be good to our Sarah Gertrude—we cherish her."[35]

Hussey also acted to protect Knott's interests in Washington. Even with the resignation of President Derthick the problems within the National Folk Festival Association remained unresolved. In January 1965, while in St. Petersburg, Knott sent an eleven-page letter to the officers and members of the board. "S. M. Hussey wrote this for me," Knott noted by hand on the top of her copy. In the message Knott insisted that most NFFA problems originated from "the assumption of control by a surprisingly few newcomers, initially welcomed as administrators" who had tried to take control of the program: "Lacking experience in the field of folklore, and without understanding of or respect for the basic philosophies which have made the Association pre-eminent, they have led us into dangerous areas, which threaten the support of the recognized folklorists, our greatest strength. I have been subjected to a series of calculated personal affronts which have seriously affected the effectiveness of my work and created widespread resentment on the part of those folklorists and festival participants who observed what was happening."[36] Knott then described how in 1961 she had insisted that during festival periods she should be relieved of all business and administrative responsibilities. Consequently, Derthick called her into his office and presented her with a contract that demoted her from the director to consultant ("I never signed such a contract," Knott scribbled down the side of the letter). Emphatically stating that her "status as Director of Programs must be accepted and respected," Knott added that were changes not made she would resign and organize a new association, in which "pure logic would require that we include that great majority of our present supporters whose views are currently being ignored or rejected." Ending on a positive note she said, "Our prestige has been enormously raised as a result of the enactment of the 'Arts' legislation. Sponsorship is now being developed for at least one National Folk Festival in each of the next four or five years, plus an integrated program of regional festivals in a number of widely scattered cities."

Meanwhile, Knott and Hussey held firm control of the National Folk Festival in St. Petersburg. Although the press provided extensive coverage, the festival fell far short of the expected profits and made only slightly more than half of the anticipated $36,450.[37] Gray, sorely disappointed, reacted with fury when Knott asked whether he had given bad reports about the festival to interested parties in St. Louis. Hussey attempted to cool him off and commiserated about finances, trying to outline some unanticipated expenses. He also suggested that they needed to audit the figures, adding, "I wish the [Chamber of Commerce] would go over the figures again. I feel confident that another hard look would produce a different result. Is there any way you can tactfully suggest it?"[38] The letter took a dramatic turn when Hussey described recent events at the National Folk Festival Association:

> Well, on the 24th of July we had our all-decisive meeting, and I can happily report that we knocked 'em dead. The opposition (the "bad guys") collapsed entirely, and the National Folk Festival Association is now back in the hands of those who have its welfare at heart, and are not going to wreck it. It was a close call, because they have blocked all progress for the past three years at least, and had we not eliminated them, neither SGK nor I would have continued.
>
> Now that I have been confirmed in the Presidency for the next three

years, and am faced with the tremendous problem of rehabilitation—
especially in the matter of finances—you can understand my deep disappointment at the result of the St. P. affair. Had it come out as we planned,
I would have started off with a respectable treasury. (The old bunch had
run it dry.)

I have instituted a membership drive which should soon start to show
results. Also, with dues starting to come in from existing members and
contributions over and above dues from many of them, I am hopeful that
the financial strain will be somewhat eased. Still, I am faced with a big
problem.

"It is a long, long time since I have felt as well as I do now," Hussey
concluded, "and the only danger is that I may overdo things. I must be
careful." A month later, on September 9, 1965, Melville Hussey died of
a heart attack.

His death was not totally unexpected. The previous year Knott fretted
over his health in letters to a new ally, Forrest Coggan, who was appointed
to the board shortly before Hussey's death. Earlier in 1965 Knott had
written of plans to find foundation support, adding, "Mr. Hussey has the
courage and ability to do it—but he's not well enough. I don't want him
to work at it."[39] After Joe Blundon resigned from the presidency of the
NFFA she reported, "That put Melville as Pres. Until we can straighten
things out. He's not well enough to be bothered—but he will."[40]

Hussey's death must have been a blow, but Knott, always a trouper,
continued to attend to folk festival business, including an upcoming board
meeting. She managed to be both emotional and telegraphic in a letter
to Coggan: "It can't be true—that Melville has left us—but it is!! . . . He
had full agenda worked out for meeting on 18th—last detail. Think he
knew—and prepared us! He has done a real job! A truly courageous one."[41]
In another letter she briskly discussed the foundation plans as well as
tentative locations for a western and eastern center for the National Folk
Festival Association. The five-page message to Coggan concluded with
a single sentence: "It's hard to move on without Melville."[42] Whether
from emotional attachment or simple self-interest, Knott moved into
Hussey's apartment, which was located in the same building as hers.
"Have moved down to Melville's apt," she reported to Coggan, "and have
it looking nice—just had to do it. Other place just wouldn't do."[43] In yet
another letter to Coggan, written on Hussey's personal stationary, Knott
said, "I've moved to 306—and its [sic] much more restful and colorful.
Wish you could see it."[44]

As many other visionaries did, Knott leaned heavily on others to get
things done. She had her practical-minded younger sister Gladys to look

after her personal affairs and many loyal female friends who dutifully served as National Folk Festival foot soldiers. For help with business matters she relied on men, first Major Pickering and later Hussey. Before Hussey's death she mentioned to Coggan, "I'm good up to a certain spot in salesmanship—but there's a point where I think a man is needed."[45] Three years later Knott observed, "The world is out of joint! It's hard for us all—but we must hold on! . . . We surely need a man in the office. Since Mr. Hussey left us—there's no one who takes that responsibility."[46] Her letters suggest that she leaned on Coggan for emotional support, but Knott no longer had the day-to-day practical assistance that Hussey had provided.

Despite the crushing blow of Hussey's death, 1965 had been an optimistic year. With the arts legislation finally passed Knott looked forward to some federal support for her enterprises. Her plans were ambitious—a series of regional festivals as well as two centers, one in the west, either in Colorado or New Mexico, and the other in either Indiana or Kentucky. As she told Coggan, "What I have in mind as to regionals at the very first, is to make them the ones that require the least money, the ones most ready to start right now, with friends and advisors whose slant and opinions I know—I believe in starting with a few, three or four at first." She added, "I believe, as I have always said to you—the University or educational institution should be behind our efforts for permenence [sic]."[47]

Knott had hoped that the 1965 festival might be hosted by one of the large universities in either Michigan or Wisconsin. Although Florida was chosen as the site for the twenty-eighth annual National Folk Festival, she continued to have misgivings about affiliation with the Chamber of Commerce. "I 'hanker' to get under Univ. *somewhere*," she wrote on a postcard to Coggan in May 1965.[48] A few months later she said, "Forever, I'm through with *just* C of C etc. That's fatal Forrest. We have to have people who see it for own sake—not tourist only—It can serve tourism—but it must be secondary—I'm sure of that!"[49]

In May, Knott traveled to Indianapolis at the invitation of the Indiana Lieutenant Governor's Office. While there she asked to meet with Richard Dorson and Edson Richmond of Indiana University.[50] She also informed Coggan of plans to visit Governor Edward T. Breathit of Kentucky: "You see Ky and Indiana might fit in together—mightn't they— that would put Bill Jansen in there with us. . . . He's friend of Edson Richmond, Dick Dorson and others at Univ. of Indiana. This could be best possible overall combination of scholars and practitioners—built real respect. Give right guidance—all around."[51]

Despite the possibility of an alliance with academic folklorists at the university Knott had reservations about Indiana. She did not wish to locate the festival in a smaller city unless doing so came with university sponsorship. "We can't go 'to highest bidder.' We have found from Covington and St. Pete—that the small places are not as effective—as larger ones," she maintained. Later she added, "I'm not altogether sure Indiana is the place. If their interest is chiefly—or *first*, in tourism, it's wrong!" Knott also mentioned to Coggan that she took advantage of her stay in Indianapolis to meet with an officer from the Lilly Endowment, who asked how much money it would take to stabilize the movement. She admitted, "I'd like a grant—maybe even a personal one—to give me real freedom, so I can do as I feel best regardless."[52]

Knott's final four festivals would be difficult ones. Several years later she informed Campa, "For several years since Denver, I wanted to turn things over—but it would have been the end if I had."[53] In 1966 Denver had been chosen as the site of the National Folk Festival, the chief advantage being the presence of Arthur Campa, who became NFFA president after Hussey's death. Knott had every reason to be optimistic about the 1966 festival. She had longed for a western venue, and federal support finally came in the form of a $39,500 grant from the National Council on the Arts. Yet Denver, too, disappointed. Knott believed that the publicity manager failed and those in charge spent too freely.

By the early summer of 1967, grant money nearly gone, the festival had yet to find a home for that year. Knott had planned to hold the thirtieth National Folk Festival once again in her home state and with Jansen at the University of Kentucky in charge.[54] The event, however, failed to materialize. Into the void stepped Edward R. Place, a public relations man who had an enthusiasm for barbershop quartet singing. Place's pitch to Knott and the NFFA must have been impressive for within the month he, as acting executive director of the organization, was enlisting support for the festival from Washington socialite friends.[55] By the end of July he had secured a possible venue as part of the National Centennial Convention of the Grange in Syracuse, New York.

Despite Place's impressive feat in pulling off a festival so late in the year, the Syracuse National Folk Festival, held November 14–17, 1967, at the Onandaga War Memorial Auditorium, was fraught with troubles. Place, who had connections to the Grange, Rotary, the Society for the Preservation and Encouragement of Barber Shop Quartet Singing in America, and the Republican National Committee, lacked the skills to court a youthful market for folk music. Knott had weathered the McCarthy years, but the fragile alliance of conservative and leftist interests could not withstand the polarizations of the Vietnam War era. Once again Pete

Seeger was a lightening rod. According to Andy Wallace, who performed at the festival, "Pete was a very controversial figure at that point in time. And the VFW picketed the festival, the auditorium, and essentially delivered an ultimatum to Sarah. That if he appeared on the festival, they were going to do everything they possibly could to disrupt it. It's one of the few occasions that I know about where Sarah backed down. She went to Pete and asked him not to perform."[56] Knott's willingness to retreat without a fight may indicate how vulnerable she felt during this period, although pragmatic choices rather than politics had always guided her. Wallace added:

> She was basically non-political. Though she was a superb politician. She didn't choose sides politically, by and large. Not in any orthodox fashion, you know. You couldn't label her, I don't think, as a Republican or a Democrat or anything. She was single-minded in what she was doing and she didn't care [laughed] what your politics were. If you had a good song or fit her mold of, of what she wanted to work with, then to hell with everything else. She didn't care. You know, she was not a part of the liberal left, that whole folk music movement. Not at all.

Although Knott managed to avoid the potential of bad press brought on by the VFW's protest, the festival unfortunately managed to avoid all publicity, good or bad. Furthermore, it rained and snowed each night, making the decision to hold a festival in upstate New York in mid-November questionable in itself. The $5,000 budget supplied by the Grange was tiny compared to funding for previous festivals in St. Petersburg and Denver. Within days of the end of the festival Place terminated his consultant services at the NFFA. As with almost everyone ever associated with the event, he had not been reimbursed for personal expenses incurred while organizing the festival, and he needed to turn his attention to his own business. "My only regret," he said in his letter of resignation, "is that I could not have served the association during the period when adequate funds were available from the Federal grant instead of coming into the picture when the grant was virtually used up." Campa thanked Place for his efforts and added, "Let us hope that the National Arts and Humanities Foundation sees fit to give another grant, at least large enough for Sarah to clean up the details and be back in black before closing the year now in progress. What will happen after that, I am not able to predict, but I must confess that I am not too optimistic."[57]

The National's failure to capture the hearts and minds of the folk revival had much to do with how Knott conceptualized her audience. She always considered it to be composed of families, a cross-section of America. Folk revivalists and younger academic folklorists, at best, saw the National as "quaint." Of his first National, the 1963 festival in Covington, Joe Hickerson recalled, "Here was a festival with kids from Milwaukee all dressed up in costumes and doing Polish stuff, sponsored by Pabst Blue Ribbon. And that kind of made me scratch my head."[58] Andy Wallace, who shared office space with Knott in the late 1960s and eventually took over as festival program director, commented, "As Sarah grew older she became less able to manage the organization on an organizational level. And the festival got—frankly, it got more and more irrelevant to what was happening. Newport Folk Festival came along and totally revolutionized festivals and then a host of others after it. And the National was kind of left in the dust."[59]

Others, however, viewed Newport as more problematic. Charles "Chuck" Perdue, president of the National Folk Festival Association in the 1970s, grew disillusioned with Newport in the mid-1960s after witnessing how fans of big-name revival acts often treated traditional performers rudely. Nancy Martin-Perdue recalled, "We were really, really angry at that. And what we observed was in the festival situation, when you mixed that kind of person, the interpreter, with the traditional person, that was the response you got; you didn't get the appreciation or the understanding or any educational background as to where is this coming from. Because people didn't take the time to listen. They didn't want to hear that old stuff."[60]

In 1967 a challenger arrived on the folk festival scene. Although the Smithsonian's Festival of American Folklife featured a number of revivalists during its early years, it could afford to be less commercial and eventually experimented with new, less theatrical, modes of presentation. In effect, it invented a new genre, the "folklife"—as opposed to "folk"—festival.[61] In many ways the Smithsonian was a far greater threat to Knott than Newport. Located in her home base, it garnered the federal financial support and support of academic folklorists, which Knott craved.

One formerly active member did return to the fold in 1967. In September of that year Ben Botkin attended the Scholars and Practitioners Washington conference and subsequently proposed a panel on NFFA policies and activities for the next National Folk Festival, scheduled for Milwaukee. Botkin advocated strengthening and broadening the base of the organization and suggested that the panel discuss the fifteen activities and services he had advocated in his "Proposal for an Applied Folklore Center," which had been published in New York Folklore Quarterly in 1961. Many of his suggestions, such as providing in-service courses for teachers and training community leaders, became standard practice for public folklorists years later. Botkin also made it clear that he saw a role for folklore in promoting world peace: "During World War II folklorists were concerned with the morale and propaganda uses of folklore. If folklore can be used for waging war, can it not also be used for peace?"[62]

Despite Botkin's involvement, Knott kept to fairly conservative rhetoric in the Milwaukee festival. In the program's introduction, she wrote, "While protests and picket lines grab public attention and paint the United States as a cauldron of discontent, there are thousands who present a totally different picture of this country. They are the conservative, but rural and urban people, who are helping to hold the balance as they have done in other times and in other countries." Still, the program emphasized "diverse cultural heritages," and Pete Seeger once again took part, sponsoring the participation of Dan Smith, an African American blues performer.[63]

Only a few days after the Milwaukee festival Knott thanked its participants and added that Knoxville, Tennessee, would host the 1969 event and become its "Eastern Center."[64] She later observed that some board members felt that commitment to the center's location should have been postponed until the organization had more money and had clearly defined what a "center" meant. Knott, however, thought that "if Tennessee wanted the 'Center' that should be a part of the bargain." Unfortunately, the Knoxville National Folk Festival was not a success. Attendance was low, and the Knoxville supporters lost a great deal of money. Knott cited several causes. She felt that the program needed great diversity, especially "Negro spirituals and Negro blues," and stretched out too long. In addition the festival lacked a school committee, and arrangements for school children came too late. Primarily, however, she felt that the festival failed because of a lack of the right kind of publicity.[65]

Alfred W. Humphreys, president of Knoxville's Folk Arts Council, took exception to Knott's laying of blame. He suggested that the presence of both Senator Edmund S. Muskie and Liberace in town may have affected attendance, and over-all "publicity, length and school business were just excuses."[66] Clearly, the possibility of Knoxville becoming the eastern center of the National Folk Festival Association had begun to disintegrate. In preparing her final report Knott focused on what the NFFA could do to improve the festival, including more rigid control of program length and greater selectivity in choosing performers. Surprisingly, she also suggested providing some means of financial assistance for performers unable to pay their way.[67] In her earlier memo Knott had bragged that the National was "about the only Festival left which does not pay participants. This influences the nature of the program and we believe gives the NFF real meaning to participants. It is their own."[68]

Throughout the late 1960s Knott wished for federal support and a man to help run the business aspects of the festival. Perhaps she should have been more careful what she wished for. Both wishes came at the expense of her authority and, ultimately, her position. The National Park Service developed an interest in supporting the festival and offered a potential site at a new park just outside Washington, Wolf Trap, devoted to the performing arts. Knott was increasingly unable to cope, and a couple of people on the NFFA's board took initiative, Wallace recalled. "So what they essentially did was cut a deal with Sarah. They basically, to put it bluntly, forced her to retire. They gave her an honorary title. . . . But they got her to step down in exchange for a cooperative agreement with the National Park Service. . . . That's how, how that relationship began. They brought in, Harlow Dean brought in, a man named Leo Bernache . . . he was an old crony from Columbia Artist management."[69]

Knott was not eager to step down. Bernache began as the NFFA's first full-time executive director in November 1970, and she stayed on in Washington until 1971. That year she complained to Arthur Campa, "All this year, I've been 'under' Leo in everything—and I took it. He doesn't know about programs anyway."[70] The year 1970 came and went without a National Folk Festival. Knott had lined up more than half a dozen prospective sites, including Wichita, Santa Fe, Dallas, Indianapolis, Detroit, and Champaign-Urbana, Illinois. She believed, however, that Washington, D.C., remained the most "logical" place for the event.[71] Despite the preliminary planning, anticipated support from the Council on the Arts did not materialize, and the festival was canceled.

When Knott proved unwilling to relinquish the reins of the organization to Leo Bernache, members of the NFFA Executive Board felt they had to resort to more dramatic action to forcibly push her into retirement. The opportunity arose when Knott began to experience health problems. Preliminary plans had already been drawn up for the 1971 festival at Wolf Trap. In her proposed program Knott included a "traditional music gathering" featuring Kentuckians John Lair and Bradley Kincaid. While visiting in Kentucky a few months before the festival, however, she began to experience heart problems, and a specialist in Louisville ordered bed rest. The NFFA Executive Board notified members and festival participants that Knott, for her own good, had been relieved of all duties. On June 18, 1971, she received a letter from John Whisman, chair of the executive committee, stating that she must "not send any communications to the Board or participants in the Festival exercising your ideas about the program."[72]

Knott spent much of the remaining year explaining to friends and acquaintances that she had suffered mostly from exhaustion. To Forrest Coggan she was more explicit: "The Doctor has never said I could not return to work at all. He did say when I first went into hospital—not to bother me about business but after I left hospital—Dr. Barnes said 'work at home' as usual."[73] A few weeks later Knott again contacted Coggan: "I believe it might just have been constant strain—so long, maybe a special 'heart ache'—of a kind not considered an illness. 'Just a heartache' of another kind. Now, I want to be home or I don't want to be in DC under the present set up the Board has put me in—under Leo. Did you finally understand that?"[74]

With Knott safely out of the way the board brought in new and younger people to develop the program, although the 1971 festival remained a curious hybrid because Knott had already invited a number of the regulars to participate. The new planners divided the daytime programming into separate "workshops" spread about among the woods at Wolf Trap, and evening programs, organized around different themes each night, took place at the new open-air Filene Center. The real rebellion came over the printed program. A far cry from the stolid and predictable programs of the past, it catered to the youth culture and included images of Janis Joplin and a stereotypical, and fat, southern law officer.

Despite assertions to Coggan, Knott chose to attend the festival and eagerly threw herself back into things. As Yvonne Dodge, who traveled to Washington with Sarah and Gladys Knott, recalled, "She was interviewed by the *Washington Post*. We stayed in her apartment. She called a lot of her friends and she was glad to be back there, to her phone, to call people in Washington at that time. She did a lot of talking on the phone, had some people in for dinner, and was very, . . . anticipating the festival, how it would be since she was not directing that year." On Saturday evening of the festival Knott was honored as its founder. "I think they had her stand and announced that she was there," Dodge said. "And I was impressed with the National Folk Festival. . . . Everybody seemed to know Sarah. She walked around, everybody was running up talking to her."[75]

Despite the honors Knott could not be happy with all she saw. Many loyal helpers and performers also expressed displeasure. Although organizers hoped to make the festival more up-to-date and "authentic," Knott's regulars saw an effort to replace grass-roots performers with professional musicians. After the 1971 festival, Elizabeth Jaderborg of the Lindsborg, Kansas, Swedish Folk Dancers commented to Bernache that grass-roots was vital, but it "is a tender plant which is frightened away by professionals, fakes, mobs, harsh treatment and protocol."[76] Privately to Knott, she also admitted having problems with the youth culture that had taken over the festival. Jaderborg added that for the first time she had witnessed adults sharing drugs, and she was afraid for her children: "Not that it doesn't happen everywhere, perhaps, but I think we'll work up other territories."[77] Ray Calkins of the Wisconsin lumberjacks reported, "I also had a nice letter from Jennie [sic] Vincent, from New Mexico, she also noticed all the strange crowd. We all wish you would take over and have some more Festivals like St Louis."[78]

Jaderborg also complained to Bernache that the western United States was not represented at the festival. "America was not all there," she maintained.[79] Of the 1972 festival another friend asked, "Wasn't that extraordinary that the American Indian participants appeared at no time on stage programs!"[80] The new organizers felt no obligation to make the National Folk Festival the geographically comprehensive pageant that Knott had striven for. They did, however, expand into other genres, especially the blues, which Newport had helped legitimize as part of the folk revival.

At least some of inclusion of new forms seemed motivated by gleeful willingness on the part of the new directors to shock their elders. Andy Wallace described the 1971 festival as being composed of about 70 percent blues and African American music. Knott, her sister, and some of their friends "were all sitting in the front row of the Filene Center when this woman, Zula Van Hunt, her name was. And she was a porch singer from Memphis . . . she sang in bordellos for years [laughed]. Came out, hit the microphone with a kind of music that had never been there and you could hear the collective gasp go off across the front row [laughed]. This was new stuff and, and things were going to be different than they'd been in the past." Of course, weeding out old regulars proved a more difficult chore. "There were all these people who had been on the festival for thirty years," Wallace recalled, "and just assumed that they were going to continue to be on the festival and I had to tell them no, that things are changing."[81]

Throughout the late 1960s Knott had publicly worried that newcomers to the NFFA would alienate academic folklorists. Her concern may have rung hollow with many because Knott herself hardly stood at the mainstream of the academic discipline undergoing revolutionary changes. The 1971 festival, however, did alienate one important academic folklorist: Kenneth S. Goldstein of the University of Pennsylvania, who had taken an active role since the Kentucky festivals. In 1971 the new directors brought Goldstein in as a consultant, but his name appeared nowhere on the program. He reacted with fury. Although Knott had not always been good about giving credit in programs she did her best to smooth his ruffled feathers. In September she observed, "If we lose the interest of the real folklorists now—you among them, I can't see the NFFA of the future, no matter how much money might be forthcoming."[82] Goldstein was not to be mollified. Although offered the presidency, he resigned from the NFFA's board.

Had he stayed on Goldstein might have been an influential link to the changing world of academic folklore. Most of Knott's academically trained advisors were themselves getting on in years. In 1971 the NFFA pressed Ben Botkin into service as president of the association, although due to his failing health he served primarily in an honorary capacity. Arthur Campa had stepped down from the presidency in 1969 and resigned from the board at the same time as Goldstein. Other older folklorists were alienated not only from the festival but also from the academic discipline itself. In 1973 Wayland Hand of UCLA informed Knott that she was not alone in noting a radical change in folklore over the past decade. "Good luck, Sarah," he said, "and do not be too dispirited by what has taken place before everyone's eyes."[83] Bill Jansen was also disillusioned with the discipline. "For the young bucks, collectors and preservers are passé. Structural analysis and social context theory are all the rage in what is now called folkloristics," he wrote in 1977.[84]

Although she attended the 1971 festival and attempted to intervene in the Goldstein affair Knott no longer held an official role in the NFFA. She frantically tried to keep board members she trusted from resigning, but those in charge made short work of weeding out many who had served for a long time. As Wallace recalled, "The first thing we really did was . . . restructure the board of directors again. And bring in people, frankly, of the caliber that she had had when she was starting out. . . . We restructured it with people who really knew what was going on out there."[85]

Knott retaliated by urging Coggan to start a festival in the West. In one letter she promised, "I will help get them started. Have contacts in every state. Could bring—we don't have to tie in with NFFA."[86] She tried the same tactic on Campa, urging, "I wish a Western Festival could start in Denver—with Colorado leadership headed by you and Lucile [*sic*]. I can turn the west to you and not leave here! Someone should do that job!" In the same letter Knott continued to agonize over accepting an offer from John Whisman during her illness, to take half her annual salary of $12,000 plus an additional $1,000 in travel expenses and work at home in Kentucky as a "consultant." "I haven't answered," she said, "but I have taken the money thus far. But the way they treated NFFA participants at the last Festival wasn't right. Under circumstance, then—I wasn't asked—because Board thought I was ill—and in a way I was, but the entire Festival changed. You see I can't be 'consultant' to the tear up

of NFFA." Surprisingly, Knott, always open to a variety of political philosophies, worried, "I wonder If [sic] I can stay if things keep moving to
the left."[87]

The "consultant" title rankled. When asked shortly after the first
Wolf Trap festival about her future role with the National Folk Festival,
Knott responded, "Well, I'll tell you, I don't like the name consultant.
And I have not yet accepted that particular title, because I don't think I
could sit still and wait for somebody to consult me."[88]

Settling back into life in western Kentucky proved difficult as well.
Knott had no intention of retiring in any normal sense of the word. As
Yvonne Dodge explained, the festival was at the "main core of her existence," and "you sensed with her, kind of a nervous energy, 'something's
happening and I'm responsible for it.' . . . that was kind of inbred in her
over so many years that—it's not something you would just come home
and say, 'well, I don't do this anymore.'" After Knott returned to the
"Little Green House" built by her sisters in Princeton, Kentucky, she
immediately ordered new stationary. As Dodge recalled, "She always had
a letterhead, that was very important to her."[89] The local public library
provided an office, and she employed secretaries to help with projects and
reams of correspondence. Still, she found it difficult to settle in. Several
years later she told Coggan, "I've been away from home so long—I'm not
really at home—at home."[90]

When John Whisman offered Knott half her salary to return to Kentucky, it was, essentially, a bribe to keep her out of the way. "I don't
think John W. really thought I had to do anything special," she said.[91]
The board eventually settled on asking Knott to work on an update of
the *Handbook for the National Folk Festival*. As Wallace recalled:

> The significance of the book, was not the book. Which never really had
> any possibility of ever being published. It wasn't, it just wasn't there . . .
> there were several transitional board members, board members mostly
> from this area who had been associated with Sarah for quite some time.
> . . . They're kind of the ones, and God bless 'em for doing it, who kind of
> nurtured Sarah along on the book, and made her feel that the book was
> important. Even though [finishes in a whisper] they knew it wasn't. . . .
> But I, I wouldn't underestimate its importance to her, because I think it
> was what kept her going for that last six, seven, eight years.[92]

After retiring, Knott attempted to become more active in the American Folklore Society and in the fall of 1971 gave a paper at the AFS meeting on "The Folk Festival Movement in the U.S., 1934–1971." Two years
later she was outraged when the American Folklore Society agreed to sup-

port the Smithsonian festival for the next three years. A decade earlier, despite the urging of MacEdward Leach, the society had refused to stand behind the National Folk Festival. She had not spoken up at the earlier meeting because she was in awe of the scholars, but this time she did. "There was a meeting with most of them absent but enough there that the Society got behind Smithsonians [*sic*] free wheeling plan, to make it legal," she wrote. "I was there, and believe it or not, I spoke up and was not afraid. I guess that is what Watergate has done for me—and maybe for many of us."[93]

In October of 1972, just over a year after her forced retirement, the NFFA terminated Knott's salary.[94] This did not stop her from attempting to intervene in the NFFA's business, and she remained frustrated by changes taking place in the festival. Several months earlier she had written, "It seems to me to be rudderless now. It's hard for me to know what stand to take. . . . I feel sure that those who have stood by—participants and leaders—would still come as they always did—to NFFA—at my beck and call—but, I *could* be mistaken. *I really know I'm not.*"[95] A year later she reported to friends in eastern Kentucky, "I just returned from the thirty-fifth National Folk Festival in Washington D.C. She didn't look like my child or grown-up daughter."[96]

The absence of Knott in a leadership position did not, as it turned out, ease divisions within the NFFA board. The new affiliation with the National Park Service did allow the festival to pay performers who might otherwise be unable to afford the trip, but in the eyes of Leo Bernache and some others the funding was more important in allowing the hiring of professionals who had box-office appeal. Although many were happy with the "Newport" model others were not, and bitter fights broke out among the board members. Chuck and Nancy Perdue were among those who fought against the preponderance of revival musicians. "We felt," he said, "Nan and I felt, and a few others, that we should do what the constitution and the by-laws said that the National Festival was going to do. Which was to find the best of traditional culture in America and present that in a national forum. And, but we always said if, if the board decided it didn't want to do that and it wanted to present revival musicians, then change the constitution." With so many revivalists going only to jam with others, Nancy Perdue described the National Folk Festival in the early 1970s as "a great urban party . . . at government expense." Chuck Perdue became president of the NFFA in 1973, and three years later, with the help of several board members, staged a "midnight coup" that resulted in the firing of Executive Director Leo Bernache for lack of "sensitivity to the aesthetics of folk culture."[97]

The 1976 hiring of Joe Wilson as the executive director eased some of Knott's feelings about the festival. Wilson weeded out many urban revival performers and emphasized the festival's continuity with its early years under Knott, although, of course, he never adopted the "cross-section of America" pageantry approach. Without the baggage of the transition years Wilson and Knott were able to start on a friendly basis. He gave Knott her due as founder of the organization, and she, in turn, was grateful that someone willingly listened to her opinions. After the 1977 festival she said to Jansen, "I'm so glad I went because somehow things seem to fall in place right with a warmth I have not felt since I left."[98]

Not all Wilson did met with Knott's approval, however. She was particularly incensed when the organization's name changed from the National Folk Festival Association to the National Council on the Traditional Arts. Despite Wilson's emphasis on the continuity of the event, Knott still had doubts. As she commented to Leonard Roberts about the introduction to the 1979 National Folk Festival program, "I question the statement that I am Founder of this—I am Founder of NFFA 1934–71 but where are objectives of NCTA?"[99]

The late 1970s was a difficult time for Sarah Gertrude Knott. Finally deciding to give up her writing projects, true retirement came with the decision to donate her papers to an archive. The day after her eighty-second birthday she informed Coggan, "I am packing up things to send either to the Library of Congress Archives or to West[ern] Kentucky University Archives. It's hard! I've never felt that I quit! And I don't even now!"[100] Perhaps under the influence of Gladys Knott, an alumna, Western Kentucky received the lion's share of the material, with a smaller portion going to Washington.

Although she generally approved of the direction the National Folk Festival took in the late 1970s, close friends felt her despair. Don Urner, who sat backstage with her at some of her last festivals, recalled:

> When I talked with her last, at Wolf Trap, she was very depressed and pessimistic because she'd saved no money. And she was losing energy. She was losing the fight. . . . It happens to a lot of people who are pioneers and they give and then don't have a way out. It's very tragic. . . . So, she stayed with me, because she didn't want the other people to know how bad she felt. She knew I wasn't going to talk to anybody except Priscilla. But the last times she was in Wolf Trap, she was in what Thoreau would call "quiet desperation."[101]

She assured other friends, however, that she had no financial problems. "I'm glad that we have this little house and that we both do get a rather good monthly check—more than I really ever got—for any job—especially NFFA," she commented to Forrest Coggan.[102]

Yvonne Dodge questioned whether Knott's life, taken as a whole, should be considered tragic: "We think she loved her life as it was and was very satisfied with it. I don't think she would have traded it all, I think she had a good time. Up to the time that maybe she retired. I think . . . the other life was the busy, bursting life of putting on the festival . . . that was Sarah. That's what she liked."[103] In 1976, when asked whether, given the chance, she would do everything in her life the same, Knott replied, "No, I don't think everything was exactly the way I wanted. . . . But I wouldn't know how, I wouldn't know how to change it."[104]

In 1980, three months after cataract surgery, Knott suffered a major stroke, and her sister moved her to a nursing home. She recovered partially but was often confused about her surroundings. Having spent much of her life on the road, she often believed she was in a hotel rather than a nursing facility. Even during these times the National Folk Festival never strayed far from her mind. Dodge recalled, "Miss Gladys would say that even in her unconscious moments, you could hear her . . . something about the National Folk Festival would come out. That was, that was the first thing on her mind."[105]

On November 20, 1984, two months short of her ninetieth birthday, Sarah Gertrude Knott died. Perhaps she would have been pleased to know that an heir to a local musical tradition attended to her body at the funeral home. The two never formally met, but Eddie Pennington played guitar in the thumb-picking tradition of Mose Rager, Merle Travis, and others. A decade later he would play at the National Folk Festival and the Smithsonian's Festival of American Folklife, and in 2001 he won a National Heritage Award from the National Endowment for the Arts. That agency that might not have included folk arts in its purview had it not been for the lobbying effort of Sarah Gertrude Knott.

Although the visitation for Knott was in Princeton, Kentucky, services took place back in Kevil at the Spring Bayou Baptist Church. The worlds of academic and public folklore paid little attention to her passing. Gladys Knott, her only surviving close relative, let it be know that nursing home expenses had taken much of the sisters' savings and asked former colleagues for help in paying for a memorial for Knott's grave.[106] Support was not forthcoming. Other than a small, metal, funeral home plaque, two decades later Sarah Gertrude Knott's grave remained unmarked.

7 Things Have Changed in Renfro Valley

> Gone were old familiar faces, All the friends I used
> to know
> Things have changed in Renfro Valley, Since the days
> of long ago.
> —"Take Me Back to Renfro Valley," John Lair

A year after Sarah Gertrude Knott celebrated her silver anniversary with the 1961 National Folk Festival, John Lair declared his own silver jubilee. He took the opportunity of an invitation to the Kentucky State Fair to invite back all former Renfro Valley performers, hoping especially to attract those who had gone on to fame and fortune. Original Renfro partner Whitey Ford did not make the main performance but joined the cast later in the weekend. Other long-time Renfro performers such as Lily May Ledford came out of retirement. Despite the opportunity for the promotion of the Valley, the nostalgic event must have been bittersweet for Lair. Just a month earlier Slim Miller, who had been with him since the Chicago days, died.

In celebration of the silver anniversary Lair also published a new version of the *Renfro Valley Keepsake* in which he devoted much space to the history of Renfro Valley, both the place and the institution, and filled the pages with photographs of performers who had once played there. Of course, Lair also took the opportunity to boast, noting that the *Sunday Morning Gatherin'* still enjoyed a Neilson rating of 81 percent in radio homes in Minneapolis and St. Paul. "If radio is dead," he added, "it's a mightly [sic] lively corpse."[1]

The backward glance of the anniversary at the state fair set the tone of Renfro Valley in the early 1960s. Increasingly, Lair marketed Renfro Valley to older people who remembered the glory days of the Valley or were interested in history and nostalgia. Renfro Valley also appealed to fans who disliked the changes overtaking country music. In 1967, when Lair editorialized in the *Renfro Valley Bugle* about new developments in country music, he received a response from Patsy Montana, who had been at WLS at the same time as Lair. She had seen a copy of the *Bugle* while visiting George Biggar and enjoyed the opportunity to catch up on other former WLS staffers. She was tiring, she said, of the "Nashville sound" and trying to help "bring back some of the good old tunes."[2]

Country music attempted to keep up with the times, but it faced its own challenges from rock and roll. As usual, Lair said one thing but did another. He publicly abhorred the influence rock and roll had on country music but allowed it to be played on his radio station. In general, however, he preferred to remain ignorant of rock and roll. When in 1966 several Baptist churches petitioned him to ask that all Beatles albums be banned from WRVK, he replied, "So far as I know we do not have a Beetle [sic] recording anywhere on the premises of WRVK." He concluded, "Very few things, in my opinion, are as detrimental to our youngsters as being exposed to such communist propaganda. This criticism does not apply to all rock and roll music, altho [sic] most of it we could well do without. As long as parents allow their children to listen to it, and buy the records, radio stations feel called upon to play it in answer to the many requests that come in from the youngsters."[3]

If Lair could have catered to any segment of the growing youth market it would have been to the folk revival. He tried on several occasions to revive Renfro Valley's folk festival, in 1958 asking Bascom Lamar Lunsford for help in rejuvenating the event, which had not been held since 1950. Rather than strictly a folk festival, however, Lair conceptualized it as a homecoming not only for those who had performed in earlier festivals but also for "any of the acts who were ever employed here."[4] Neither Lunsford's appeal to folk enthusiasts nor Lair's to nostalgia generated enough interest to keep the event going.

Lunsford, similar to Knott, soon had his own difficulties with the folk revival. More than a decade older than Lair and considerably more conservative than Knott, he was uncomfortable with the personal and political style of youthful revivalists. In addition, a competing folk festival organized along Newport lines had its debut in Asheville in 1963 with the support of the Chamber of Commerce but, luckily for Lunsford, it lost money and did not survive. Lunsford also faced challenges from within. Attendance at the Mountain Dance and Folk Festival slumped, and some within the Chamber of Commerce felt he had become too old. At least some astute members, though, realized that Lunsford *was* the festival and suggested that publicity be built around him. He continued to be a presence at the Mountain Dance and Folk Festival until his death in 1973.[5]

Not all early folk promoters felt out of synch with the revival. The leftist wing of the previous folk revival, after surviving the era of communist witch hunts, fit more comfortably into the new folk scene. Among them was Alan Lomax, who returned from a self-imposed exile in England. If he thought harshly of Lair's influence during the 1937 Ohio Valley Folk Festival, by 1960 Lomax was calling upon Lair's expertise. "I seem to be pestering you to death with questions these days," he began a letter on March 27. Lomax was looking for a gourd banjo to use in a film and checking on a citation for a manuscript. Lair's response was cordial.[6] If Lair had any problem with Lomax's politics or was even aware of them it was not reflected in the exchange.

Nor did Lair have reservations about possible collaborations with Pete Seeger. In 1962 Harold Leventhal Management contacted Lair in reference to the song "Little Birdie," which Seeger had recorded. He wished to know whether Lair had written the tune or whether it was a folk song. Lair responded that it was an old tune but he had changed its tempo and many words. "I am pleased to know that Pete Seeger has recorded it and you may send through contract forms for it at your convenience," he wrote. "Incidentally," he concluded, "I have through the years accumulated a lot of numbers suitable to Pete's style and type of material if he is looking for more in that line."[7]

Bluegrass stars Lester Flatt and Earl Scruggs also recorded "Little Birdie." Louise Scruggs, who acted as their manager, informed Lair that the recording was so good they wanted it for a single. Apparently unaware that Seeger had already recorded the song, she asked Lair to keep the information confidential and not submit "Little Birdie" to anyone else. "Any other numbers you have would also be appreciated," Scruggs wrote.[8] Lair seemed to enjoy a cordial relationship with Flatt and Scruggs but was ambivalent about bluegrass music. Several of its pioneers had passed through Renfro Valley, including Flatt and Scruggs and Charlie Monroe, and Lair willingly acknowledged its popularity. He insisted, however, on referring to the style as "so-called bluegrass music" because he claimed to be unable to understand how it differed from the old-time music he promoted.

Compared to the electrified instruments and drums of Nashville's country music, Lair did not dislike bluegrass, although its success mystified him and caused him jealousy. That was especially apparent after Bill Monroe played Renfro Valley in 1967 as one of the acts Lair had contracted with Hal Smith to book. The gross ran under expectation, and Lair wrote to Smith, disgusted with himself for having missed an opportunity, "I had covered seven newspapers in this and surrounding counties in the section where I thought he would be most popular. I was surprised to note that we had the biggest percentage of teenagers we have had in any audience. I talked with some of these after the show and found many of them from the University of Kentucky and Eastern [Kentucky University]. It seems that the college kids accept Monroe much as the [*sic*] do Flatt and Scruggs, as folk singers."[9] Lair felt he had learned a lesson, but he never fully succeeded in capitalizing on the youth market for bluegrass and old-time music.

In 1963 and 1964 Robert Grant, a young businessperson from Mt. Vernon, Kentucky, rented out the Renfro Valley barn on Friday nights for a "hootenanny," but that was about the extent of catering to the folk revival. At least one of Lair's associates, Roy Starkey, was actively hostile to revivalists. In early 1965, Starkey, who had left performing for advertising, complained to Lair that the caterwauling of the "snotty-nosed kids" who had taken over folk music made him want to vomit. Starkey wanted to get into a promotion business of "true early Americana" and could think of no better place to do so than Renfro Valley.[10] Lair in turn saw Starkey as a potential successor who could enable him to finally retire. Later the same year, however, Starkey suffered a heart attack onstage at the Barn Dance and died shortly thereafter.

In 1965 Starkey had proposed opening a combination store and promotional material display area stocked with nothing but handmade objects from the local region. Lair, however, had recently been down that road. In the early 1960s he had eagerly jumped on the bandwagon when Governor Bert Combs began to promote Kentucky arts and crafts. In January 1962 the *Bugle* announced the opening of a new handicraft school, funded by the John Lair Foundation and "free to all young folks who want to make salable articles from native materials." Under the name "Cabin Craft, Inc.," a shop as well as a mail order business would market the school's products. On June 8, Governor Combs officially opened the new handicraft center at Renfro Valley, but the enterprise lasted only a short while. The school never got off the ground. According to the *Bugle*, qualified instructors could not be found.[11]

Lair also followed with interest the governor's initiatives in the area of performing arts, which brought together a number of individuals who had been involved with folklore. In the spring of 1962 Jean Thomas wrote to Lair in anticipation, she said, of meeting him for the first time.[12] Thomas began by mentioning their mutual friend Pleaz Mobley, who had worked at Renfro Valley and been *"the* Star of my American Folk Song Festival, for lo! These many years." He had, the ever-media-conscious Thomas added, also appeared with her on the *Today Show.* Finally, Thomas got to the point—Lair was invited to the thirty-second annual American Folk Song Festival. She would be proud for him to have a seat in her "Court-of-Honor" and speak about his radio show as well as about the Kentucky Council of Performing Arts. Perhaps Lair could also bring a singer or two. "Anyway," Thomas concluded, "we can discuss it when we meet in Frankfort for the first annual meeting of the Directors of the Council." Lair's scribbled note on the back suggests his reply ("Thanks for your very kind invitation. Hope I can attend"), but his papers do not indicate whether he attended Thomas's festival that year.[13]

Governor Combs's interest in the folk arts, of course, also brought Sarah Gertrude Knott back to Kentucky. In preparation for her survey of Kentucky folk arts, she wrote a collective letter to John Lair and Edith James. Addressing Lair, she advised, "What I am thinking of is to especially feature these inherited kinds of songs—on TV and radio and on some festival programs. In fact I am thin[k]ing of having a Kentucky festival where we just feature the real folk songs, the banjo pickers, harmonica and other instruments." Knott also suggested that country musicians might be used to promote folk music. "And John," she added, "for several years I have had in mind the idea of having noted country singers on tv and radio cross the country—feature the genuine folk music they know—giving a shot in the arm—just show how many still know these traditional songs, and play the instruments in the traditional way. What about starting this at Renfro Valley?" Lair's draft of his response was encouraging: "Think your idea a good one. We are still plugging along with the old-time songs."[14]

Aside from Lair's modest involvement in the 1963 and 1964 National Folk Festivals, Lair and Knott apparently did not collaborate. Although both still had loyal followers they had largely lost their audiences due to vastly changed public perceptions of folk and country music. Lair could not deliver the country music audience to folk music because he no longer understood the market for country music, and he, similar to Knott, did not fully understand the folk revival.

Surprisingly, it was Lily May Ledford who benefitted from the revival. Some Renfro Valley performers saw Ledford, under Lair's management for more than twenty years, as his favorite and the heart of Renfro Valley's happy family. Underneath it all, however, she resented the fact that her career had never quite taken off after the glory days of the late 1930s. Of course, Lair did not deserve all the blame. Unlike musicians who used Renfro Valley as a stepping stone, Ledford tied herself there through family commitments. She would come to believe that Lair did not fully promote the Coon Creek Girls, but his business correspondence suggests that he would eagerly have made Ledford a country music recording star had he means to do so.

In the late 1950s Lily May Ledford retired in order to spend more time with her family, yet retirement does not come easy to those who have been onstage for decades—as Lair would discover a decade later. In 1966 the folklorist Ralph Rinzler invited the Coon Creek Girls to come out of retirement and play at the Newport Folk Festival, where Ledford discovered an audience composed not of the old and nostalgic but of young and appreciative college students. The group played a number of other folk festivals in the early 1970s, including the Smithsonian's, and Ledford launched a solo career after the death of her sister, Rosie Foley. Newfound popularity and freedom made it possible for her to express years of frustration with Lair's management. Rather than criticize Lair directly, in performances and interviews she told humorous stories that cast him as controlling and manipulative. Her resentment was to some degree just, but Lair may have unfairly received the brunt of her anger. Ledford had two failed marriages to controlling men, but even in her final years she did not feel she could publicly speak of them. Lair was an easier target.[15]

Whatever her personal motivations, Ledford's audiences were receptive to stories of John Lair. In recasting the early recording and radio artists of country music as authentic folk musicians, members of the folk revival encountered a certain amount of dissonance. Early country music was rife with artifice, much of which smacked of hillbilly stereotypes. Revivalists dealt with their discomfort by viewing musicians such as Ledford as passive victims of money-grubbing managers. Lair, therefore, was not a promoter of folk music but a huckster who forced musicians from their authentic roots.

Other Renfro Valley performers also found work on the folk circuit, but not all fit as comfortably into the revival scene. Fiddler Jim Gaskin, at Renfro Valley since the 1950s, recalled that in the 1960s "the folk music craze started hitting the colleges and universities. . . . We did, I wouldn't know how many, concerts in colleges and universities and a lot of times, these were with other performers like Doc Hopkins, Lily May." Gaskin played the National Folk Festival two years in a row in the 1970s and recorded with Rounder Records in Boston. Although thrilled by the level of enthusiasm for old-time fiddling found among college students, the mix of music labeled *folk* at festivals troubled him:

> Looking back on it now, the thing that it, that sticks in my mind the most is the contrasts that we had within those shows. You had your traditionalists, your people my age and older, people Asa [Martin]'s age, much older than I. And Lily May, who were playing the real folk music. And then you had your counterfeits, your college kids, and this is not putting down college kids it tickled us to death to see them interested in it. But . . . they were writing songs trying to take, even some of the ideas from the old, real folk songs and develop protest songs out of them and things like that. And in every concert that we'd go to, almost, you'd have that, that contrast. You'd have your authentic and then your counterfeit stuff. They tried to intermingle that.[16]

Asked about "counterfeits," Gaskin added, "Wolf Trap was overrun with them. It was like a dumping ground for the world there for a while."

If he ultimately would be seen as too commercially oriented to be a folk promoter, Lair found himself too much of a traditionalist within country music to be successful in the new, Nashville-dominated business. In the early 1960s things indeed looked bleak for Renfro Valley despite all Lair's projects and promotions. In 1963 he received a letter from an old WLS friend, Jack Holden, who had heard from George Biggar about the taped version of the *Sunday Morning Gatherin'*. Lair forwarded a tape to Holden and told him: "We make no actual charge for this tape as long as the show is sustaining. If you should happen to sell it locally we have a small graduated fee based on your city population (not the surrounding area). Or, some of the stations carry the show with the understanding that we might later use a minute of it to plug some of our own activities or products, not anything else, giving the other minute spot to sell or use as they see fit, barring liquor or other objectionable products." He was also uncharacteristically honest about the show's quality: "There isn't much to it in the way of quality or production and if we auditioned the show for somebody who had never heard of it we probably couldn't get on a station with it—but once on its [sic] hard to take it away from listeners, especially the older ones."[17]

A year and a half later Lair heard from John and Barbara DeMott, who had worked at Renfro Valley during the General Foods days. "Things still at low ebb for Renfro so far as sponsors are concerned," he informed them. "Outside of a bi-week TV show for Pillsbury a few years ago we have done nothing. Our Sunday morning show, taped is carried on twenty-two stations—mostly 50,000 watters. . . . With no agent or rep of any kind we are more or less hidden away. You can't make anybody believe that daytime radio is the biggest advertising bargain." He would send them, he added, one of the new record albums that sold well at the barn and by mail but for which he had been unable to find a distributor.[18] In 1967 Lair was giving his shows away in exchange for good new tapes and charging $4.70 per broadcast if the program were to be sold commercially. He ruefully admitted to Jack Schilla, "Incidentally, when the Gatherin' was on CBS for a good many years we got $1,500.00 per program for it. Times have changed!"[19]

For all his own hard times, John Lair was well aware that not all he helped send on the way to stardom met with happy endings. In the early 1950s his former partner Red Foley suffered through public scandal and the suicide of his wife, Eva. Merle Travis, who also hit hard times, had his first big break when working with Lair on the *Plantation Party* at WLW. In early 1965 Lair received a letter from Hank Richards in Burbank, expressing concern for Travis and wondering "if the best possible therapy for him at this moment might not be a return to Kentucky." After asking whether Lair could possibly use Travis at Renfro Valley, Richards mentioned that he was thinking of moving to Chicago and getting into television, and he saw the television potential of Lair's *Songs Lincoln Loved.* Surprisingly, Lair let the latter offer pass without comment but expressed concern and affection for Travis. "I, too, have a problem. I can't afford him," he replied. "We have waited around for radio to come back, as it is gradually doing, but we are now out of sponsors." Perhaps, though, something could be worked out: "I believe that with Merle to build a good unit on I could get all the bookings we could use. I believe I could give him a better background build-up than he has ever had and I think we would both be happy with the results but I am in no position to offer him a salary he might be interested in. We would have to work something out on a partnership basis I think he would find acceptable."[20]

Lair continued to entertain hopes that some older stars who had once worked for him might once more help pull in crowds. When Whitey Ford informed him that he was still out touring and wanted to stop by, Lair responded, "I too, want to talk about Renfro Valley's future and your possible part in it."[21] As with Travis, however, Lair realized he could hardly afford musicians whose careers he had once helped launch. In 1967 he noted that two years earlier he had to pay Homer and Jethro "fifteen hundred dollars for fifteen minutes at the State Fair," a far cry from the fifty dollars a week they earned when they started at Renfro Valley.[22]

Even in his bleakest days Lair continued to scheme. He mentioned to the DeMotts and to Richards that the one bright lining in a cloudy day was the coming of Interstate I-75, which would create an interchange right at Lair's front door. "While it is not far enough along for any certainty," he wrote, "I am presently working on a Government loan of a couple of million dollars to build a big tourism complex here."[23] Lair actively lobbied for the interstate to come through Renfro Valley. As Ann Lair Henderson recalled, "We were lucky to have [I-75] come paralleling [route] 25 and as close to Renfro Valley as it did. It wasn't originally planned that way. . . . I think I have to give my dad credit, made a lot of trips to Frankfort.[24] A few years later Lair was active in the gubernatorial campaign of the commonwealth's commissioner of highways, Henry Ward.

The new highway might make a difference, but Lair still contemplated selling out, whether literally or figuratively. Just a few months earlier he described his accomplishments to the secretary of the Ford Foundation: "In all these years devoted to preserving Early American music we have also fostered, through our radio programs and through our way of life here in 'The Valley Where Time Stands Still,' the best of an earlier way of life." Now, Lair admitted, his dream would end unless someone could lend aid: "We would set up a non-profit organization along such lines as you might require. We are not interested in making money off of Renfro Valley but we are vitally interested in seeing its usefulness continued. . . . Unless the project is aided in some way and new management gradually brought in to carry on, Renfro Valley, which has become a living American tradition, must soon come to an end."[25] He not only contemplated turning Renfro Valley into a nonprofit organization but also flirted with the forces that threatened the facility: television and Nashville's country music industry.

In 1960 Lair inquired about selling television rights to the Lincoln book he had published six years earlier. He added, "With TV inspired interest in all things Western, wouldn't now be a good time to work up my collection of folk songs on the various well-known characters, using either of my pet titles, Bullets and Ballads, or 'Ballads of Badmen'?"[26] Some years later he informed Mitch Miller, "I admire your TV show for its sensible approach to music for the masses and believe I can offer you something which will add to its interest and acceptability." Enclosing a copy of Songs Lincoln Loved, Lair offered to help provide song histories for Miller's show. "I have spent more than twenty-five years in radio specializing in music of interest to common folks," he added.[27]

In 1965 the country music performer Pee Wee King did use the Renfro Valley barn as a setting for a few episodes of a television series. Also in 1965, Lair approached yet another country musician who had his own television show, Jimmy Dean. "Homer and Jethro tell me that you have expressed some interest in Renfro Valley as the scene of one of your TV shows," he reported. "Needless to say we would be very pleased if the idea could be worked through to a conclusion."[28] The following year, no deal yet in the works, Lair attempted to get permission to syndicate the Pillsbury shows taped nine years earlier.

If Lair had little success getting back on television he did finally make a deal for a Renfro Valley movie. This was no Hollywood production; the producers, Arthur W. Stanish and James F. Sullivan, hailed from Louisville, Kentucky. As could be predicted, conflicts soon emerged between the director and Lair. As the *Bugle* recounted the situation, the director wanted "flash" and "color" whereas Lair desired "naturalism and realism."[29] The filming caused quite a stir in the Valley in 1965, but the movie itself was of poor quality. Ann Lair Henderson and a few of the performers involved readily admitted as much. *John Lair's Renfro Valley Barn Dance* premiered at two theaters in Louisville on July 20, 1966, an event that included live appearances of Lair and a number of Renfro Valley performers as well as free Kentucky Fried Chicken for the first thousand people at each venue.[30]

By the 1960s Lair also sought help from the Nashville recording industry. He chose as a sympathetic ear, Chet Atkins, one of the architects of the "Nashville sound." Atkins, Lair would claim, considered "Take Me Back to Renfro Valley" one "of the best and one of the finest of the country songs ever written."[31] In 1963 Lair observed to Atkins, "The trend in recorded music seems to have switched around to the type of thing I have been connected with for a good many years. I have some fairly decent numbers to submit to recording companies and artists. Would you take time to look them over?"[32] Two years later Lair traveled down to Nashville to meet with Atkins, who advised that he could make more money selling his records through Walgreen racks and individual record shops. Atkins also had Lair talk to RCA's "album man," who seemed enthusiastic about Lair's ideas for an album.[33]

At about the same time, Lair began to correspond with the Hal Smith Agency in Goodlettsville just north of Nashville. In September 1965 Smith asked if Lair would be interested in a syndicated Renfro Valley Barn Dance television show.[34] The following month Lair told the president of Hal Smith TV Programs, "We would welcome an opportunity to get back on radio or TV with the kind of show we once had and know how to build again."[35] The next fall Smith proposed shooting a pilot of a *Gatherin'* television show in Nashville.[36] Plans to put the *Sunday Morning Gatherin'* on television stalled, however, when Smith hesitated to take on the legal conflicts created by Lair's obligations to Seven Arts, which released the Renfro Valley movie.[37] Although plans for the television shows did not reach fruition, in the spring of 1966 Lair entered into a two-year working agreement with Smith, who would provide talent for Lair's show and have an option to purchase the Valley "where time stood still."

The difficulties of bringing Nashville to Renfro Valley soon became apparent when Ray Price played the Barn Dance. On April 20, 1966, Lair informed Smith of the many problems involved with combining Price's flashy stage act with typical Renfro Valley fare. It had been a challenge to adjust recording levels between Price and the Renfro Valley acts, and Lair did not know what to do with a stage full of equipment when the square dance groups came onstage. He also needed to develop a professional staff band because "our boys never see each other from Saturday night to Saturday night and never have a chance to rehearse and work things out together." He concluded, "Hal, I don't believe we'll be able to get a blend the way we tried it this time. Listening to the tapes sounds just like listening to two different stations, with two different concepts of Country Music. We'll either have to mix them better or make up two different program tapes. It's the difference between homefolks entertainers with a little native talent and professional musicians and singers, strictly 'Show-folks.' The difference between 'Renfro Valley' and 'Grand Ole Opry.'"[38]

Lair may have started out in a conciliatory mood, but he soon chafed under Smith's management. In July, Smith informed him that Don Reno would be performing on August 6, the night of the all-night gospel sing. Lair replied that the event had been going on for nineteen years and was the one night he did not book outside talent. Smith's response was swift and to the point: "As pointed out in my letter of last week, Don Reno is set to appear at Renfro Valley the Saturday night in question and will be there as he is definitely contracted to do so."[39]

According to Renfro employee Pete Stamper, the two transitional years proved difficult for Renfro Valley staff and performers unsure of where to place their loyalties.[40] Despite his personal feelings about Smith, Lair hoped to see Renfro Valley survive, and he worked cooperatively to plan for the future. Unbidden or not, Lair provided ideas of how Smith might develop the Valley if he exercised his option to buy. In May 1967 Smith wrote that he had received his letter in which Lair made "some worthy suggestions in how the future of Renfro should be handled, if and when we take complete possession and control."[41]

Despite periodic attempts to cooperate, Lair was not happy about the job Smith was doing. In early November of 1966 he wrote to Smith, worried that the Saturday night crowds would soon drop off. "Hope you can send up a stronger name act or two soon," he added.[42] Lair did seem to be willing to take the blame for mistakes in advertising as he did a few weeks later when he failed to anticipate Bill Monroe's appeal to college students. By the following summer, however, he was displeased that Smith tended to send the same "guest acts" too often, a practice Lair felt hurt the box office. "Honestly," he continued, "I feel that we should discontinue the whole thing. . . . We have paid you approximately $16,000.00 in talent cost, of which I would say not more than $5,000.00 had come back to us in increased box office receipts. . . . In other words, I can't afford to spend what these acts have cost me and you can't afford to pay for better ones, so maybe you were right in the first place when you advised against our entering into such an arrangement." Lair hastened to add in a postscript, "Of course any change in our working agreement would not in any way affect your option to purchase."[43]

Despite Lair's offer to terminate the working agreement, Smith continued to provide talent even beyond the agreed two years. By early July 1968 Lair was impatient to terminate the deal. "I have been allowing your acts to continue since the expiration date," he told Smith, "because I thought we were on the verge of closing the sale."[44] A month later the *Nashville Tennessean* announced the sale of Renfro Valley for an undisclosed price believed to be close to a million dollars. The purchase included the barn and country store, Lair's music collection, the *Bugle*, and WRVK but not the Pioneer Museum. Smith announced that he would invest well over two million dollars more in expansions, including a new auditorium, a new lodge, a golf course, an amphitheater, a chair lift, and a marina on a lake that would be formed by highway construction. He also intended to preserve the history of Renfro Valley: "We have bought a lot of image here as well as property, and we are going to build an ever-lasting memorial to its creator, Mr. Lair."[45]

According to the *Tennessean*, Hal Smith had asked Lair to stay on in some capacity, an offer "being considered." Lair, however, was ready to be away from the business, at least for the time-being. Virginia Lair had long pressed her husband to retire so he could pay more attention to family. When he did finally sell the property, however, Lair did not seem able to pull himself away. As Barbara Lair Smith recalls, "Mother thought that if he sold that, they would—Mother liked to travel—that they would do some of that. She, she loved the ocean, she would hope they could go to Florida for you know awhile. But all Daddy did was stand at that window of the house."[46] Virginia Lair's health became fragile at the same time, ending the couple's plans to travel.[47] The Lairs stayed in their home immediately adjacent to the Renfro Valley complex, and despite efforts to keep busy, John Lair could not help but sit and stew over the changes taking place in front of his eyes.

The new owners solved the challenge of how to continue Renfro's most enduring show, the *Gatherin'*, which Lair had written and narrated for more than two decades, by using tapes of old shows and editing out his voice. Lair was disgusted that they omitted his voice and had another person introduce numbers, leaving out the "story" that was central to the show.[48] In 1973 he complained:

> I've got letters on my desk, another came in today, I get them every day. People complaining about how they've loved Renfro Valley and how it's all been destroyed by what they see when they come here now and what they hear when they come here. It's really touching. . . . people do not realize the hold that that darn Sunday morning program had on the American public. . . . They haven't had the decency yet to tell them that it's not live. . . . They'll come down here and hang around till nine or ten o'clock, then come up here and ask me where the Sunday morning show is, why it isn't on. That's what they come down here for.[49]

After his retirement, Virginia Lair urged her husband to write, especially his history of Rockcastle County. Their daughter Ann, however, remembers him spending most of his time trying to develop the commercial potential of the Great Saltpeter Cave, purchased when Lair first began his enterprises at Renfro Valley.[50] Later, Virginia Lair's declining health also impeded his writing. Asked about not publishing more scholarly research on song histories, Lair admitted in 1975, "I can't even get this county history out. I'm, I'm terribly handicapped on writing, I'm right in the midst of too many things. . . . You see, with my wife's present condition . . . she's not well at all. And I can't neglect her too much. To write a thing like this, you just come in, lock the door, leave everybody else out and get to work. . . . I've never had two hours on this book."[51]

Despite his distractions, Lair did serve on a traditional music committee for Berea College during the early 1970s and helped develop a collection for the library there.[52] As Sarah Gertrude Knott became more active in Kentucky folk activities following her retirement in 1971, she and Lair probably crossed paths on several occasions, yet no correspondence between them survives from this period in either of their collections. In 1972 Knott informed the director of the Kentucky Bicentennial Celebration that folklorists should lead the way in planning the events, and she listed John Lair as a folk leader for eastern Kentucky.[53] Knott's papers also include a printed schedule of events for Berea's Celebration of Traditional Music in 1974; Lair is listed as both a master of ceremonies and a speaker at a symposium on old-time music.[54]

Lair apparently approved of one new feature at Renfro Valley during the early 1970s, the annual bluegrass festival started by Mac Wiseman in 1971. He still did not think bluegrass music should be considered a distinct form from old-time music, being that it was a "reversal of the old fiddle, banjo, and guitar," but he increasingly saw traditional bluegrass players as the "true" country music performers.[55] Lair believed that mainstream commercial country music had changed so much that it was no longer country. In 1975, when asked who still played country, Lair responded with the names of bluegrass stalwarts Bill Monroe and Ralph Stanley.[56]

The commercial success of bluegrass festivals was particularly impressive. As Lair told Bradley Kincaid and Loyal Jones in 1971:

> Mac's been putting on some bluegrass festivals over the country and had brilliant success, so has Bill [Monroe] for that matter. They get twenty-five and thirty thousand people out to those things. Now you can't take a country show into a theater or average booking place anymore and get that kind of business. And I said, "Mac, how do you explain it?" He said, "Well, there are so many people in the country who like the type of music that was popular back in the early radio days. And where are they going to hear it?" They can't hear it on recordings, they can't hear it on the radio, they can't hear it on the TV. So they come out to one of these things and sit there and drink their fill of the music they want. So that's the reason sure enough." Now if that's true, if there's a reversal coming in, I've seen the trend that way for a number of years. There's a reversal to the old, original type of this thing we call country music.[57]

Eventually, Lair succumbed to the urge to once again be the boss at Renfro Valley. "Daddy," Barbara Smith commented, "just couldn't not be the owner."[58] Ann Henderson conjectured, "Had [my parents] left, . . . after he'd sold it, I think he could have weaned away. But they didn't, and I guess it was hard to sit up there on the front porch and look down here at what had been yours, and it wasn't the same anymore. And so I guess he just decided he wasn't ready to retire after all and came back into it."[59]

Despite Hal Smith's Nashville connections, his grandiose schemes for making Renfro Valley commercially successful were no more successful than Lair's had been the previous decade. Pete Stamper remembers that at one point Smith became so disgusted at the lack of cooperation from local Rockcastle County officials that he threatened to dismantle every building and move it west to Cave City, north of Bowling Green.[60] Lair's first bid to buy back Renfro came in partnership with Father Ralph W. Beiting, head of the Christian Appalachian Project, but Smith kept upping the price.[61] Barbara Smith, however, was skeptical about the partnership's survival. "[They] were two willful men. Father Beiting was . . . he was a showman also. . . . So that, that didn't work," she recalled.[62]

For a brief time Lair worked as the manager of Renfro Valley for the absentee owner, Hal Smith. Glenn Pennington, a local businessman and Lily May Ledford's former husband, took over management duties when Lair left the position. Soon thereafter a sign appeared on a piece of land he still owned: "John Lair's Country Music Show" was coming. A new red barn was also built on the property.[63] Smith tried to purchase the new barn, but Pennington got it first, and soon both men were vying for control of the Valley itself. Pennington went into partnership with Alpha Smith, owner of the Renfro Valley Lodge, and in 1976 they decided to enlist Lair's help as an intermediary. "At this point," Pennington said, "Hal Smith wouldn't have spoke to me, . . . And pretty well the same way with Alfie Smith. And Lair was the only one that . . . [Smith] wasn't really mad at. So we had to bring Lair back in to, to get the thing bought. . . . it didn't happen all this fast, but that's what Lair did . . . Lair got together and bought it from him, we had the contracts arranged that when he bought it, he was immediately to sell the percentage to us."[64] With ambitions of his own, however, Lair did not sell out as expected.

Smith, and Pennington arranged to split the responsibilities of the new partnership. As Smith's son, Gary, noted, "Mr. Lair was to go ahead and run this show over here at the old barn, and do the *Sunday Morning Gatherings.* Mr. Pennington was to see to the new barn, the talent, whatever on that show. My dad was in charge of the shops, all the other buildings, keep up things, see about the insurance, things like that."[65]

The arrangement did not last long. Less than two years after the purchase of Renfro Valley, Alpha Smith died, leaving his shares to his son. Lair's alliance with Pennington must have been an uneasy one from the outset. Not two years before, Lair had told Loyal Jones that Pennington, who at that time managed Renfro Valley, "wants that loud noisy stuff because other new places, because the Opry has that loud, noisy stuff. He's not going to be left behind, he's going to be right up there with them."[66] For his part, Pennington thought Lair, although a genius from an artistic standpoint, was unqualified to handle business affairs.[67] In 1979 Pennington sold his share of Renfro Valley to Lair and Gary Smith.

Lair would have preferred to own Renfro Valley by himself, but financially he had no choice. As it was, in order to afford his share of the partnership he had to auction off his large collection of historical artifacts, which, the Associated Press reported, he estimated as being worth $100,000.[68] "He sold so many of his things that we've always regretted," Nancy Lair Griffin recalled. "So many of the things were gone that we would have liked to have kept."[69]

Whatever the costs of doing so, repurchasing Renfro Valley was vital to Lair. "The only time he was, I ever saw him seem down was after he sold the Valley," Nancy Griffin said, "for that period of time. And I'd say he just seemed to sort of age, he and Mother were going to travel, they were going to do this and that, but the spark, he just didn't have that spark. He just had to have it back." Although now eighty-two, stepping back into the limelight rejuvenated Lair. "He came back to life again when he got back in it," Griffin added. "He just had to have that, just had to have that people, and involvement, and adulation, whatever you want to call it."[70]

The joy Lair must have felt in being back in the limelight must have been tempered by the declining health of Virginia Crawford Lair, who died the year after the repurchase of Renfro Valley. The couple had been married for more than fifty years, and her death made apparent the extent to which Virginia Lair had taken care of the practical, day-to-day business of their lives. "Daddy," Barbara Smith observed, "just couldn't do anything, as far as bills or that type of thing. . . . Like you hear of a lot of widows today, you know, then the husband died, they weren't aware of their insurance policies or how to do this or—that was Daddy. And I think we realized then how much of that Mother had handled for him all those years."[71]

Even though he doted on his daughters Lair always seemed to regret not having a male heir to take over operations at Renfro Valley. Barbara Smith noted, however, "We've always felt like if he'd had a son, he [the son] would have been miserable. . . . Daddy might have really kind of pushed at him a little bit. I think because we were girls, it never entered his head that any of us would be interested or could be interested."[72] Eventually, two of the Lairs' daughters would become involved in the operation of Renfro Valley. After he repurchased the venue, their second daughter, Virginia Lee (Ginalee), began to work on public relations and arranging bus tours of the attraction.

In 1975, just months before the repurchase, local citizens had provided their own recognition in a "John Lair Day" celebration that included long-time Lair friend Colonel Harland Sanders as well as old associates such as Doc Hopkins and Bradley Kincaid.[73] "Founder's Day," said Gary Smith, began in 1977 when the state put up a historic marker, and "after that we started celebrating Mr. Lair's birthday on the Fourth of July. . . .

Ex-governors have been here, Merle Travis has been here . . . Lily May, used to be with the Coon Creek Girls."[74]

On the occasion of Lair's eighty-seventh birthday celebration in 1981 Merle Travis wrote a six-stanza song that acknowledged Lair's role in starting Travis's musical career.[75] The same year Steve Cisler, who at WLS fifty years earlier had auditioned Karl Davis and Hartford Connecticut Taylor—Karl and Harty, the Renfro Valley Boys—sent Lair a birthday tape to "remind others of when you began and how much you have done." He added in a handwritten note, "Someday your many friends will see you honored in the Country Music Hall of Fame as a genuine pioneer who has never evaded his responsibility for being real and heart warming, and whose contribution to country music of the genuine type is not capable of measurement in the synthetic rating racket of today's radio."[76]

Lair was nominated for the Country Music Hall of Fame on several occasions. In 1976 Ford Philpot of the Ford Philpot Evangelistic Association informed the Country Music Foundation, "I am convinced that Mr. Lair is more knowledgeable about country music than anyone I know of in America today . . . It would be a great thrill to me to see him nominated to the Country Music Hall of Fame."[77] Lair's outspoken criticism of the changes in country music, however, probably did not endear him to the Nashville establishment. As the years went by he grew even more appalled by its direction. Barbara Smith recalls him attending one awards ceremony: "1981 I think, he was nominated. And they just called at the office, and [said] 'Oh please be sure and be there this year. Be there,' and all this stuff. So Ann and her husband took him down . . . to the Opryland Hotel, and down the long aisle . . . and Alabama came onstage . . . Daddy turned around in a very loud voice and said, "'I thought you said this was a country music show,'. . . 'This isn't country music.'"[78]

If recognition from the country music establishment eluded John Lair, his ambition for himself and Renfro Valley did not fail him until his final years. In 1973 he told a class from Berea College, "I hate like heck to get to be eighty or ninety years old and give it up. I'm getting close, I'll be seventy-nine the first day of July, but I can use a whole lot more years yet . . . like one of my little girls said, 'It's too bad Daddy can't live twice,' said, 'he'll never get it all done this time.'"[79]

After reclaiming Renfro Valley, Lair attempted to return it to what it had once been. Buildings had been allowed to deteriorate and needed care, and Lair removed the large sound system Hal Smith put in the old barn and once again banned drums and most electrified instruments. The partners tried to offer the best of both worlds. They reserved the old barn for more traditional and bluegrass music and offered an updated version of country music at the *Jamboree* in the red barn.

Lair, as always, continued to have ambitions for expansion. His last partner, Gary Smith, recalled, "Mr. Lair wanted to put in a big theme park. Rides, a chairlift. He wanted to build an auditorium to seat 3,500 people. He had plans on it, he had the site picked out."[80] As Ann Henderson said, her father "never ran out of plans." He wanted a bigger barn, and "at one time he was talking with various architects and different people about, over in the other field that's now empty where they sometimes have festivals, of putting in there, more of an entertainment complex. But it would be . . . an enlarged old-time county fair, that sort thing, not a Dollywood."[81] Henderson noted that by adding attractions such as a farm, homestead, and petting zoo as well as more accommodations her father hoped to make Renfro Valley "more of a three- or four-day visit place instead of Saturday night."[82]

Despite his ambitions for growth, Lair hoped to take the music back to his glory days and sought out former stars. Jo Fisher left Renfro Valley in 1966 and moved to Bowling Green, Kentucky, with her husband. Coming home late one night in 1978 she found Lair's Cadillac in her driveway. "I said, 'Well what in the world are you doing in Bowling Green?' He said, 'I thought I'd . . . come and see if you would let me take you back to Renfro Valley.'" Despite her doubts, Lair convinced her that she could still play. The return was, Fisher felt, "just like going home."[83] Lair also tried to shape new performers into new permutations of his old acts. Marge and Debbie Rhoads auditioned at the Lair home in the summer of 1983 after Lair had his first stroke. Impressed by their close harmonies, he signed them as regulars at the *Barn Dance* and urged them to wear long, gingham dresses and change their names to the Sunbonnet Girls. They chose, however, to stick with Country Rhoads. "He came over there in that wheelchair and came onstage," Marge Rhoads remembered, "and he announced to the audience that he was getting some new acts and we were one of those."[84]

After an initial stroke in 1982 Lair for a time regained some strength and continued with some of his responsibilities at Renfro Valley, but by 1984 he was no longer able to attend the shows. After he became incapacitated his daughter Ginalee King took on more responsibilities and in doing so realized what an active life her father had led. "Seven days a week, writing a monthly newspaper, doing a half an hour show, being there for tapings and recordings, being there Sunday mornings, plus everything," she marveled. "I thought, how in the world this man did it, I don't know [laughed]. It was seven days, plus a week."[85]

On November 12, 1985, at ninety-one, John Lair died. Ginalee King felt she could no longer handle running Renfro Valley and turned the responsibility over to her elder sister, Ann. The Lair daughters bought out Smith's interest, but in 1989 the family sold the Valley, except for the homeplace, to Ralph Gabbard and Glenn Pennington.

Although all Lair's dreams did not come true, Nancy Griffin recalled, "When he was in his nineties, he said, 'You know Nancy, I've done everything in my life I ever wanted to do.'"[86] More than a decade earlier her father had told Loyal Jones, "I've often thought I was the only man in the world that made a living out of things that he'd had paid somebody to let him do."[87] Lair's final business partner, Gary Smith, also remembered him as a man who accomplished his dreams. With more than a half-century's age difference, Smith did not always find it easy to get along with Lair, but he did believe Lair deserved respect: "He was one of a kind. He's the only person I know besides my dad that fulfilled what he wanted to do while he was here. He had a dream and he followed it through and he seen it done. I respected that man as much as anybody I ever knew. He was a smart man. He was a hard man, he was stern when it come to Renfro Valley, he was very stern. He was set in his ways. But I don't know too many people that could have done what Mr. Lair done. I really don't."[88]

8   Staging Tradition

The Past is Prologue! Study the Past!
—Sarah Gertrude Knott

In 2001 the Country Music Foundation in Nashville inducted performers Homer and Jethro, who found their first taste of success at Renfro Valley, into the Country Music Hall of Fame. The hall already included two of Lair's original Renfro Valley partners, Red Foley and Whitey Ford, as well country music media pioneers George Hay and Connie B. Gay. Lair, a finalist three years before his death, was never so honored. In 1985 the National Endowment for the Arts awarded Lily May Ledford a National Heritage Fellowship just weeks before her death, which preceded Lair's by only a few months.

Also in 2001, Sarah Gertrude Knott's successor Joe Wilson became the first nonartist to receive the National Heritage Fellowship. No Public Folklore Hall of Fame recognizes the pioneers of public folklore. Generally, however, folklorists recognize Archie Green for his heroic efforts in lobbying Congress for the American Folklife Preservation Act, Ralph Rinzler as the architect of the Smithsonian's Festival of American Folklife, and Bess Lomax Hawes for her long reign at the helm of the National Endowment for the Arts' Folk Arts Program. Public folklorists have generally distanced themselves from the creators of early folk festivals and found common cause instead with federally employed folklorists of the New Deal. Ben Botkin, long dismissed in academic circles as a popularizer, is now considered ahead of his time for many of his opinions. Botkin, similar to most of the New Deal folklorists, used literary, not theatrical, means to "give folklore back" to the people. Botkin's long association with the National Folk Festival, however, testifies to his interest in other forms of public presentation, and he once told a mutual friend that he was "in awe" of Knott.[1]

Perhaps it should come as no surprise that the Nashville establishment has not honored John Lair, who during his lifetime openly criticized Nashville-based country music. The folk revival has also been, at best, ambivalent toward Lair. In order to reinstate the early country music artists to the role of folk musicians, the artifice and commercialism of the industry had to be blamed on someone else. Not that all criticisms of Lair were unjustified. He made money from others' art, and sometimes he was selfish or tightfisted. But a careful assessment of his career does not lead to the conclusion that his actions rose to the level of exploitation. Many musicians credited Lair for starting them out professionally, and his lack of a star system at Renfro Valley gave new musicians a chance in the limelight. Lair also offered an alternative for performers who wished to maintain a family life while pursuing a career in show business.

The attempt to cast him as an exploiter of musicians also does not do justice to the musicians themselves. Surely they knew they were in show business. Most actively participated in the creation of their own acts and did not offer themselves as passive victims to Lair. Some may have been bitter about getting a raw deal from Lair, but they seem to constitute a distinct minority. Even those reputedly victimized, such as Lily May Ledford and Doc Hopkins, were still on hand for birthday tributes to him during the final years of his life.

If not outwardly commercial, Knott has also been represented as exploitive because she did not pay performers. Self-righteousness comes perhaps too easily in a day and age when folklorists can (almost) take for granted government support for the folk arts. This support exists, in a large part, because Knott lobbied for the inclusion of folk arts in the legislation that created the National Endowment for the Arts. For more than thirty years Knott kept her festival afloat without federal support. She did receive funding from some state governments, but the majority of her support came from private interests, especially the print media. Knott made herself believe that being onstage and sharing tradition was payment enough for folk artists. But what other choices did she have? She could have sold Ballard Flour and Post Toasties like John Lair, or she could have packed up and gone home. The person Knott exploited the most was herself. She dedicated most of her adult life to her festival, and when she retired she barely had enough to live on.

In her later years Sarah Gertrude Knott also fell victim to the professionalization of folk festival work. Having more or less won the battle of professionalization on the academic front, in the 1960s and 1970s the discipline of folklore turned its attention to the professionalization of popularization. Over time, the popularization of folklore became acceptable within the discipline as long as popularizers possessed academic training. As in so many other stories of professionalization, younger professionals replaced older amateurs and, quite often, male professionals replaced female amateurs. It is tempting to speculate on the role gender played in the professionalization. Would the takeover of the National Folk Festival have been handled differently if Knott were a man? Would she have seemed less threatening, less irritating, or less subject to ridicule?

Although the emerging class of academically trained public folklorists and professional folk revivalists did not always constitute mutually exclusive groups, they tended to have different agendas and, ultimately, different notions of authenticity. Knott's retirement brought more, not less, conflict from within the National Folk Festival Association as the board struggled to define who publicly funded folk festivals should serve. Ultimately, the festival came back to a vision not dissimilar to Knott's original. During the invention (or reinvention) of public folklore, however, more attention was paid to what its predecessors did wrong rather than what they did that was right. Surely contemporary public folklorists would approve of Knott's tireless efforts to involve local schools, both public and private, in her festival. She also worked ceaselessly at bringing academic folklorists and "practitioners" together, and these dialogs took place in the context of the festival itself. If ultimately practitioners came to predominate, that probably reflects the degree to which each group willingly participated in the festival. Finally, one dream never came true. For thirty-five years Knott searched for an academic base for her festival. Had that come about, surely it would have included, as proposed in the 1930s, an integrated university curriculum that taught both academic folklore and its public presentation.

To the extent that modern public folklorists do acknowledge Knott's achievements it is typically for the diversity and authenticity of her early festivals. Although Knott's earliest festivals are usually the ones noted with approval, the National Folk Festival during that period still excluded "recent Americans." Ironically, the trend toward greater diversity in the early Washington years opened the floodgates for revivalists and professional ethnic and international dance troupes. The strength of the early festivals lay in the willingness of folklorists, whether academics or notable collectors, to identify and bring folk artists to the festival and provide both written and oral interpretation. The motivations of these individuals were varied. Physical attraction lured Vance Randolph, whereas Zora Neale Hurston hoped for favorable attention from academic folklorists.

The reasons Knott could not sustain this level of involvement are equally as varied. She was no longer young and attractive; moreover, her festival no longer had the same prestige. Change also came from the attitudes of folklorists themselves. Despite Richard Dorson's willingness to have his name publicly associated with the festival, many members of the generation of academic folklorists trained during the wave of academic professionalization of the 1950s and early 1960s may not have seen public involvement with a festival as a positive career move.

Perhaps if Knott had the federal funding she helped make possible for a younger generation of public folklorists she could have afforded to pay performers as well as fieldworkers to identify artists and traditions, and that information would have kept her festival vibrant and on the cutting edge. Small local festivals were an innovative means of identifying folk artists, but they, too, tended to fall by the wayside during the National Folk Festival's long tenure in St. Louis. Limited funding made Knott vulnerable to one form of revivalism and resistant to another. She seemed well aware of the issues of authenticity the dance revival posed for her festival, yet the dance contingent provided its loyalest supporters during the lean postwar years. The declining audiences for the National Folk Festival during the 1950s and 1960s may have made Knott willing to court the emerging folk music revival, but she could scarce afford the new breed of professional folk singers.

The conflicts that arose following Knott's retirement point to the slippery nature of the concept of authenticity. Although the younger generation criticized Knott for not paying her performers they were also horrified by her willingness to accept commercial sponsors. If a beer company would cover the expenses of a dance group from Milwaukee, Knott was all for it. The elimination of the professional and amateur dance groups from the National Folk Festival did not necessarily presage an immediate shift to authenticity, and Knott's friends were not entirely unjustified in their belief that the grassroots had been left behind. Were the Lindsborg Swedish dancers really less authentic than John Prine or David Bromberg?

The issue of diversity was also disputed. The new National Folk Festival no longer tried to represent the broad sweep of America and deemphasized the western United States and Native Americans. The event's new programmers, however, were proud of their growing emphasis on African American vernacular music, especially genres that had been overlooked by the old National. It is true that Knott's notions of African American folklore were limited and all too often romantic and patronizing. Yet she did consult the leading African American folklorists of her day, individuals such as Zora Neale Hurston and J. Mason Brewer, and her efforts to present African American folklore in the festival's early days, especially at the Texas Centennial and at Constitution Hall, were nothing less than heroic. If Knott shied away from most forms of the blues (beyond W. C. Handy), that probably reflected the predilections of the African American church and educational leaders to whom she frequently turned for mediation. The new organizers rightly wanted to expand their presentation of African American expression, but they were also more than a little gleeful at being able to shock their elders.

In the end, the issue was not about authenticity but audience and a generation's popular tastes. Knott understood the cultural milieu of the depression and World War II. She rode the crest of the folk dance revival, but the folk music revival defeated her. It had numerically expanded the audience for folk music, but it presented a far narrower demographic. Knott envisioned her festival as wholesome family entertainment. Pageantry, nationalism, and kiddie dance groups, however, generally made the Woodstock generation gag. So did, for that matter, prima donnas in ball gowns. The generation gap was ultimately impossible for Knott to bridge. In 1971 she wrote bitterly to Irwin Silber, editor of *Sing Out!* "I'm from the 'Establishment' you thought. You said you were the 'radical.' Looking deeper, you were not radical, that is no more radical than I."[2]

Issues of professionalism and authenticity are threaded through John Lair's career as well. His imaginative vision allowed his radio programs to transcend the medium's aural nature, and his talent for sounding warm and authentic while selling a product put him at the cutting edge just as commercial sponsorship became the solid base of country radio. Lair appealed to listeners because they felt they knew and could trust him. That vision, however, could not foresee the impact of the recording industry, and ultimately television, on live country-music radio. Nor did it prepare him for changes in media advertising. By the time of the General Mills and Pillsbury contracts in the 1950s, Lair was already well out of his league. When the bottom fell out of his sponsor base, Lair could always fall back on the notion of authenticity. Privately, he may have been willing to cut a deal with Hollywood or Nashville, but publicly he decried their influence on country music, which was, he argued, no longer "real" country music at all.

In their latter years both Knott and Lair sustained relentless optimism despite tumbles from the pinnacle of success. Perhaps their optimism had made them successful in the first place, but each cushioned their fall by wrapping themselves in the blanket of authenticity. Both undoubtedly knew that their productions were in danger of becoming uncomfortably close to amateur talent shows in their declining years, but they comforted themselves with their own notions of tradition. If Knott could not attract the popular revival folk artists to her show, that was fine. The National Folk Festival was really about "diamonds in the rough." If the audience was sparse or inattentive, well, the festival existed for the performers anyway, not the audience. Lair's claim that Renfro Valley was the star of his show served more than one purpose. In the early days of success it kept Lair firmly at center stage and in control; in the latter years the notion covered for the fact that Lair, or Renfro Valley, no longer had the ability to create stars.

Lair walked the tightrope of authenticity all his career. He possessed genuine fascination for American vernacular music and wished to preserve country music's traditional roots. He was also a showman, however, and willingly manipulated tradition to punch up a show. Lair was genuinely proud of his role in making instruments such as the string bass and the Hawaiian guitar acceptable within country music, although he would later be outspoken about the use of drums and the dominance of electrified instruments. If vaudeville-derived humor helped bring in an audience, Lair happily obliged, but he also knew how far he could push country stereotypes without offending the sensibilities of his rural-based audience.

John Lair's reputation ought to be as both an innovator and a traditionalist. Unfortunately, he was too much of a traditionalist to be remembered fondly by the country music establishment and too much of an artificer to be in good stead with the folk establishment. The latter's critique is in some sense contradictory. They complained that Lair manipulated authenticity for commercial success and did not bring enough commercial success to performers. Ultimately, Lily May Ledford's chief criticism lay not in the fact that Lair dressed her in long dresses and high-top boots but that he did not make her a star. Ledford felt that doing so was clearly in Lair's power, but no evidence supports the conclusion that he ever deliberately stood in the way of a performer's success. The bad choices he made for them, he also made for himself and the valley. From the late 1940s onward Lair wanted nothing more than recording contracts for Lily May Ledford and the other performers. The fact was, however, that Renfro Valley performers who wanted to be stars had to leave the valley, and perhaps their ties to tradition, behind.

Lair's lack of business ability to some extent belies him being cast as a greedy manipulator. His talents were those of a visionary and a showman, not a businessperson. By the accounts of his daughters, Lair did not have a head for money, and he left financial details to his wife,

Virginia, and a handful of business associates. From the late 1930s to the mid-1950s Lair had far less business control over his organization than his performers imagined. Freeman Keyes, and later General Foods and Pillsbury, called the shots.

The staging of tradition and authenticity binds together the histories of country music and the folk festival. Scholars often pose the two as oppositions. The noted country music historian Bill Malone, for example, suggests, "In the decades since the 1920s, however, two conceptions of "mountain music" have contested for legitimacy in American life, each supported basically by two very different audiences. Scholars' concert recitalists; folk festival promoters like Jean Thomas, John Powell, and Annabel Morris Buchanan; and the record labels that catered to a specialized, academic audience promoted one approach; while the other was popularized by the hillbilly musicians of radio and recording."[3] According to a commonly accepted narrative, folk festivals were reconciled to early country music only after revivalists discovered the recordings included in Harry Smith's *Anthology of American Folk Music.* Ironically, during the same period the leftist associations of the revival caused the country music establishment to distance themselves from the label *folk.*

Different audiences did exist for folk festivals and country music radio, but the two did not operate in parallel universes. Nor is it necessarily true that creators of folk festivals all wished to combat the evils of hillbilly music. Of the early folk festival entrepreneurs, Annabel Morris Buchanan and John Powell, the creators of White Top, used rhetoric that was more purist, yet a number of performers at White Top were influenced by—and in some cases performed on—radio. Surely, some of the audience at White Top also listened to "hillbilly music" on the radio, although as John Lair indirectly suggested many others were just as happy to stay home and listen to "ole WLS."[4] Jean Thomas of the American Folk Song Festival also officially took a purist line, but her Hollywood background was evident. Every bit as much an artificer as John Lair, she more than happily used a radio personality as the emcee for her festival and sought spots for her performers on radio and later television.

Bascom Lamar Lunsford and Sarah Gertrude Knott did not usually take such purist positions. Lunsford abhorred hillbilly stereotypes but had no problem working for Lair as dance director at the beginning of the Renfro Valley Barn Dance or later directing Lair's folk festivals. Knott occasionally wrote of the nefarious effect radio had on folk tradition, but she did so primarily in articles targeted to academic folklorists. She had quite a few associates who abhorred hillbilly music, but she maintained a relatively open mind. She willingly called on WLS for help with her Chicago festival and enlisted John Lair as a board member. She also defended hillbilly musicians as bearers of folk tradition to some of her more purist associates. The relationship of country music to folk tradition "pestered" her throughout her career, and when she finally read Bill Malone's *Country Music U.S.A.* she rejoiced.

Other folk music entrepreneurs were also open to some forms of country music long before Harry Smith's anthology made it respectable. Alan Lomax may have derided hillbilly music's influence at the Ohio Valley Folk Festival, but two years later he willingly shared the stage with Lair's Coon Creek Girls at the White House, and in the 1940s he featured Lily May Ledford in two folk-based radio dramas. During the same decade Lomax also recorded the folk repertoire of country performer Cousin Emmy (Cynthia Mae Carver). Ralph Rinzler also discovered country music before the folk revival was in full swing. In 1954 he attended Sunshine Sue's (Mary Arlene Higdon's) revue in New York, where he, too, discovered the music of Lily May Ledford.[5]

For their part country music radio stations took keen interest in folk festivals. If Knott used WLS to locate talent in the Upper Midwest, that radio station had raided the National for performers. Certain performers had a natural crossover appeal for folk and country audiences. WLS probably discovered cowboy performer Romaine Lowdermilk at the Second National Folk Festival, and in the late 1950s Jimmie Driftwood secured interest from both folk festival and mainstream country music audiences. Although the label *folk*, at least until the 1950s, may have had business appeal for those in country music interested in courting middle-class audiences, some early entrepreneurs held a sincere interest in traditional music. Charles Wolfe argues that WSM's George Hay "understood the full dimension of Southern folk tradition better than did most of the respectable 'academic' folklorists of the day."[6] Of all the early country music radio entrepreneurs, no one had their feet more firmly planted in the folk realm than John Lair.

Both Lair and Knott held academic folklorists in high esteem. Aside from Frederick Koch and Paul Green, Knott's most important mentors were academically trained folklorists. All her life she craved respect, as well as support for her festival, from the academic discipline of folklore. Lair did not try as hard to cultivate connections within the discipline, but in many ways he was more the folklorist at heart. Had he come from a slightly different economic and social milieu he might well have become an academic himself. Lair's passion for tracing the histories of songs through written and oral sources went well beyond any economic gain he derived from the activity. Unfortunately, he found little outlet for such research. Even his much-loved format, which put Lair in the role of genial professor explaining the history of individual songs, found little interest among commercial sponsors. With the exception of *Songs Lincoln Loved*, most of his publications had specific commercial purposes, and Lair was not above using even that as a premium offer or a gift to attract new sponsors.

Had he found an academic audience for his research Lair would have been well ahead of his time in understanding the permeability of the labels *folk* and *popular* in American vernacular music. Whatever claims he made for traditionality and authenticity for music on his shows, Lair had a sharp sense of how songs passed in and out of oral tradition. Perhaps, however, he would have had difficulty finding a comfortable home within the fairly restricted field of vernacular music research in the first half of the twentieth century. Late in life he would admit that "folk" music was not his primary passion: "I've never said this before, I don't believe, but my favorite music was old popular, actually what I enjoyed listening to most . . . I liked the folk songs because of their culture and their words and the stories that they opened up, but as far as the musical sounds went, I liked things like 'Silver Threads among the Gold' and stuff like that better."[7]

Lair may have been something of a frustrated academic, but there is no doubt that he found his life's calling. Most of all, Lair, similar to Sarah Gertrude Knott, wanted to be onstage. He knew he lacked musical ability, and perhaps Knott did not have the talent to succeed as an actress, but both spent the majority of their adult lives in the limelight. The desire to stay center-stage fueled their long and active careers. Whatever they wrote, whatever ideologies they espoused, they seemed driven by personal need. To state this is not to denigrate their achievements or excuse their sins but only to insist on the necessity of understanding them as real people. Critical histories falter at the failure to recognize the complexity of human needs and motivations that drive all of us.

A critical element that distinguishes the careers of John Lair and Sarah Gertrude Knott are the theatrical models they used to stage tradition. Lair's exposure to theater came through vaudeville during World War I and quite probably the medicine shows and other popular entertainments that may have passed through the Rockcastle County of his youth. Although undoubtedly sincere in his interest to preserve folk traditions, Lair fundamentally understood that he was in the entertainment business. That realization freed his imagination to enhance and manipulate authenticity in order to create a better show. If Lair could include a history lesson or two all the better, but he never forgot that he was involved in a commercial enterprise.

Sarah Gertrude Knott's attraction, even as a young woman, was to serious drama. She inherited the legacy of pageantry filtered through the academic playwriting program at the University of North Carolina. This was theater with a didactic purpose. Although American pageantry expressed a wide variety of nationalistic concerns, Knott absorbed the social liberalism of the Carolina Playmakers. In 1934 she took a giant leap beyond the folk drama of "Proff" Koch and Paul Green by seeing folk culture not as source material but as performance in itself. Still, the influence of Koch and Green allowed Knott to break free of the narrow monocultural vision of predecessors in the folk festival field.

Folklorist Timothy Lloyd has explored the role "social therapeutics" played in the creation of the National Folk Festival.[8] Although concern for social issues did motivate many of Knott's associates and definitely made up part of the milieu of the festival, she was not motivated by a specific ideology. Not that she spurned ideologies—in fact, she loved them, the more the better as long as they justified her festival. This is not to attribute cynicism to Knott because she was anything but cynical. She was sincere in embracing ideas that justified her festival. Ultimately, however, those ideas were so numerous, contradictory, and mutable that they canceled each other out.

Despite the differences in their theatrical models, Lair and Knott were not so different in their efforts. Lair had a didactic aim within his enter-tainment model, and Knott had a simple passion for the stage within a theatrical form replete with social and educational purposes. Ultimately, both models failed them because they fell out of favor with the public. Now it is easy to see how theatrical conventions alter traditions. But is the public presentation of tradition not inescapably theatrical in nature? Contemporary folklife festivals have generally moved away from the big stage to emphasize smaller, more intimate venues. Folklife festivals, how-ever, have changed with, not against, theatrical convention. In breaking down the barriers between the stage and audience Knott toyed with the notion of theater in the round in the 1960s. Modern festivals are perhaps just a more avant-garde form of theater.[9]

The National Folk Festival under Knott always included exhibits of material culture although she was far more drawn to the performance genres and so did not bring much imagination to displays of material folk art. Since Knott's time the Smithsonian's Festival of American Folklife has made pioneering efforts in the inclusion of nonperformance genres in its format. Whether this move escapes the conventions of theater or theatricalizes all of life remains a question. And what is the alternative to the theatrical presentation of tradition? An equally old, and equally problematic, model does exist: the zoological model. There is a certain dignity to being onstage not conferred on the inmates of zoos. Despite exhortations to folk artists to act and dress naturally (the theatrical conventions of the present-day folklife festival), we know full well that the most successful participants are those who figure out how to stage their own culture.

In the early twenty-first century the institutions that John Lair and Sarah Gertrude Knott created still survive. Renfro Valley, country music's first auto-tourism site, is now one among many. Within Renfro, Lair is "museumized" in a Disneyland sort of way. Now that he is gone, a red-check-shirted, audio-animatron tells the story, in Lair's voice, of Renfro Valley. Although things have indeed changed in Renfro Valley, its history and Lair's personal history remain a central theme of the complex. Nearby, the Lairs' home, privately owned, is now on the National Register of Historic Places. Their stable, also on the National Register, is now the site of Kentucky's Music Hall of Fame, which opened in 2002. John Lair was included in the first group of inductees.

After the Filene Center at Wolf Trap burned in 1982, the National Folk Festival once again took to the road, staying a few years in each location and hoping to leave behind a locally based yearly event. Since 1976 the National has made efforts to acknowledge ties to its past, even while changing with the times. The National Folk Festival is still a more performance-driven event than some folklife festivals, although the influence of the Smithsonian festival is evident. Closer to home, Knott has also received some acknowledgment for her accomplishments. For the past several years her home state has awarded a folk heritage award in Knott's name at the Kentucky Folklife Festival. In Princeton, Kentucky, the Little Green House has also been listed on the National Register, and the town sponsors an annual festival honoring National Heritage Award winner Eddie Pennington and other local musicians. Whether or not she would recognize them, Knott's "grown-up daughter" and her countless grown-up grandchildren seem to be alive and well, going strong in the National Folk Festival and the many festivals it has spawned.

NOTES

Chapter 1: Tradition, Ambition, and the Theater

1. "Clinton I. Knott of County Dead," *Paducah Evening Sun*, 25 Feb. 1918.
2. Knott, letter to Paul Green, 1937, PGC.
3. Henderson interview, 6 Dec. 1985.
4. Knott, "A Dream Come True—in Sight," manuscript fragment, 1971, SGKC.
5. *History and Families, McCracken County, Kentucky.*
6. Knott interview, 6 Mar. 1976.
7. Pezzuti, "Sarah Gertrude Knott House."
8. Dodge interview, 29 July 1996.
9. Davis interview, 25 June 1999.
10. A. M. Easterling, "Religious Drama Would Fill the Empty Church Pews Says This Promoter of Amateur Dramatics," *St. Louis Globe-Democrat Sunday Magazine*, 25 May 1930.
11. Knott, undated manuscript fragment, SGKC.
12. *The Chowanoka* 26, Yvonne Dodge Collection, Chowan College, Murfreesboro, N.C.
13. Knott interview, 6 Mar. 1976.
14. Ibid.
15. Dodge interview, 29 July 1996.
16. Lair, "The Renfro Valley Music Library," 10.
17. Lair, tape-recorded talk, 23 June 1973.
18. Lair interview, 30 April 1974.
19. Smith interview, 3 Mar. 1995.
20. "Frank Tinney Shines in 'Atta Boy,'" *New York Times*, 24 Dec. 1918.
21. Lair, typed manuscript on microfiche, CMF.
22. Ibid.
23. Some histories state that Lair attended art school. In an interview late in life, however, he dismissed that as "just one of these commercial art things, it didn't amount to much, I went to one summer." Lair interview, 15 April 1975.
24. Smith interview, 25 Oct. 1996.
25. Lair, *Renfro Valley Then and Now*, 31.
26. Ibid., forward.
27. Lair interview, 15 April 1975.
28. Henderson interview, 22 May 1997.
29. Esma Baker Maher, letter to John Lair, 20 Aug. 1933, box 70, JLC.

30. Griffin interview, 1 Mar. 1995.
31. Smith interview, 3 Mar. 1995.
32. Griffin interview, 1 Mar. 1995.
33. Smith interview, 3 Mar. 1995.
34. Griffin interview, 1 Mar. 1995.
35. Smulyan, *Selling Radio*.
36. Wolfe, *A Good-Natured Riot*, 7–11.
37. Evans, Prairie Farmer *and WLS*, 177.
38. Lair interview, 30 April 1974.
39. Ibid.
40. Lair interview, 26 Oct. 1967.
41. Lair, letter to Clyde [Red] Foley, 24 Feb. 1931, box 19, JLC.
42. Lair interview, 26 Oct. 1967.
43. Rice, "Renfro Valley on the Radio, 1937–1941," 18.
44. Wolfe, *A Good-Natured Riot*, 11–15.
45. For histories of Lunsford's career see Jones, *Minstrel of the Appalachians*; Whisnant, "Finding the Way between the Old and New"; and Williams, *Great Smoky Mountains Folklife*, 26–29.
46. Wolfe, *Kentucky Country*, 73.
47. Whisnant, *All That Is Native and Fine*, 183–252.
48. Bendix, *In Search of Authenticity*, 215–16.
49. Whisnant, *All That Is Native and Fine*, 184–85.
50. Buchanan, "The Function of a Folk Festival."
51. Green, "The National Folk Festival Association."
52. Knott's copy of the program is located in KFC1/D1/F112, SGKC.
53. Knott, letter to Annabel Morris Buchanan, 26 Oct. 1973, KFC2/D1/F13, SGKC.
54. Knott, letter to Dr. Webster, 18 Dec. 1936, NFFC.
55. Glassberg, *American Historical Pageantry*, 242–43.
56. Koch, "Making a Native Folk Drama."
57. Avery, ed., *A Southern Life: Letters of Paul Green, 1916–1981*, xiii–xxxiii; Roper, "Paul Green and the Southern Literary Renaissance."
58. Knott interview, 6 Mar. 1976.
59. Knott, letter to Green, 3 Jan. 1964, PGC.
60. Knott, letter to Green, 28 Aug. 1978, KFC2/D1/F46, SGKC.

Chapter 2: "Something Big": The Birth of the National Folk Festival

1. A. M. Easterling, "Religious Drama Would Fill the Empty Church Pews Says This Promoter of Amateur Dramatics," *St. Louis Globe-Democrat Sunday Magazine*. 25 May 1930, 2, 15.
2. Knott, letter to Dr. Willard Rhodes, 22 Jan. 1973, KFC2/D1/F113, SGKC.
3. Knott, manuscript fragment for "The National Folk Festival USA," unprocessed material, SGKC.
4. Knott interview, 1971.
5. Knott, interoffice communication to Frank N. Watson et al., Jan. 25, 1936, CC.

6. Knott, manuscript fragment, "Folk Festival Movement in the U.S., 1934–1976," 17, unprocessed material, SGKC.

7. Alexander, "The Return of the Troubadours," 10.

8. Knott, manuscript fragment, "Folk Festival Movement in the U.S., 1934–1976," 17, SGKC.

9. Knott, manuscript fragment, "Folk Festival Movement in the U.S., 1934–1976," SGKC.

10. Knott interview, 6 Mar. 1976.

11. Alexander, "The Return of the Troubadours," 11.

12. Knott, letter to Green, 25 June 1933, PGC.

13. Avery, ed., *A Southern Life*, 217–18.

14. Originally Green's title was "national chairman," while St. Louis business-man Maurice Weil was given the title of president.

15. Avery, ed., *A Southern Life*, 219.

16. Ibid., 228.

17. Ibid.

18. "Talent Scout Combs the Hills," *Daily Oklahoman*, 7 April 1957.

19. Kaplan, ed., *Zora Neale Hurston*, 295–96.

20. Boyd, *Wrapped in Rainbows*, 253.

21. Hemenway, *Zora Neale Hurston*, 255–56.

22. Wilson, *The Myth of Santa Fe*, 156–57.

23. Rourke, "The National Folk Festival," *The New Republic*, 30 May 1934, 72–73; Rourke, "The National Folk Festival," *The New Republic*, 5 June 1935, 102–3.

24. Knott, letter to Wayland Hand, 25 April 1974, KFC2/D1/F51, SGKC.

25. Hirsch, "Cultural Pluralism and Applied Folklore."

26. Knott, letter to Hawes, 5 July 1973, KFC2/D1/F53, SGKC.

27. Knott, manuscript fragment in unprocessed material, SGKC.

28. Randolph, "Ballad Hunters in North Arkansas," 5–6.

29. Cochran, *Vance Randolph*, 129–40.

30. Ibid. 135–38.

31. Selections of McCord's columns are found in the scrapbooks of Otto Ernest Rayburn, UAK. Two volumes are devoted to McCord. The dates are cut off the columns.

32. McCord, "Hillbilly Heartbeats," undated, Otto Ernest Rayburn Scrapbooks, UAK.

33. Knott, manuscript fragment from "Folk Festival Movement in the U.S., 1934–1976," 21–22, unprocessed material, SGKC.

34. McCord, "Hillbilly Heartbeats," undated, Otto Ernest Rayburn Scrapbooks, UAK.

35. "Ozarkan Ballads with Sea Chanteys at Folk Festival," *St. Louis Daily Globe-Democrat*, 1 May 1934.

36. Knott, "Questions That Pester Me," NFFC. 1939[?] is written in hand on the document, but mention of the upcoming seventh International Folk Festival would place it in the early 1940s.

37. Knott, letter to Karpeles, 13 June 1956, unprocessed material, SGKC.

38. Knott, letter to Malone, 28 April 1972, KFC2/D1/F88, SGKC.

39. Knott, letter to Wilgus and Hand, 15 Feb. 1972, KFC2/D1/F139, SGKC.

40. *St. Louis Post Dispatch,* 30 April 1934.

41. Knott interview, 6 Mar. 1976.

42. Becker, *Selling Tradition,* 213.

43. "Folklore History Vividly Painted by Display of Relics," *St. Louis Daily Globe-Democrat,* 30 April 1934.

44. Knott, letter to Frank N. Watson, 27 Nov. 1935, KFC1/D1/F60, SGKC.

45. "Indians on Opening Program of National Folk Festival Today at New Municipal Auditorium," *St. Louis Post-Dispatch,* 29 April 1934.

46. "Indians on Opening Program of National Folk Festival"; "Sea Chanteys and Ozark Folk Songs at Festival," *St. Louis Post-Dispatch,* 1 May 1934; "Lumberjacks at Festival Sing of Their Mighty Men," *St. Louis Post-Dispatch,* 2 May 1934.

47. "Ozarkan Ballads with Sea Chanteys at Folk Festival," *St. Louis Daily Globe-Democrat,* 1 May 1934.

48. Knott, letter to Hugh Jansen and Leonard Roberts, 23 Jan. 1973, KFC2/D1/F65, SGKC.

49. 1937 NFF stationary, KFC1/D1/F61, SGKC.

50. Knott, "Folk Gatherings in Tennessee," from manuscript, "Folk Festival Movement in the U.S., 1934–1976," 40, KFC1/D2/F4, SGKC.

51. Pickering, memo to Messrs. Hatfield and Weil, 7 Dec. 1936, KFC1/D1/F59, SGKC.

52. Knott, "Folk Gatherings in Tennessee," 41, SGKC.

53. Knott, interoffice communication to Bolton et al., 25 Jan. 1936, CC.

54. Gillespie, *Folklorist of the Coal Fields,* 41–44.

55. Hemenway, *Zora Neale Hurston,* 22–23.

56. Yuhl, "High Culture in the Low Country," 241–45.

57. Williams, *Great Smoky Mountains Folklife,* 33–37, 55–57.

58. "Program for the National Folk Festival and Cooperating Agencies," box 77, TJC.

59. Pickering, letter to Mssrs. Hatfield and Weil, 1 Jan. 1937, unprocessed material, KFC3/D2, SGKC.

60. Knott, "The First International Folk Dance Festival—London, 1935," manuscript fragment from "Folk Festival Movement in the U.S., 1934–1976," SGKC.

61. Pickering and Knott, memo to Messrs. Hatfield and Weil, 7 Dec. 1936, KFC1/D1/F59, SGKC.

62. Botkin, letter to Fletcher, 20 Nov. 1935, John Gould Fletcher Collection, UAK.

63. Knott, letter to Watson, 27 Nov. 1935, CC.

64. Pickering, letter to Watson, 29 Nov. 1935, CC.

65. "Contract between Texas Centennial Central Exposition and National Folk Festival" (draft), CC.

66. Knott, interoffice communication to C. E. Turner et al., CC.

67. Press Release, Mar. 1936, TCR.

68. Knott, memo to Smith, 6 May 1936, unprocessed Texas file, SGKC.

69. Knott, manuscript fragment, KFC1/D1/F60, SGKC.

70. Knott, "Texas—the Happy Hunting Ground," manuscript fragment, KFC1/D2/F4, SGKC.

71. Mooney, "Texas Centennial 1936."

72. Knott, letter to Watson, 27 Nov. 1935, CC.

73. Owens, *Tell Me a Story, Sing Me a Song,* 119.

74. Knott, "Stage Requirements for National Folk Festival," memo to A. L. Vollman, 27 April 1936, unprocessed Texas file, SGKC.

75. Pickering, memo to Paul Massman, 22 June 1936, unprocessed Texas file, SGKC.

76. Knott, "Stage Requirements for National Folk Festival," memo to A. L. Vollman, 27 April 1936, KFC1/D1/F60, SGKC.

77. Owens, *Texas Folk Songs,* 18–19. Owens recounts the same story in *Tell Me a Story, Sing Me a Song,* 118–19.

78. Knott, manuscript fragment, "Texas—the Happy Hunting Ground," KFC1/D2/F4, SGKC.

79. Knott and Pickering, Memo to Messrs. Hatfield and Weil, 7 Dec. 1936, KFC1/D1/F59, SGKC.

80. Hatfield, letter to Throop, 9 Dec. 1936, KFC3/D2, SGKC.

81. Gerling, letter to Throop, 21 Dec. 1936, KFC1/D1/F49, SGKC.

82. Pickering, letter to Messrs. Hatfield and Weil, 1 Jan. 1937, KFC3/D2, SGKC.

83. Knott, script for WCFL, 3 April 1937, KFC1/D1/F61, SGKC.

84. Ibid.

85. "U.S. Folklore Traced, Says Festival Director," *Chicago Daily News,* 9 April 1937.

86. Leary, "Otto Rindlisbacher and the Wisconsin Lumberjacks."

87. Lloyd, "A Brief History of the National Folk Festival," 10.

88. Knott, script for WCFL, 3 April 1937, KFC1/D1/F61, SGKC.

89. Knott, "The National Folk Festival—Its Problems and Reasons," 121.

90. Pickering, letter to Messrs. Hatfield and Weil, 1 Jan. 1937, KFC3/D2, SGKC.

Chapter 3: John Lair, Student of the Origins of American Folk Music

1. George C. Biggar, "Mountain Music Plus: Capers at Folk Festival Show Nation Has Rich Heritage of Song, Story and Dances," *Stand By,* 8 June 1935, 4–5, 11; George C. Biggar, "Music That Lives: Texas Centennial Shows Why American Folk Tunes Outlive Tin Pan Alley," *Stand By,* 8 Aug. 1936, 3, 15.

2. Biggar, memo to Harold Safford, 12 May 1937, Biggar, letter to Knott, May 11, 1937, Safford, memo to Art Page, 12 May 1937, and WLS program sheet for 23 May 1937, all in box 5, JLC.

3. "Folk Music Comes to Town: National Folk Festival Offers Song Variety," *Stand By,* June 19, 1937.

4. *1931 WLS Family Album,* 44, box 24, JLC.

5. John Lair, "High Jinks on White Top," *Stand By,* 14 Sept. 1935, 5, 11.

6. Jones, *Minstrel of the Appalachians,* 36, 70.

7. Lair interview, 30 April 1974.

8. Script for *Aladdin Barn Dance Frolic,* 13 Dec. 1930, box 31, JLC.

9. Script for *Aladdin Barn Dance Frolic,* 10 Jan. 1931, box 31, JLC.

10. Script for *Aladdin Barn Dance Frolic*, 21 Feb. 1931, box 31, JLC.

11. Lair, *Swing Your Partner*, 1931, box 23, JLC.

12. Script for the Olson Rug folk song program, 4 April 1931, and handwritten script for the special Abraham Lincoln edition, 25 April 1931, both in box 31, JLC.

13. Script for Thursday noon show, 25 Feb. 1932, box 31, JLC.

14. Untitled script, *Prairie Farmer* Programs, 1931, box 31, JLC.

15. Lair, letter to Clyde [Red] Foley, 24 Feb. 1931, box 19, JLC. Lair frequently spelled Hopkins's name as "Dock," although most printed references spell it "Doc."

16. George C. Biggar, "Time Out," in Lair, *Swing Your Partner*, 1931.

17. McCusker, "Dear Radio Friend.'"

18. Lair interview, 26 Oct. 1967.

19. Lair, letter to Ernest Hodge, 22 Oct. 1930, box 7, JLC.

20. Cisler, letter to Lair, 16 Jan. 1931, box 7, JLC.

21. *1933 WLS Family Album*, 21, box 24, JLC.

22. *1936 WLS Family Album*, 30, box 24, JLC.

23. Lair, "Notes from the Music Library," *Stand By*, 12 Oct. 1935.

24. Lair, "A Plan for Extending the Activities of the WLS Music Department" [undated, probably 1936], box 12, JLC.

25. Lair, "A Plan for Extending the Activities."

26. Lair, "Proposed Plan for Making Certain Musical Compositions from the WLS Music Library Available to Other Radio Stations" [undated, probably 1936], box 12, JLC.

27. Thomas, registered letter to Manager Station W.L.S., 17 Jan. 1934, box 7, JLC.

28. Lair, tape-recorded talk, 23 June 1973.

29. Henderson interview, 16 May 1995.

30. Lair, tape-recorded talk, 23 June 1973.

31. McCusker, "'Bury Me Beneath the Willow.'"

32. Lair interview, 15 April 1975.

33. Koehler, "Silent Singer," box 70, JLC.

34. Ledford, *Coon Creek Girl*, 10–11.

35. Yarger, "Banjo Pickin' Girl," 70–76.

36. *Stand By*, 21 Mar. 1936, 16.

37. Lair, letter to Frankie Moore, 19 Sept. 1935, box 7, JLC.

38. Lair, letter to Cousin Emmy, 12 Aug. 1937, box 7, JLC.

39. Cousin Emmy, letter to Lair, 11 Feb. 1941, and Lair, letter to Cousin Emmy, 21 Feb. 1941, both in box 19, JLC.

40. *Stand By*, 2, 9, 16, 23 Mar. 1935.

41. *Stand By*, 14, 21, 28 Mar. 1936.

42. "Flashes—Renfro Valley Folks Going on Network Program in October," *Stand By*, 14 Sept. 1935, 3.

43. "Listeners' Mike," *Stand By*, 17 Oct. 1936.

44. Sophia Germanich, "Notes from the Music Library," *Stand By*, 18 Sept. 1937, 11.

45. Lair interview, 30 April 1974.

46. Lair interview, 26 Oct. 1967.

47. Lair interview, 20 Nov. 1971.

48. Williams and Morrisey, "Constructions of Tradition."

49. Lichty, "'The Nation's Station.'"

50. Lair, "The Renfro Valley Barn Dance," prospectus for sponsors, 1939, box 16, JLC.

51. Keyes, letter to Lair, 8 June 1938, box 16, JLC.

52. Keyes, letter to Lair, 20 June 1938, box 16, JLC.

53. Keyes, letter to Lair, 29 Dec. 1938, box 16, JLC.

54. Lange, letter to Lair, 11 Aug. 1937, box 16, JLC.

55. Perry interview, 13 Aug. 1993.

56. Ibid.

57. Bufwack and Oermann, *Finding Her Voice*, 38.

58. Margaret Lillie, letter to Lair, 29 Jan. 1937, Lair, letter to Lillie, 11 Feb. 1937, Lair, letter to Lillie, 26 Aug. 1937, all in box 19, JLC.

59. Lair, letter to Neal Tomy, WJR Detroit, 28 Oct. 1938, box 7, JLC.

60. Mrs. T. A. Timmons, letter to Lair, 23 Sept. 1938, box 7, JLC.

61. Pickering, letter to Lair, 4 Feb. 1938, box 7, JLC.

62. Lunsford, printed stationary, box 7, JLC.

63. "Ohio Will Send Two Folk Groups to D.C. Festival," *Washington Post*, undated clipping, 1938.

64. "Appoint Judges for Local Folk Festival, Recordings Will Go to Library of Congress," *Cincinnati Times-Star*, 23 Mar. 1938.

65. Alan and Elizabeth Lomax, entry for 27 Mar. 1938, Journal of the Indiana Field Trip, Archive of Folk Song, Library of Congress.

66. Knott, letter to Lair, 30 Mar. 1938, box 7, JLC; "Festival," *Cincinnati Post*, 26 Mar. 1938.

67. "Kentucky Will Send Four Musical Belles to Festival," *Washington Post*, National Folk Festival special edition, 1938.

68. Lair, letter to Knott, 11 April 1938, box 7, JLC.

69. Lair, letter to Knott, 13 April 1938, box 7, JLC.

70. Lair, letter to Knott, 11 April 1938, box 7, JLC.

71. Lair interview, 30 April 1974.

72. Pickering, letter to Green, 24 Nov. 1943, PGC.

73. Ledford, *Coon Creek Girl*, 24; Perry talking tape, 30 May 1994.

74. Lair interview, 30 April 1974.

75. Kirk, *Music at the White House*, 242–45; Lair interview, 30 April 1974; Perry interview, 13 Aug. 1993; Ledford, *Coon Creek Girl*, 24–25.

76. White House program, 8 June 1939, box 5, JLC.

77. Yarger, "Banjo Pickin' Girl," 110. Yarger notes that "Buffalo Gals" was not actually performed at the concert.

78. Eva Travis, letter to Lair, 25 Mar. 1939, box 7, JLC.

79. Lee Thomas, letter to Lair, 10 Feb. 1939, box 7, JLC.

80. Perry interview, 13 Aug. 1993.

81. Keyes, letter to Lair, 8 June 1938, box 16, JLC.

82. Keyes, letter to Lair, 20 June 1938, box 16, JLC.

83. Lair interview, 26 Oct. 1967.

84. Keyes, letter to Lair, 1 Sept. 1938, box 16, JLC.

85. Paul Kennedy, "Guitars Throb Thunder as War Wages along Hillbilly Front," *Cincinnati Post*, 29 Sept. 1938, 22.

86. Keyes, letter to Lair, 1 Sept. 1938, box 16, JLC.

87. Lair, "The Renfro Valley Barn Dance" (presentation sent to Mr. Widdifield), box 16, JLC.

88. *Renfro Valley Keepsake*, 1941, box 23, JLC.

89. Lair, "The Renfro Valley Barn Dance" (presentation sent to Mr. Widdifield), box 16, JLC.

90. Lair, letter to Keyes, 23 Sept. 1940, box 16, JLC.

91. Harry VanNoy, letter to Lair, 22 Jan. 1941, box 7, JLC.

92. Lair, letter to Keyes, undated fragment, box 16, JLC.

93. Lair interview, 26 Oct. 1967.

Chapter 4: Tooting the Horn: The Heyday of the National Folk Festival *and* Renfro Valley Barn Dance

1. Knott, manuscript fragment, ca. 1938, KFC1/D1/F62, SGKC.

2. Knott interview, 6 Mar. 1976.

3. "D.C. Leaders Accept Places on Folk Festival Committee," *Washington Post*, undated [1941], clipping from SGKC.

4. Tom Zito, "The Festival's Folk," *Washington Post*, 25 Aug. 1971.

5. Anderson, *The Daughters*, ch. 5.

6. Ibid., 133.

7. Ibid., 115.

8. Knott, "The National Folk Festival—Its Problems and Reasons."

9. Becker, *Selling Tradition*, 25.

10. Knott, "The National Folk Festival after Twelve Years," 83.

11. "Folk Festival to Draw upon Maryland Lore," *Washington Post*, 20 Feb. 1938.

12. "Field Worker," letter to Sanderson, 7 Feb. 1938, KFC2/D3/F5, SGKC.

13. Knott, letter to Sanderson, undated, NFFC.

14. Knott, "The National Folk Festival after Twelve Years," 88.

15. Knott, letter to Clinton P. Anderson, 3 May 1939, KFC2/D2/F18, SGKC.

16. Glen, *Highlander*, 66.

17. Knott, letter to A. J. Campbell, 26 Mar. 1940, KFC1/D1/F64, SGKC.

18. Pickering, letter to Green, 13 May 1940, PGC.

19. Cantwell, *When We Were Good*, 112–13.

20. Knott, letter to Botkin, 28 Sept. 1943, NFFC.

21. Pickering, letter to Botkin, 9 Sept. 1943, NFFC.

22. Botkin, "The Function of a Folk Festival," *Washington Post* [1939], unprocessed material, KFC1 D4, SGKC.

23. Knott, letter to Green, undated, PGC. The letter was written on stationery from the Seventh National Folk Festival and therefore probably dates from spring 1940.

24. Knott, letter to Green, 1939, PGC.

25. "Folk Festival Hailed as Spur to Scholars," *Washington Post* [1941], KFC1/D1/F66, SGKC.

26. Knott, "Some Questions which Pester Me! What Are Yours? Send a List," NFFC.

27. *Washington Post*, 17 Mar. 1941.

28. Knott, "Chart of NFFs in Eighteen Locations," unprocessed materials, SGKC.

29. Knott, "Cultures of Many Lands to Be Represented at National Folk Festival," *Washington Post*, 22 Mar. 1942.

30. Carl Albert, "An Experience in Cultural Relations," reprinted in manuscript from the "Reconstructionist," KFC1/D1/F69, SGKC.

31. Knott, radio broadcast interview with Mary Margaret McBride, 1 May 1942, Motion Picture, Broadcasting and Recorded Sound Division, Library of Congress.

32. Knott, "Chart of NFFs in Eighteen Locations," unprocessed materials, SGKC.

33. John Martin, "Folk Festival Draws Twenty-two Thousand to Garden," *New York Times*, 12 May 1942, 16.

34. Alessandroni, letter to Sanderson, 12 Jan. 1943, NFFC.

35. Laura Lee, "Folk Festival Here Is Expected to Be a Symbol of Unity," *Philadelphia Bulletin*, 3 May 1943.

36. Knott, "The National Folk Festival after Twelve Years," 85.

37. Botkin, memo "Re: Project for Duplicating Recordings of the National Folk Festival," 2 Sept. 1943, NFFC.

38. Botkin, letter to Knott, 2 Sept. 1943, Pickering, letter to Botkin, 9 Sept. 1943, Knott, letter to Botkin, 28 Sept. 1943, Botkin, memo, 30 Sept. 1943, Pickering, letter to Botkin, 2 Dec. 1943, Botkin, letter to Pickering, 7 Dec. 1943, and Pickering, letter to Botkin, 22 Jan. 1944, all NFFC.

39. Laura Lee, "Folk Festival Here Is Expected to Be a Symbol of Unity," *Philadelphia Bulletin*, 3 May 1943.

40. Pickering, letter to Botkin, 26 Dec. 1944, NFFC.

41. Knott, letter to Botkin, 15 Feb. 1945, NFFC.

42. Knott, "Chart of NFFs in Eighteen Locations," unprocessed materials, SGKC.

43. National Folk Festival Newsletter 1944, NFFC.

44. Knott, manuscript fragment, KFC1/D1/F71, SGKC.

45. Urner interview, 1 Mar. 1995.

46. Knott, manuscript fragment, KFC1/D1/F71, SGKC.

47. Knott, "Feet That Dance and Hearts That Sing."

48. Knott, *Folk Festival Handbook* (Philadelphia: Evening Bulletin, 1945), KFC1 D5, SGKC.

49. Knott, "The National Folk Festival after Twelve Years," 83, 86.

50. Knott, "The National Folk Festival—Its Problems and Reasons," 123.

51. Knott, "The National Folk Festival after Twelve Years," 90.

52. "Historical and Industrial Review of Rockcastle County Commemorating the Opening of Renfro Valley," supplement to the *Mount Vernon Signal*, 30 Nov. 1939.

53. Listener Correspondence 1940–41, and Gregory, "'I'm So Anxious to See Renfro Valley,'" both in box 70, JLC.

54. Ibid.

55. Byrd interview, 14 Feb. 1997.

56. Ibid.

57. Bray interview, 14 April 1995.

58. Bray interview, 22 May 1997.

59. Bray interview, 14 April 1995.

60. Lair, letter to Keyes, 23 Sept. 1940, box 16, JLC.

61. Rice, "Renfro Valley on the Radio 1937–1941," 18.

62. Scripts, Monday night show, 5, 19 Aug., 9 Sept. 1940, box 41, JLC.

63. Homer and Jethro, "From Moonshine to Martinis," 4–5.

64. Lair, letter to Keyes, 14 Feb. 1941, box 16, JLC.

65. Smith interview, 3 Mar. 1995.

66. Lair, letter to M. L. Stover, 18 Jan. 1941, box 7, JLC.

67. O. A. Brock, letter to Keyes, 3 Mar. 1941, box 16, JLC.

68. McCluskey, letter to Lair, 20 Jan. 1941, box 12, JLC.

69. E. G. Bentley, letter to Lair, 12 Dec. 1940, box 7, JLC.

70. Lair, letter to Keyes, 12 Feb. 1941, box 16, JLC.

71. Kurtze, letter to Lair, 14 Sept. 1939, and Lair, letter to Kurtze, 18 Sept. 1939, both in box 1, JLC.

72. Kurtze, letter to Lair, 24 July 1940, and Lair, letter to Kurtze, 21 Aug. 1940, both in box 7, JLC.

73. Kurtze, letter to Lair, 16 Sept. 1940, and Lair, letter to Kurtze, 7 Oct. 1940, both in box 7, JLC.

74. Wolfe, *A Good-Natured Riot*, 60, 77–78.

75. Kettlewell, letter to Lair, 8 Sept. 1939, box 16, JLC.

76. Lair, letter to Keyes, 14 Feb. 1941, box 16, JLC.

77. Lair, letter to Kurtze, 7 Oct. 1940, box 7, JLC.

78. Rice, "Renfro Valley on the Radio, 1937–1941," 22–23.

79. Griffin interview, 1 Mar. 1995.

80. Martin interview, 16 May 1995.

81. Clark interview, 18 May 1995.

82. Rice, "Renfro Valley on the Radio, 1937–1941," 23.

83. Helen Marie Strain, letter to John Lair, 11 Feb. 1941, box 70, JLC.

84. Mr. and Mrs. Robert Wright, letter to John Lair, 10 Feb. 1941, box 70, JLC.

85. Rena Niles, letter to John Lair, 4 Aug. 1941, box 7, JLC.

86. Smith interview, 3 Mar. 1995.

87. Jack Ryan, "Minstrels . . . in the Mountains," *Highway Traveler* 19 (Oct.–Nov. 1946): 28–29, 34.

88. "Renfro Valley Festival," *Louisville Courier-Journal*, 28 April 1946.

89. *Renfro Valley Bugle*, Dec. 1947.

90. Clark interview, 18 May 1995.

91. Clark interview, 5 Dec. 1985.

92. J. Richardson, letter to Lair, 26 April 1941, box 16, JLC.

93. Keyes, letter to Lair, 10 Mar. 1942, box 16, JLC.

94. Lair, letter to Keyes, 18 Mar. 1942, box 16, JLC.

95. Lair, letter to Si and Fannie Otis, 7 Feb. 1942, box 19, JLC.

96. Malone, *Country Music, U.S.A*, 18.

97. Grantham, letter to Lair, 10 Oct. 1943, box 71, JLC.

98. Cobb, letter to Lair, 2 Nov. 1943, box 24, JLC.

99. Martin interview, 16 May 1995.

100. Baxter, "John Lair House and Stables"; Baxter, "Structures, Images and Words: John Lair as Architect."

101. Williams and Morrisey, "Constructions of Tradition," 166.

102. Henderson interview, 22 May 1997.

103. Smith interview, 25 Oct. 1996.

104. Ibid.

Chapter 5: The Changing Scene

1. Mary Bryant, "Folk Dancers Back with Song, Color," *St. Louis Star-Times,* 12 April 1950.

2. Knott interview, 6 Mar. 1976.

3. Urner interview, 1 Mar. 1995.

4. Dodge interview, 29 July 1996.

5. Knott interview, 6 Mar. 1976.

6. Knott, "Chart of NFFs in Eighteen Locations," unprocessed material, SGKC; Knott, manuscript fragment, KFC1/D1/F73, SGKC.

7. Program, Twelfth Annual National Folk Festival, 22–26 May 1946, KFC1/D1/F73, SGKC.

8. Knott, manuscript fragment, KFC1/D1/F73, SGKC.

9. Mary Bryant, "Folk Dancers Back with Song, Color," *St. Louis Star-Times,* 12 April 1950.

10. Program, Thirteenth Annual National Folk Festival, 21–24 May 1947, KFC1/D1/F74, SGKC.

11. Knott interview, 6 Mar. 1976.

12. Knott, letter to Green, 1952, PGC.

13. Pickering, letter to Green, 1954, PGC.

14. Knott, letter to Chris [Sanderson?], summer 1955, NCTA.

15. Knott interview, 6 Mar. 1976.

16. McDermott, letter to Mackenzie, 22 Feb. 1954, NCTA.

17. Bascom, letter to McDermott, 3 Mar. 1954, Kurath, letter to McDermott, 23 Feb. 1954, and Dorson, letter to McDermott, 24 Feb. 1954, all in NCTA; Dorson, "Folk Arts," 363.

18. Baron, "Postwar Public Folklore and the Professionalization of Folklore Studies"; Thompson, *Four Symposia on Folklore.*

19. Leach, letter to McDermott, 17 Nov. 1953, NCTA.

20. 1954 conference correspondence, NCTA.

21. Program of the Folklore Conference of the National Folk Festival Association, 27–28 April 1955, Missouri Historical Society.

22. Knott, Report of Meeting of the American Folklore Society, attached to letter to Dr. Lawrence G. Derthick and Members of NFFA Executive Board, [early 1960s], KFC2/D1/F28, SGKC.

23. McDermott, letter to Mackenzie, 22 Feb. 1954; Mackenzie, letter to McDermott, 5 Mar. 1954, NCTA.

24. Knott, letter to Chris [Sanderson?], undated, NCTA.

25. Seeger interview, 30 Aug. 1995.

26. Ibid.

27. "Folk Festival Opens before Young Audience," *St. Louis Globe-Democrat,* 14 April 1955.

28. "Pete Seeger Will Return as Folk Festival Balladeer," *St. Louis Globe-Democrat,* 4 April 1955.

29. Seeger interview, 30 Aug. 1995. Edwin Edward Willis, who represented his congressional district in Louisiana from 1949 to 1969, was one of three representatives who questioned Seeger on 18 August 1955.

30. Ibid.

31. Knott, letter to McDermott, undated; McDermott, letter to Knott, 29 Mar. 1957, NCTA.

32. Seeger interview, 30 Aug. 1995.

33. *Viltis* 7 (May–June 1949).

34. Knott, letter to "Festival Friends," undated [spring 1951], KFC1/D1/F78, SGKC.

35. Knott, letter to Maude Longwell, 25 June 1956, KFC2/D2/F32, SGKC.

36. Karpeles, letter to Knott, 27 Jan. 1956, KFC2/D2/F53, SGKC.

37. Knott, manuscript fragment, KFC2/D2 /F35, SGKC.

38. Seeger interview, 30 Aug. 1995.

39. Tate, letter to Knott, 24 June 1976, KFC2/D2/F2, SGKC.

40. Knott, letter to John and Mary Stephanie McDermott, 7 May 1957, NCTA.

41. Knott, letter to McDermott, [received 14 Feb. 1957], NCTA.

42. Austin, letter to Knott, 17 Mar. 1957, KFC2/D1/F1, SGKC.

43. Beers, letter to Knott, 27 Feb. 1957, KFC2/D1/F5, SGKC.

44. Knott, "Folksongs and Dances, U.S.A.: The Changing Scene."

45. Ibid.

46. Howard [?], letter to Knott, 6 Aug. 1961, unprocessed material, SGKC.

47. "Renfro Valley to Have Record Factory," *Renfro Valley Bugle,* 15 Dec. 1946, 1, 4.

48. Lair, letter to W. M. Ellsworth, 25 Aug. 1947, box 13, JLC.

49. Lair, letter to Keyes, 27 April 1948, box 13, JLC.

50. Lair, letter to Keyes, 20 Nov. 1948, box 13, JLC.

51. Lair, letter to Keyes, 13 Dec. 1949, box 16, JLC.

52. Lair, letter to Chick Kimball, 8 June 1948, box 8, JLC.

53. Lair, letter to Jake Salisbury, 20 Sept. 1948, box 8, JLC.

54. Lair, letter to Pleaz Mobley, 26 Aug. 1948, box 8, JLC.

55. Lair, letter to Reconstruction Finance Corporation, 13 Nov. 1948, box 8, JLC.

56. Lair, letter to Jones, 16 Dec. 1948, and John Lair, letter to Englehard, 16 Dec. 1948, both in box 16, JLC.

57. Lair, letter to Al Stass, 23 Dec. 1948, box 8, JLC.

58. Stamper, *It All Happened in Renfro Valley,* 33–34.

59. Keyes, letter to Lair, 23 Mar. 1949, box 16, JLC.

60. King interview, 27 Feb. 1996.

61. Martin interview, 16 May 1995.

62. Lair, letter to Keyes, 23 May 1949, box 16, JLC.

63. Keyes, letter to Lair, 19 Dec. 1949, box 16, JLC.

64. Keyes, letter to Lair, 16 Feb. 1950, box 8, JLC.

65. Lair, letter to George Patterson, 25 May 1949, box 8, JLC.

66. Lair to William E. Jones, 26 Nov. 1949, box 16, JLC.

67. Lair, letter to Glenn Snyder, 29 Dec. 1949, box 16, JLC.

68. Buttram, letter to Lair, 27 Nov. 1950, box 8, JLC.

69. Hargis, letter to Lair, 10 May 1950, box 8, JLC.

70. Lynne, letter to Lair, 3 Nov. 1949, box 8, JLC.

71. Lair, letter to Howe, 20 April 1950, box 8, JLC.

72. Lair, letter to Howe, 19 Jan. 1950, box 8, JLC.

73. Tom Wood Scrapbook, 9 May 1994, box 2, JLC.

74. Renfro Valley Presentation Materials, 1950, box 16, JLC.

75. "Suggested Program Titles," box 16, JLC.

76. CBS promo for Renfro Valley programs, 21 Dec. 1950, box 16, JLC.

77. Behrens, letter to Lair, 2 Aug. 1949, box 19, JLC.

78. Lair to Behrens, 18 Nov. 1950, box 19, JLC.

79. Edmund B. Abbott, letter to Lair, 29 Mar. 1951, box 17, JLC.

80. Lair to Carl W. Stursberg Jr., 30 April 1953, box 18, JLC.

81. Wood, "Summary Report on the Office and Radio Operation of Renfro Valley," 10 May 1951, box 17, JLC.

82. Lair, letter to Phil Bottfeld, 30 Jan. 1951, box 17, JLC.

83. Wood, "Summary Report on the Office and Radio Operation of Renfro Valley," 10 May 1951, box 17, JLC.

84. John Lair, letter to Tom McDonnell, 21 April 1952, box 17, JLC.

85. Thomas M. McDonnell, letter to Lair, 14 May 1952, box 17, JLC.

86. Wood, "Summary Report on the Office and Radio Operation of Renfro Valley," 10 May 1951, box 17, JLC.

87. Wood, memo to Lair, 4 Sept. 1951, box 17, JLC.

88. Lair, letter to Carl W. Stursberg Jr., 30 April 1952, box 17, JLC.

89. Lair, letter to Frank Edwards, 13 Mar. 1948, box 8, JLC.

90. Wood, "Summary Report on the Office and Radio Operation of Renfro Valley," 10 May 1951, box 17, JLC.

91. John DeMott, letter to Barbara DeMott, 11 Nov. 1952, box 18, JLC.

92. Lair, to Phil Bottfeld, 24 Feb. 1951, box 17, JLC.

93. "TV Pilot Script on Darling Nellie Gray," 1953, box 14, JLC.

94. Lair, letter to Eleanor Corrigan, 13 Feb. 1951, box 17, JLC.

95. Lair, letter to Olga Edmond, 17 Sept. 1949, box 8, JLC.

96. Lair, letter to George Pullen Jackson, 16 Oct. 1951, and letter to Francis Lee Utley, 31 Oct. 1951, box 11, JLC.

97. Wood, letter to Edward A. Russell, 4 Sept. 1951, box 17, JLC.

98. M. W. Alderman, letter to Lair, 15 Feb. 1955, box 18, JLC.

99. Wood, "Summary Report on the Office and Radio Operation of Renfro Valley," 10 May 1951, box 17, JLC.

100. Tom Wood Scrapbook, 9 May 1994, box 2, JLC.

101. Lair, letter to Keyes, 3 Mar. 1955, box 18, JLC.

102. Lair, letter to Wood, 3 Mar. 1955, box 18, JLC.

103. Lair, letter to McBride, 10 May 1955, box 18, JLC.

104. Lair, letter to Keyes, 27 May 1955, box 18, JLC.

105. Lair, letter Edwin W. Ebel, 1 July 1955, box 18, JLC.

106. Lair, letter to Hargis, 4 Mar. 1955, box 18, JLC.

107. CBS, letter to Lair, 15 June 1955, box 18, JLC.

108. Bidwell, letter to Lair, 8 Dec. 1955, box 18, JLC.

109. Lair, letter to Bidwell, 16 July 1956, box 18, JLC.

110. Bidwell, letter to Lair, 18 July 1956, box 18, JLC.

111. Lair to Hargis, 31 July 1956, box 12, JLC.

112. Bidwell, letter to Lair, 2 Oct. 1956, box 18, JLC.

113. Lair, letter to Bidwell, 6 Oct. 1956, box 18, JLC.

114. Bidwell, letter to Lair, 10 Oct. 1956, box 18, JLC.

115. Lair, letter to Bidwell, 12 Jan. 1957, box 18, JLC.

116. Lair, letter to Dodd, 22 Jan. 1957, box 4, JLC.

117. Lair, letter to Bidwell, 12 Jan. 1957, box 18, JLC.

118. Reid H. Ray, letter to Lair, 22 Jan. 1957, box 14, JLC.

119. Lair, letter to Bidwell, 13 Feb. 1957, box 18, JLC.

120. Henderson interview, 16 May 1995.

121. Stamper, *It All Happened in Renfro Valley*, 62–76.

122. Peterson, *Creating Country Music*, ch. 12.

123. Robert Cantwell, *When We Were Good*, ch. 6.

Chapter 6: The Prima Donna of Folk

1. Knott, typewritten report to *Viltis*, 26 Oct. 1960, KFC1/D1/F86, SGKC. The original is in capital letters.

2. Ibid.

3. Knott, letter to Lawrence J. Derthick, undated, KFC2/D1/F28, SGKC.

4. Knott, letter to the President, Officers, and Members of the Board of Directors, NFFA, Inc., 18 Jan. 1965, KFC1/D1/F91, SGKC.

5. Silber, letter to Knott, 25 Jan. 1963, KFC2/D3/F48, SGKC.

6. Bob Karlman, "Folk Singing: A Deep Thing That Gets into the Soul," *Kentucky Enquirer*, 25 Mar. 1964.

7. Seeger interview, 30 Aug. 1995.

8. Sommer, letter to Knott, 28 Aug. 1963, KFC2/D1/F127, SGKC.

9. Knott, letter to Leach, 18 Aug. 1961, KFC2/D1/F73, SGKC.

10. Coffin, letter to Knott, 12 Dec. 1963, KFC2/D2/F3, SGKC.

11. Leach, letter to Knott, 9 Dec. 1966, KFC2/D1/F73, SGKC.

12. "Council of Performing Arts Surveying Kentucky Folklore," *Lexington Herald*, 27 Nov. 1962.

13. Knott interview, 6 Mar. 1976.

14. Knott, letter to McLain, Lair, James, Edna and Jean Ritchie, and Thomas, 21 Mar. 1963, unprocessed material, KFC1/D4, SGKC.

15. Wilgus, letter to Knott, 21 Feb. 1963, KFC2/D2/F15, SGKC.

16. Lair, letter to Knott, 23 April 1963, box 9, JLC.

17. Knott, letter to Lair, undated [1963], box 9, JLC.

18. Lair, letter to Knott, 23 April 1963, box 9, JLC.

19. Knott, draft of letter to members of the Board and National Advisory Council, NFFA, undated [late 1963 or early 1964], KFC1/D1/F89, SGKC.

20. Knott, letter to Charlotte Horowitz "and the Gang," [1963], KFC2/D2/F15, SGKC.

21. Knott, letter to the President, Officers, and Members of the Board of Directors, NFFA, Inc., 18 Jan. 1965, KFC1/D1/F91, SGKC.

22. Knott interview, 6 Mar. 1976.

23. Hussey, letter to "Velma," undated [1963 or 1964], unprocessed material, SGKC.

24. Knott interview, 6 Mar. 1976.

25. Biddle, *Our Government and the Arts*, 30.

26. Knott, letter to Frank G. Dickey, Bill Jansen, and Dr. Seay, 10 June 1963, KFC2/D1/F28, SGKC.

27. Knott, "Search for Folk Dancers, Singers, Tale Tellers, Customs—Ohio, Kentucky," [1964], KFC1/D1/F89, SGKC.

28. Hussey, letter to Editor of the *St. Petersburg Independent*, 5 Nov. 1964, KFC1/D1/F92, SGKC.

29. James Lewis, "Our Folk Heritage: How We're Preserving It," *St. Petersburg Times*, 4 April 1965.

30. "Folk Festival Communist Tie Held Untrue," undated clipping, KFC1/D1/F91, SGKC.

31. Gray, letter to Hussey, 4 Nov. 1964, KFC1/D1/F92, SGKC.

32. Hussey, letter to Gray, 9 Nov. 1964, KFC1/D1/F92, SGKC.

33. Gray, letter to Hussey, 9 Dec. 1964, KFC1/D1/F92, SGKC.

34. Gray, letter to Hussey, 10 Feb. 1965, KFC1/D1/F92, SGKC.

35. Hussey, letter to Gray, 8 Feb. 1965, KFC1/D1/F92, SGKC.

36. Knott, letter to the President, Officers, and Members of the Board of Directors, NFFA, Inc., 18 Jan. 1965, KFC1/D1/F91, SGKC.

37. Knott, "Chart of Nffs in Eighteen Locations," unprocessed material, SGKC.

38. Hussey, letter to Gray, 8 Aug. 1965, KFC1/D1/F92, SGKC.

39. Knott, letter to Coggan, dated "6th" [month unknown, 1965], Coggan Donation, SGKC.

40. Knott, letter to Coggan, dated "19th" [unknown month, 1965], Coggan Donation, SGKC.

41. Knott, letter to Coggan, no date, Coggan Donation, SGKC.

42. Knott, letter to Coggan, no date, Coggan Donation, SGKC.

43. Knott, letter to Coggan, dated "28th" [on Twenty-eighth Annual National Folk Festival letterhead], Coggan Donation, SGKC.

44. Knott, letter to Coggan, undated, Coggan Donation, SGKC.

45. Knott, letter to Coggan, undated [1965], Coggan Donation, SGKC.

46. Knott, letter to Coggan, undated [probably 1968], Coggan Donation, SGKC.

47. Knott, letter to Coggan, undated [1965], Coggan Donation, SGKC.

48. Knott, postcard to Coggan, postmarked 19 May 1965, Coggan Donation, SGKC.

49. Knott, letter to Coggan, undated [1965], Coggan Donation, SGKC.

50. Knott, letter to Dorson and Richmond, 7 May 1965, Coggan Donation, SGKC.

51. Knott, letter to Coggan, undated, Coggan Donation, SGKC.

52. Knott, letter to Coggan, undated, Coggan Donation, SGKC.

53. Knott, letter to Arthur Campa, 28 July 1967, SGKC.

54. Knott, "Part of the Proposed Program (almost Definite) Thirtieth Annual National Folk Festival, Louisville, Kentucky," KFC1/D1/F96, SGKC.

55. Place, letter to Mrs. Astrid J. Highfield, 28 July 1967, KFC2/D1/F106, SGKC.

56. Wallace interview, 27 Feb. 1995.

57. Campa, letter to Place, 29 Nov. 1967, KFC2/D1/F106, SGKC.

58. Hickerson interview, 24 Feb. 1995.

59. Wallace interview, 27 Feb. 1995.

60. Perdue interview, 2 Mar. 1995. The specific incident recalled was an incident where Maybelle Carter was booed and hissed by Joan Baez fans.

61. Gerald E. Parsons Jr. and Chuck Perdue originally came up with the "folklife" designation for the Smithsonian Festival in order to distinguish it from the National Folk Festival. Perdue, letter to Michael Ann Williams, 9 Feb. 2005.

62. Botkin, "Proposal for a Panel on NFFA Policies and Activities of the NFFA at the Thirty-first Annual Folk Festival, Milwaukee, July 19–21, 1968," no date, KFC1/D2/F97, SGKC.

63. Program of the Thirty-first National Folk Festival, KFC1/D1/F98, SGKC.

64. Knott, letter to National Folk Festival participants, 25 July 1968, KFC1/D1/F97, SGKC.

65. Knott, "The Thirty-second National Folk Festival in Retrospect," no date, KFC1/D1/F99, SGKC.

66. Humphreys, letter to Sarah Knott, 18 Nov. 1969, KFC1/D1/F100, SGKC.

67. Knott, memo to Board of Directors, NFFA, no date, KFC1/D1/F100, SGKC.

68. Knott, "The Thirty-second National Folk Festival in Retrospect," no date, KFC1/D1/F99, SGKC.

69. Wallace interview, 27 Feb. 1995.

70. Knott, letter to Campa, 7 Dec. 1971, KFC2/D1/F16, SGKC.

71. Knott, memo to Leonard Roberts, Jack Batham, and John Whisman, 9 Dec. 1969, KFC1/D1/F99, SGKC.

72. Whisman, letter to Knott, 18 June 1971, KFC2/D1/F143, SGKC.

73. Knott, letter to Coggan, 21 July 1971, Coggan Donation, SGKC.

74. Knott, letter to Coggan, undated [summer 1971], Coggan Donation, SGKC.

75. Dodge interview, 29 July 1996.

76. Jaderborg, letter to Bernache, 29 Oct. 1971, KFC2/D1/F63, SGKC.

77. Jaderborg, letter to Knott, undated, KFC2/D1/F63, SGKC.

78. Calkins, letter to Knott, 15 Jan. 1972, Unprocessed Subject Files [Wisconsin], SGKC.

79. Jaderborg, letter to Leo Bernache, 29 Oct. 1971, KFC2/D1/F63, SGKC.

80. Pat Parmelee, letter to Knott, 12 Aug. 1972, KFC2/D1/F101, SGKC.

81. Wallace interview, 27 Feb. 1995.

82. Knott, letter to Goldstein, 27 Sept. 1971, KFC2/D1/F43, SGKC.

83. Hand, letter to Knott, 21 Nov. 1973, KFC2/D1/F51, SGKC.

84. Jansen, letter to Knott, 8 Mar. 1977, KFC2/D1/F65, SGKC.

85. Wallace interview, 27 Feb. 1995.

86. Knott, letter to Coggan, 21 July 1971, Coggan Donation, SGKC.

87. Knott, letter to Campa, 7 Dec. 1971, KFC2/D1/F16, SGKC. The deal offered to Knott turned out to be $5,000 plus $1,000 in expenses.

88. Knott interview, 1971.

89. Dodge interview, 29 July 1996.

90. Knott, letter to Coggan, July 1975, Coggan Donation, SGKC.

91. Knott, letter to Campa, 7 Dec. 1971, KFC2/D1/F16, SGKC.

92. Wallace interview, 28 Feb. 1995.

93. Knott, letter to Willard Rhodes, [1973], KFC2/D1/F113, SGKC.

94. Whisman, letter to Knott, 18 June 1971, KFC2/D1/F143, SGKC.

95. Knott, letter to Humphrey[s], 8 June 1972, KFC2/D1/F49, SGKC.

96. Knott, letter to Loyal Jones, Ethel Capps and Raymond McLain, 13 Aug. 1973, KFC2/D1/F62, SGKC.

97. Perdue interview, 2 Mar. 1995.

98. Knott, letter to Jansen, 12 Aug. 1977, KFC2/D1/F65, SGKC.

99. Knott, handwritten comments to Roberts on typed copy of the introduction from the Forty-first National Folk Festival Program, [1979], KFC1/D1/F116, SGKC.

100. Knott, letter to Coggan, 31 Jan. 1977, Coggan Donation, SGKC.

101. Urner interview, 1 Mar. 1995.

102. Knott, letter to Coggan, [1978], Coggan Donation, SGKC.

103. Dodge interview, 29 July 1996.

104. Knott interview, 6 Mar. 1976.

105. Dodge interview, 29 July 1996.

106. Gladys Knott, form letter to former friends and colleagues of Sarah Gertrude Knott, 19 Mar. 1985, letter in possession of Yvonne Dodge.

Chapter 7: *Things Have Changed in Renfro Valley*

1. *Renfro Valley Keepsake Commemorating the Twenty-fifth Anniversary and Homecoming of the Renfro Valley Folks at the 1962 Kentucky State Fair,* box 23, JLC.

2. Montana, letter to Lair, 29 Mar. 1967, box 19, JLC.

3. Lair, letter to Freedom Baptist Church, Fairview Baptist Church, and Roundstone Baptist Church, 1966, box 9, JLC.

4. "Folk Music Festival Installed," *Renfro Valley Bugle* 11 (May 1958).

5. Jones, *Minstrel of the Appalachians,* 84–85, 96–97.

6. Lomax, letter to Lair, 27 Mar. 1960, and Lair, letter to Lomax, no date, both in box 10, JLC.

7. Leventhal, letter to Lair, 19 May 1962, and Lair, letter to Leventhal, 23 May 1962, both in box 9, JLC.

8. Mrs. Earl [Louise] Scruggs, letter to Lair, 3 Dec. 1963, box 9, JLC.

9. Lair, letter to Hal Smith, 21 Nov. 1967, box 14, JLC.

10. Starkey, letter to Lair, 5 Feb. 1965, box 9, JLC.

11. *Renfro Valley Bugle,* Jan., April, June, Oct. 1962, Oct. 1964; see also Stamper, *It All Happened in Renfro Valley,* 82.

12. Photographs in the Lair Collection show John Lair and George Biggar at the American Folk Song Festival in the mid-1930s.

13. Thomas, letter to Lair, 17 April 1962, box 9, JLC.

14. Knott, letter to Lair and Edith James, 10 Oct. [1962], and Lair, draft of letter to Knott, undated, both in box 9, JLC.

15. Yarger, "Banjo Pickin' Girl," 159–72.

16. Gaskin interview, 5 Dec. 1985.

17. Holden, letter to Lair, 8 Aug. 1963, and Lair, letter to Holden, 26 Aug. 1963, both in box 9, JLC.

18. John and Barbara DeMott, letter to Lair, 2 Feb. 1965, and Lair, draft of letter to John and Barbara DeMott, undated, both in box 9, JLC.

19. Lair, letter to Jack Schilla, 12 May 1967, box 9, JLC.

20. Richards, letter to Lair, 25 Feb. 1965, and Lair, letter to Richards, 1 Mar. 1965, both in box 9, JLC.

21. Lair, draft of response to letter from Ford dated 16 June 1964, box 9, JLC.

22. Lair interview, 26 Oct. 1967.

23. Lair, letter to Richards, 1 Mar. 1965, box 9, JLC.

24. Henderson interview, 22 May 1997.

25. Lair, letter to Joseph M. McDaniels Jr., 31 Nov. 1964, box 18, JLC.

26. Lair, letter to Duell, Sloane and Pearce, 26 July 1960, box 11, JLC.

27. Lair, letter to Miller, 10 Jan. 1962, box 9, JLC.

28. Lair, letter to Dean, 25 Sept. 1965, box 9, JLC.

29. "Renfro Valley Movie," *Renfro Valley Bugle*, July 1965, 1.

30. "Gala World Premiere!" advertisement, *Louisville Courier-Journal*, 20 July 1966.

31. Lair interview, 26 Oct. 1967.

32. Lair, letter to Chet Atkins, 9 Dec. 1963, box 9, JLC.

33. John Lair, Notes on Nashville Trip—Thurs., 9 Sept 1965, box 13, JLC.

34. Smith, letter to Lair, 14 Sept. 1965, box 14, JLC.

35. Lair, letter to A. O. Stinson, 11 Oct. 1965, box 14, JLC.

36. Smith, letter to Lair, 8 Nov. 1966, box 14, JLC.

37. Lair, letter to Arthur Stanish, 26 Nov. 1966, box 9, JLC.

38. Lair, letter to Smith, 20 April 1966, box 14, JLC.

39. Smith, letter to Lair, 15 July 1966, Lair, letter to Smith, 19 July 1966, and Smith, letter to Lair, 22 July 1966, all in box 14, JLC.

40. Stamper, *It All Happened in Renfro Valley*, 99–100.

41. Smith, letter to Lair, 15 May 1967, box 14, JLC.

42. Lair, letter to Smith, 1 Nov. 1966, box 14, JLC.

43. Lair, letter to Smith, 11 Aug. 1967, box 14, JLC.

44. Lair, letter to Smith, 8 July 1968, box 14, JLC.

45. Albert Carson, "Music Publisher Buys Renfro Valley," *Tennessean*, 4 Aug. 1968.

46. Barbara Smith interview, 25 Oct. 1996.

47. Henderson interview, 6 Dec. 1985.

48. Lair interview, 15 April 1975.

49. Lair interview, 30 April 1974.

50. Henderson interview, 22 May 1997.

51. Lair interview, 15 April 1975.

52. Lair, tape-recorded talk, 23 June 1973.

53. Knott, letter to Charles Helman, 20 Nov. 1972, KFC2/D2/F59, SGKC.

54. Unprocessed material, SGKC.

55. Lair interview, 20 Nov. 1971.

56. Lair interview, 15 April 1975.

57. Lair interview, 20 Nov. 1971.

58. Smith interview, 25 Oct. 1996.

59. Henderson interview, 6 Dec. 1985.

60. Stamper, *It All Happened in Renfro Valley*, 125.

61. Lair interview, 30 April 1974.

62. Smith interview, 25 Oct. 1996.

63. Stamper, *It All Happened at Renfro Valley*, 133–34.

64. Pennington interview, 4 Dec. 1985.

65. Smith interview, 6 Dec. 1985.

66. Lair interview, 30 April 1974.

67. Pennington interview, 4 Dec. 1985.

68. Bob Cooper, "Bidding Goodbye, Lair Will Auction Off Items Collected at Renfro Valley," *Louisville Courier-Journal*, 26 Sept. 1975, A10.

69. Griffin interview, 1 Mar. 1995.

70. Ibid.

71. Smith interview, 25 Oct. 1996.

72. Ibid.

73. Stamper, *It All Happened in Renfro Valley*, 139.

74. Smith interview, 6 Dec. 1985.

75. Travis, "To John Lair on His Eighty-seventh Birthday," John Lair microfiche, CMF.

76. Cisler, letter to Lair, 28 June 1981, box 9, JLC.

77. Philpot, letter to Jo Walker, 30 April 1976, Lair microfiche, CMF.

78. Smith interview, 3 Mar. 1995.

79. Lair, tape-recorded talk, 23 June 1973.

80. Smith interview, 6 Dec. 1985.

81. Henderson interview, 16 May 1995.

82. Henderson interview, 22 May 1997.

83. Simunick interview, 17 Jan. 1997.

84. Rhoads interview, 15 July 1986.

85. King interview, 27 Feb. 1996.

86. Griffin interview, 1 Mar. 1995.

87. Lair interview, 20 Nov. 1971.

88. Smith interview, 6 Dec. 1985.

Chapter 8: Staging Tradition

1. Rennick interview, 21 July 1995.

2. Knott, letter to Silber, 5 Oct. 1971, KFC2/D3/F48, SGKC.

3. Malone, "Appalachian Music and American Popular Culture," 464.

4. Lair, "High Jinks on White Top," *Stand By*, 14 Sept. 1935, 5, 11.

5. Yarger, "Banjo Pickin' Girl," 140.

6. Wolfe, *A Good-Natured Riot*, 13.

7. Lair interview, 30 April 1974.

8. Lloyd, "Whole Work, Whole Play, Whole People," 239–59.

9. Kirshenblatt-Gimblett, *Destination Culture*, 203–48.

WORKS CITED

Archival Collections Consulted

CC   Centennial Collection, Dallas Historical Society.
CMF   Frist Archive of the Country Music Hall of Fame and Museum.
JLC   John Lair Collection, Southern Appalachian Archives, Berea College.
KOHC   Kentucky Oral History Commission, Kentucky Historical Society,
        Frankfort.
NCTA   National Council for the Traditional Arts, Silver Spring, Md.
NFFC   National Folk Festival Collection, Archive of Folk Song, Library of
        Congress.
PGC   Paul Green Collection, Southern Historical Collection, Wilson Library,
        University of North Carolina at Chapel Hill.
SGKC   Sarah Gertrude Knott Collection, Department of Library Special
        Collections, Folklife Archives, Western Kentucky University.
TCR   Texas Centennial Records, Center for American History, University of
        Texas at Austin.
TJC   Thomas Jones Collection, Special Collections, Fisk University.
UAK   Special Collections, University of Arkansas.

Interviews Cited

Virginia Sutton Bray, tape-recorded interview with David Baxter, Renfro Valley,
    Ky., 14 April 1995. KOHC.
———, tape-recorded interview with Larry Morrisey, Mt. Vernon, Ky., 22 May
    1997. KOHC.
Jerry Byrd, tape-recorded telephone interview with Larry Morrisey, 14 Feb. 1997.
    KOHC.
Manuel "Old Joe" Clark, tape-recorded interview with John Rumble, Berea, Ky.,
    5 Dec. 1985. CMF/KOHC.
———, tape-recorded interview with David Baxter, Berea, Ky., 18 May 1995.
    KOHC.
Holbert Davis, tape-recorded interview with Michael Ann Williams, Kevil, Ky.,
    25 June 1999. KOHC.
Yvonne Dodge, tape-recorded interview with Michael Ann Williams, Princeton,
    Ky., 29 July 1996. KOHC.
Jim Gaskin, tape-recorded interview with John Rumble, Berea, Ky., 5 Dec. 1985.
    CMF/KOHC.

Nancy Lair Griffin, tape-recorded interview with Hillary Glatt, Annandale, Virginia, 1 March 1995. KOHC.

Ann Lair Henderson, tape-recorded interview with John Rumble, Renfro Valley, Ky., 6 Dec. 1985. CMF/KOHC.

———, tape-recorded interview with David Baxter, Renfro Valley, Ky., 16 May 1995. KOHC.

———, tape-recorded interview with Larry Morrisey, Mt. Vernon, Ky., 22 May 1997. KOHC.

Joe Hickerson, tape-recorded interview with Hillary Glatt, Washington, D.C., 24 Feb. 1995. KOHC.

Virginia Lee King, tape-recorded telephone interview with Larry Morrisey, 27 Feb. 1996. KOHC.

Sarah Gertrude Knott, radio broadcast interview with Mary Margaret McBride, May 1, 1942, Motion Picture, Broadcasting and Recorded Sound Division, Library of Congress.

———, tape-recorded interview with Shirley Shanahan, for the United States Information Agency, 1971. SGKC.

———, tape-recorded interview with Patty Harrington, Princeton, Ky., 6 Mar. 1976. Transcript in possession of Charles Perdue.

John Lair, tape-recorded interview with Reuben Powell, Renfro Valley, Ky., 26 Oct. 1967. Special Collections, Berea College.

———, tape-recorded interview with Loyal Jones [and Bradley Kincaid], Renfro Valley, Ky., 20 Nov. 1971. Special Collections, Berea College.

———, tape-recorded talk to Loyal Jones's class, Renfro Valley, Ky., 23 June 1973. Special Collections, Berea College.

———, tape-recorded interview with Loyal Jones, Renfro Valley, Ky., 30 April 1974. Special Collections, Berea College.

———, tape-recorded interview with Loyal Jones, Renfro Valley Ky., 15 April 1975. Special Collections, Berea College

Linda Martin and Emory Martin, tape-recorded interview with David Baxter, Mount Vernon, Ky., 16 May 1995. KOHC.

Glenn Pennington, tape-recorded interview with John Rumble, Berea, Ky., 4 Dec. 1985. CMF/KOHC.

Charles Perdue and Nancy Martin Perdue, tape-recorded interview with Hillary Glatt, Charlottesville, Va., 2 March 1995. KOHC.

Evelyn "Daisy" Lange Perry, tape-recorded interview with Lisa Yarger, Frankfort, Ind., 13 Aug. 1993. Tape in possession of Lisa Yarger.

———, talking tape made for Lisa Yarger, 30 May 1994. Tape in possession of Lisa Yarger.

Robert Rennick, tape-recorded interview with Michael Ann Williams, Prestonburg, Ky., 21 July 1995. KOHC.

Marge and Debbie Rhoads, tape-recorded interview with John Rumble, Nashville, Tenn., 15 July 1986. CMF/KOHC.

Pete Seeger, tape-recorded telephone interview with Michael Ann Williams, 30 Aug. 1995. KOHC.

Jonelle [Fisher] Simunick, tape-recorded telephone interview with Larry Morrisey, 17 Jan. 1997. KOHC.

Barbara Lair Smith, tape-recorded interview with David Baxter, Hopkinsville, Ky., 3 March 1995. KOHC.

————, tape-recorded interview with Larry Morrisey, Hopkinsville, Ky., 25 Oct. 1996. KOHC.

Gary Smith, tape-recorded interview with John Rumble, Renfro Valley, Ky., 6 Dec. 1985. CMF/KOHC.

Priscilla Urner and Don Urner, tape-recorded interview with Hillary Glatt, McLean, Va., 1 March 1995. KOHC.

Andy Wallace, tape-recorded interview with Hillary Glatt, Silver Spring, Md., 27 Feb. 1995. KOHC.

Printed Sources and Dissertations

Alexander, T. H. "The Return of the Troubadours." *The Rotarian,* April 1939.

Anderson, Pegg. *The Daughters: An Unconventional Look at America's Fan Club—the DAR.* New York: St. Martin's Press, 1974.

Avery, Laurence G., ed. *A Southern Life: Letters of Paul Green, 1916–1981.* Chapel Hill: University of North Carolina Press, 1994.

Baron, Robert. "Postwar Public Folklore and the Professionalization of Folklore Studies." In *Public Folklore,* edited by Robert Baron and Nicholas R. Spitzer, 307–37. Washington, D.C.: Smithsonian Institution Press, 1992.

Baxter, David. "John Lair House and Stables." Nomination for the National Register of Historic Places, 1995.

————. "Structures, Images and Words: John Lair as Architect." Paper for Appalachian folklife class, Western Kentucky University, April 1995.

Becker, Jane S. *Selling Tradition: Appalachia and the Construction of an American Folk, 1930–1940.* Chapel Hill: University of North Carolina Press, 1998.

Bendix, Regina. *In Search of Authenticity: The Formation of Folklore Studies.* Madison: University of Wisconsin Press, 1997.

Biddle, Livingston. *Our Government and the Arts: A Perspective from the Inside.* New York: ACAD Books, 1988.

Boyd, Valerie. *Wrapped in Rainbows: The Life of Zora Neale Hurston.* New York: Scribner, 2003.

Buchanan, Annabel Morris. "The Function of a Folk Festival." *Southern Folklore Quarterly* 1, no. 1 (1939): 29–34.

Bufwack Mary A., and Robert K. Oermann. *Finding Her Voice: The Saga of Women in Country Music.* New York: Crown Publishers, 1993.

Cantwell, Robert. *When We Were Good: The Folk Revival.* Cambridge: Harvard University Press, 1996.

Cochran, Robert. *Vance Randolph: An Ozark Life.* Urbana: University of Illinois Press, 1985.

Dorson, Richard M. "Folk Arts." *The American Peoples Encyclopedia Yearbook.* Editor-in-chief Franklin J. Meine. Chicago: Spencer Press, 1953.

Evans, James F. *Prairie Farmer and WLS: The Burridge D. Butler Years.* Urbana: University of Illinois Press, 1969.

Gillespie, Angus K. *Folklorist of the Coal Fields: George Korson's Life and Work.* University Park: Pennsylvania State University Press, 1980.

Glassberg, David. *American Historical Pageantry: The Uses of Tradition in the Early Twentieth Century.* Chapel Hill: University of North Carolina Press, 1990.

Glen, John M. *Highlander: No Ordinary School,* second edition. Knoxville: University of Tennessee Press, 1996.

Green, Archie. "The National Folk Festival Association." *John Edwards Memorial Foundation Newsletter* 11 (Spring 1975): 23–32.

Gregory, Brian. "'I'm So Anxious to See Renfro Valley': Traditional Music, Modern Architecture, and the Semiotics of Attraction at an Early Site of Auto Tourism." Paper presented at the annual meeting of the Southeast Chapter, Society of Architectural Historians, Lexington, Ky., 1999.

Hemenway, Robert E. *Zora Neale Hurston: A Literary Biography.* Urbana: University of Illinois Press, 1977.

Hirsch, Jerrold. "Cultural Pluralism and Applied Folklore: The New Deal Precedent." In *The Conservation of Culture,* edited by Burt Feintuch, 46–67. Lexington: University Press of Kentucky, 1988.

History and Families, McCracken County, Kentucky. Paducah: Turner Publishing, 1989.

Homer and Jethro. "From Moonshine to Martinis." *Journal of Country Music* 16, no. 1 (1995): 4–5.

Jones, Loyal. *Minstrel of the Appalachians: The Story of Bascom Lamar Lunsford.* Boone, N.C.: Appalachian Consortium Press, 1984.

Kaplan, Carla, ed. *Zora Neale Hurston: A Life in Letters.* New York: Doubleday, 2002.

Kirk, Elise K. *Music at the White House: A History of the American Spirit.* Urbana: University of Illinois Press, 1986.

Kirshenblatt-Gimblett, Barbara. *Destination Culture: Tourism, Museums, and Heritage.* Berkeley: University of California Press, 1998

Knott, Sarah Gertrude. "Feet That Dance and Hearts That Sing." *Recreation* 38 (Dec. 1944): 455–59, 494.

———. "Folksongs and Dances, U.S.A.: The Changing Scene." *Southern Folklore Quarterly* 25 (June, 1961): 184–91.

———. "The National Folk Festival after Twelve Years." *California Folklore Quarterly* 5 (Jan. 1946): 83–93.

———. "The National Folk Festival—Its Problems and Reasons." *Southern Folklore Quarterly* 3 (June 1939): 117–25.

Koch, Frederick H. "Making a Native Folk Drama." *Southern Folklore Quarterly* 1, no. 3 (1937): 29–33.

Lair, John. "The Renfro Valley Music Library." *1965 Country Music Who's Who* (1965): 10.

———. *Renfro Valley Then and Now.* Self-published, 1957.

Leary, Jim. "Otto Rindlisbacher and the Wisconsin Lumberjacks." Paper presented at the American Folklore Society, Oct. 1995.

Ledford, Lily May. *Coon Creek Girl.* Reprint. Berea: Berea College Appalachian Center, 1991.

Lichty, Lawrence Wilson. "'The Nation's Station': A History of Radio Station WLW." Ph.D. diss., Ohio State University, 1964.

Lloyd, Timothy. "A Brief History of the National Folk Festival." *1999 Michigan Folklife Annual.* East Lansing: Michigan State University, 1999.

———. "Whole Work, Whole Play, Whole People: Folklore and Social Therapeutics in 1920s and 1930s America." *Journal of American Folklore* 110 (1997): 239–59.

Malone, Bill C. "Appalachian Music and American Popular Culture: The Romance That Will Not Die." In *Appalachia Inside Out*, vol. 2: *Culture and Custom*, edited by Robert J. Higgs, Ambrose N. Manning, and Jim Wayne Miller, 462–69. Knoxville: University of Tennessee Press, 1995.

———. *Country Music, U.S.A.* Rev. ed. Austin: University of Texas Press, 1985.

McCusker, Kristine M. "'Bury Me beneath the Willow': Linda Parker and Definitions of Tradition on the National Barn Dance, 1932–1935." *Southern Folklore*. 56, no. 3 (1999): 223–43.

———. "'Dear Radio Friend': Listener Mail and the National Barn Dance, 1931–1941." *American Studies* 39 (Summer 1998): 173–95.

Mooney, Kevin. "Texas Centennial 1936: African-American Texans and the National Folk Festival." *Journal of Texas Music History* 1 (Spring 2001): 36–43.

Owens, William A. *Tell Me a Story, Sing Me a Song: A Texas Chronicle*. Austin: University of Texas Press, 1983.

———. *Texas Folk Songs*. Austin: Texas Folklore Society and the University Press in Dallas, 1950.

Peterson, Richard A. *Creating Country Music: Fabricating Authenticity*. Chicago: University of Chicago Press, 1997.

Pezzuti, Michele. "Sarah Gertrude Knott House." Nomination for the National Register of Historic Places, 1999.

Randolph, Vance. "Ballad Hunters in North Arkansas." *Arkansas Historical Quarterly* 7 (Spring, 1948): 5–6.

Rice, Harry. "Renfro Valley on the Radio, 1937–1941." *Journal of Country Music* 19, no. 2 (1997): 18.

Roper, John Hebert. "Paul Green and the Southern Literary Renaissance." *Southern Cultures* 1 (Fall 1994): 75–89.

Rourke, Constance. "The National Folk Festival." *New Republic*, May 30, 1934, 72–73.

———. "The National Folk Festival." *New Republic*, June 5, 1935, 102–3.

Smulyan, Susan. *Selling Radio: The Commercialization of American Broadcasting 1920–1934*. Washington: Smithsonian Institution Press, 1994.

Stamper, Pete. *It All Happened in Renfro Valley*. Lexington: University Press of Kentucky, 1999.

Thompson, Stith. *Four Symposia on Folklore*. Indiana University Folklore Series, no. 8. Bloomington: Indiana University Press, 1953.

Whisnant, David E. *All That Is Native and Fine: The Politics of Culture in an American Region*. Chapel Hill: University of North Carolina Press, 1983.

———. "Finding the Way between the Old and New: The Mountain Dance and Folk Festival and Bascom Lamar Lunsford's Work as a Citizen." *Appalachian Journal* 7 (1979–80): 135–54.

Williams, Michael Ann. *Great Smoky Mountains Folklife*. Jackson: University Press of Mississippi, 1995.

Williams, Michael Ann, and Larry Morrisey. "Constructions of Tradition: Vernacular Architecture, Country Music, and Auto-Ethnography." In *People, Power, Places: Perspectives in Vernacular Architecture VIII*, edited by Sally McMurry and Annmarie Adams, 161–75. Knoxville: University of Tennessee Press, 2000.

Wilson, Chris. *The Myth of Santa Fe: Creating a Modern Regional Tradition.* Albuquerque: University of New Mexico Press, 1997.

Wolfe, Charles K. *A Good-Natured Riot: The Birth of the Grand Ole Opry.* Nashville: Country Music Foundation Press and Vanderbilt University Press, 1999.

———. *Kentucky Country: Folk and Country Music of Kentucky.* Lexington: University Press of Kentucky, 1982.

Yarger, Lisa J. "Banjo Pickin' Girl: Representing Lily May Ledford." M.A. thesis, University of North Carolina at Chapel Hill, 1997.

Yuhl, Stephanie Eileen. "High Culture in the Low Country: Arts, Identity and Tourism in Charleston, South Carolina, 1920–1940." Ph.D. diss., Duke University, 1998.

INDEX

Abbey Theater, 14
ABC, 120
Acadian Bicentennial Festival, 102–3, 105–6
A. C. Bilbrew Negro Chorus, 72
Acuff, Roy, 89
Adult Education Council (Chicago), 37
Aladdin Barn Dance Frolic, 41–43
Alessandroni, Judge Eugene V., 69, 71
All Florida Folk Festival. *See* Florida Folk Festival
Allis-Chalmers, 58
All-Ozark Festival, 23
Amburgey Sisters, 79
American Council on Education, 31
American Folk Dance Society, 67
American Folklife Preservation Act, 171
American Folklore Society, 22, 67, 70, 98–100, 130–31, 148
American Folk Song Festival, 11–12, 46, 156, 177
American Humor: A Study of National Character (Rourke), 21
American Indian Pageant, 105
Anadarko, Okla., 105
Anderson, Clinton P., 66
Anderson, Marion, 62–63
Andrews, Elizabeth, 68
Anthology of American Folk Music (Smith), 125, 130, 177–78
A'nt Idy and Little Clifford, 53, 60, 83
Appalachians: displaced, 50; stereotypes of, 28
Archive of Folk Song. *See* Library of Congress

ASCAP, 46
Asheville Chamber of Commerce, 11, 24, 27, 153–54
Ashland, Ky., 11
Associated Realtors of St. Louis, 96
Atkins, Chet, 161
Atta Boy (show), 6
Austin, Leonard, 107
auto-tourism, 50, 181
Autry, Gene, 113, 121

Back Where I Came From (radio program), 66
Ballard and Ballard Flour, 83, 90, 110–11, 121
Ball, John W., 100
barbershop quartets, 140
Barkley, Alben, 2, 63
Bascom, William, 98–99
Beatles, 153
Beck, Earl, 21
Beckwith, Martha, 22, 65
Beers, Robert "Fiddler," 108, 132
Behrens, Jerry, 115–16
Beiting, Father Ralph W., 166
Belden, H. M., 22
Beliajus, Vyts, 38, 64, 104, 107
Bentley, E. G., 81
Benton and Bowles Advertising Agency, 114, 118
Berea College, 75, 86, 122, 164–65, 168
Bernache, Leo, 144–45, 149
Bethune-Cookman College, 20
Biddle, Livingston, 134–35
Bidwell, Oakley, 114, 121, 123
Big Ben tobacco, 76

MICHAEL ANN WILLIAMS is a professor and head of the Department of Folk Studies and Anthropology at Western Kentucky University. She is also the author of *Great Smoky Mountains Folklife* and *Homeplace: The Social Use and Meaning of the Folk Dwelling in Southwestern North Carolina.*

Only a Miner: Studies in Recorded Coal-Mining Songs   *Archie Green*
Great Day Coming: Folk Music and the American Left   *R. Serge Denisoff*
John Philip Sousa: A Descriptive Catalog of His Works   *Paul E. Bierley*
The Hell-Bound Train: A Cowboy Songbook   *Glenn Ohrlin*
Oh, Didn't He Ramble: The Life Story of Lee Collins, as Told to Mary
    Collins   *Edited by Frank J. Gillis and John W. Miner*
American Labor Songs of the Nineteenth Century   *Philip S. Foner*
Stars of Country Music: Uncle Dave Macon to Johnny Rodriguez
    Edited by Bill C. Malone and Judith McCulloh
Git Along, Little Dogies: Songs and Songmakers of the American West
    John I. White
A Texas-Mexican *Cancionero:* Folksongs of the Lower Border
    Américo Paredes
San Antonio Rose: The Life and Music of Bob Wills   *Charles R. Townsend*
Early Downhome Blues: A Musical and Cultural Analysis   *Jeff Todd Titon*
An Ives Celebration: Papers and Panels of the Charles Ives Centennial
    Festival-Conference   *Edited by H. Wiley Hitchcock and Vivian Perlis*
Sinful Tunes and Spirituals: Black Folk Music to the Civil War
    Dena J. Epstein
Joe Scott, the Woodsman-Songmaker   *Edward D. Ives*
Jimmie Rodgers: The Life and Times of America's Blue Yodeler
    Nolan Porterfield
Early American Music Engraving and Printing: A History of Music
    Publishing in America from 1787 to 1825, with Commentary on Earlier
    and Later Practices   *Richard J. Wolfe*
Sing a Sad Song: The Life of Hank Williams   *Roger M. Williams*
Long Steel Rail: The Railroad in American Folksong   *Norm Cohen*
Resources of American Music History: A Directory of Source Materials
    from Colonial Times to World War II   *D. W. Krummel, Jean Geil,
    Doris J. Dyen, and Deane L. Root*
Tenement Songs: The Popular Music of the Jewish Immigrants
    Mark Slobin
Ozark Folksongs   *Vance Randolph; edited and abridged by Norm Cohen*
Oscar Sonneck and American Music   *Edited by William Lichtenwanger*
Bluegrass Breakdown: The Making of the Old Southern Sound
    Robert Cantwell
Bluegrass: A History   *Neil V. Rosenberg*
Music at the White House: A History of the American Spirit
    Elise K. Kirk
Red River Blues: The Blues Tradition in the Southeast   *Bruce Bastin*
Good Friends and Bad Enemies: Robert Winslow Gordon and the Study of
    American Folksong   *Debora Kodish*

Burn, Baby! BURN! The Autobiography of Magnificent Montague
  Magnificent Montague with Bob Baker
Way Up North in Dixie: A Black Family's Claim to the Confederate
  Anthem   *Howard L. Sacks and Judith Rose Sacks*
The Bluegrass Reader   *Edited by Thomas Goldsmith*
Colin McPhee: Composer in Two Worlds   *Carol J. Oja*
Robert Johnson, Mythmaking, and Contemporary American Culture
  Patricia R. Schroeder
Composing a World: Lou Harrison, Musical Wayfarer   *Leta E. Miller and
  Fredric Lieberman*
Fritz Reiner, Maestro and Martinet   *Kenneth Morgan*
That Toddlin' Town: Chicago's White Dance Bands and Orchestras,
  1900–1950   *Charles A. Sengstock Jr.*
Dewey and Elvis: The Life and Times of a Rock 'n' Roll Deejay
  Louis Cantor
Come Hither to Go Yonder: Playing Bluegrass with Bill Monroe
  Bob Black
Chicago Blues: Portraits and Stories   *David Whiteis*
The Incredible Band of John Philip Sousa   *Paul Edmund Bierley*
"Maximum Clarity" and Other Writings on Music   *Ben Johnston,
  edited by Bob Gilmore*
Staging Tradition: John Lair and Sarah Gertrude Knott
  Michael Ann Williams

*The University of Illinois Press
is a founding member of the
Association of American University Presses.*

---

*Composed in 9.5/12.5 Trump Mediaeval
by Jim Proefrock
at the University of Illinois Press
Manufactured by Thomson-Shore, Inc.*

*University of Illinois Press
1325 South Oak Street
Champaign, IL 61820-6903
www.press.uillinois.edu*